Praise for Jack D. Coombe's

GUNFIRE AROUND THE GULF

"Although the Navy contributed enormously to Union victory, books on the land war outnumber naval books by hundreds to one. Mr. Coombe's blood-and-thunder narrative helps redress the balance."
—*The Wall Street Journal*

"A well-done study, clearly written . . . a worthwhile addition to Civil War collections."
—*Library Journal*

"Mr. Coombe makes fine use of those anecdotes and details that turn up in Civil War records . . . and brings his own experience [as a Navy veteran] to bear on the Civil War navies. . . . an effective approach to history."
—*The Atlantic Monthly*

THUNDER ALONG THE MISSISSIPPI

"Essential for anyone with an interest in Civil War naval operations or the war in the West."
—*Library Journal*

"Fascinating . . . Coombe is a skilled writer. . . . This work will be a delight for Civil War buffs, but there is also much here for the well-informed general reader too."
—*Booklist*

Books by Jack D. Coombe

The Temptation

Derailing the Tokyo Express

Thunder Along the Mississippi

Gunfire Around the Gulf

GUNSMOKE
OVER THE
ATLANTIC

FIRST NAVAL ACTIONS
OF THE CIVIL WAR

Jack D. Coombe

BANTAM BOOKS

New York Toronto London Sydney Auckland

GUNSMOKE OVER THE ATLANTIC
A Bantam Book

PUBLISHING HISTORY
Bantam hardcover edition published April 2002
Bantam trade paperback edition / April 2003

Published by
Bantam Dell
A Division of Random House, Inc.
New York, New York

ISBN 0-553-38073-7

Manufactured in the United States of America
Published simultaneously in Canada

BVG 10 9 8 7 6 5 4 3 2 1

To the late Jean Makas,

who awoke my slumbering love

for the wonderful world of

American/English literature

CONTENTS

NAVAL CHRONOLOGY
1860–1865

1860

November 6:   Lincoln elected president.

November 20:   South Carolina secedes from Union.

1861

January 9:   South Carolinians fire on *Star of the West*.

February 18:   Jefferson Davis inaugurated as president of the Confederacy.

March 4:   Lincoln inaugurated as president; Gideon Welles appointed secretary of the navy.

April 12:   Fort Sumter bombarded by Confederates.

April 19:   Lincoln proclaims blockade of Confederate ports.

April 20:   Gosport Navy Yard abandoned by Union.

July 5:   Blockade Board issues report.

August 29:   Union amphibious forces take Forts Hatteras and Clark.

November 7:   Union amphibious forces take Port Royal, South Carolina.

November 8:   The *Trent* affair.

1862

March 8:   C.S.S. *Virginia* sinks U.S.S. *Congress* and U.S.S. *Cumberland*.

March 9:   C.S.S. *Virginia* and U.S.S. *Monitor* battle in Hampton Roads.

April 4:   McClellan launches Peninsula Campaign.

April 11:   Union forces take Fort Pulaski.

May 10:   Confederates abandon Gosport Navy Yard.

May 11:   C.S.S. *Virginia* is destroyed by crew.

August 24:   Raphael Semmes becomes captain of C.S.S. *Alabama*.

December 31:   U.S.S. *Monitor* lost in Atlantic storm.

1863

April 7:	Union ironclads repulsed in Charleston Harbor.
June 17:	C.S.S. *Atlanta* surrenders at Warsaw Sound, Georgia.
July 10:	Union monitors bombard Battery Wagner, South Carolina.

1864

February 2:	C.S.S. *Underwriter* is captured by Union navy.
February 17:	Confederate sub *H. L. Hunley* sinks U.S.S. *Housatonic*.
April 19:	U.S.S. *Southfield* sunk by C.S.S. *Albemarle*.
June 19:	C.S.S. *Alabama* sunk by U.S.S. *Kearsarge* off France.
October 27:	C.S.S. *Albemarle* sunk by Lt. Cushing's task force.
December 21:	Savannah taken by General Sherman.
December 24–25:	Union naval forces make first assault on Fort Fisher, North Carolina.

1865

January 13–15:	Union naval and amphibious forces capture Fort Fisher.
February 17:	Wilmington, North Carolina, abandoned by Confederates.
April 9:	Lee surrenders at Appomattox Court House.

INTRODUCTION

In actuality, the naval aspects of the Civil War began on the East Coast of the United States. It was born out of the necessity of maintaining a blockade of southern ports ordered by President Lincoln after the states of South Carolina, Mississippi, Florida, Alabama, Louisiana, and Texas had seceded from the Union. Although a viable navy existed in 1861, it was in pitiful condition, many ships having been depleted by inaction and lack of maintenance due to a parsimonious Congress under the Buchanan administration. As a matter of fact, only 42 ships were in active service, with most of them scattered around the world at various foreign posts. By the end of the Civil War, however, the U.S. Navy had grown to an impressive 650 ships consisting of powerful single- and double-turreted monitors, screw frigates, sloops, and a vast array of supply vessels. This navy grew out of its birth pangs early on when Lincoln's secretary of the navy, Gideon Welles, inaugurated an ambitious shipbuilding program needed to enforce the blockade.

Before that was accomplished, a great deal of naval activity took place along the eastern seaboard, consisting mainly of countering Confederate blockade-runners and raiders. The naval activity accelerated when a fleet of warships assaulted Port Royal, South Carolina, in the war's first amphibious landing operation and later in the famous battle of ironclads at Hampton Roads, Virginia.

We will attempt to cover select naval activities on the East Coast between 1861 and 1865, with the Union enforcing the blockade and meeting the feeble but growing Confederate naval threat. However, all this had had ignominious beginnings: a pathetic attempt to use Federal warships to prevent the calamity at Fort Sumter, and a disgraceful betrayal of the garrison there by apathetic politicians. The shame was further compounded by the monumental loss of the Gosport Navy Yard at Norfolk, Virginia, which gave the Confederacy the hull of a warship with which to build the iron-clad C.S.S. *Virginia* (formerly the U.S.S. *Merrimack*). This famous warship was thrown into a duel with the equally famous Union ironclad U.S.S. *Monitor* in a March 1862 surface battle that was to change the course of naval history forever by sounding the death knell of sail-powered wooden ships and ushering in the iron ship age.

The struggles of the fledgling Union and Confederate navies resulted in strategic but sometimes brutal naval actions along the numerous rivers and coastal waterways of the Atlantic coast, from Virginia to Florida. The climax of this activity came with the massive amphibious landing, supported by overwhelming naval gunfire, to capture the Confederate stronghold at Fort Fisher, off Wilmington, North Carolina, in January 1865. The awesome landings of World War II would equal this operation.

Finally, the vital Confederate ports of Norfolk, Charleston, Wilmington, Savannah, New Orleans, and Mobile closed the naval chapter of the Civil War, thereby hastening the surrender of the Confederacy. But this conclusion was not accomplished without substantial fighting with heavy casualties on both sides.

I am aware that this theater of the Civil War saw a great deal of naval action between 1861 and 1865, and to cover every event and the detailed movements of particular warships would constitute a ponderous volume. Therefore, as with my previous works, I have been selective in my narrative and have highlighted the most important and meaningful events that occurred along the Atlantic seaboard—events that nevertheless contributed to the conclusion of the war.

As with my previous works, this book entailed intensive research at both well-known historical archives and not-so-well-known archival sites and museums, plus extensive personal visits to the actual historical sites for atmosphere and color. A great deal of emphasis has been placed on eyewitness accounts culled from diaries, journals, and letters. I am also grateful for new dimensions added to research—that of the Internet and the amazing technology of CD-ROMs, which contain impressive amounts of information.

This book will augment my previous books: *Thunder Along the Mississippi,* which dealt with naval actions along the Mississippi River that split the Confederacy, and *Gunfire Around the Gulf,* which treated the final naval actions of the Civil War that occurred in the Gulf of Mexico. This work, summarizing important naval actions along the Atlantic coast, completes the trilogy containing the entire naval history of the Civil War, from the Atlantic to the Gulf.

Once again, I have taken some liberties with respect to naval terms. Unlike the terms used by sailors on the riverine fleets, nomenclature has not changed much in Atlantic fleets. The term *hurricane deck* was in use, although today it has been replaced by *quarterdeck,* as was *poop deck,* which is known today as *fantail.* The archaic ordnance term *gun* has been replaced by *naval rifle,* because today's ordnance is all rifled, as opposed to only a few in Civil War navies. The terms *starboard* and *port* remain today, as they were in fleets of yesteryear, although *larboard* was used in riverine fleets instead of *starboard.* I have included in this work a section on nomenclature that explains the terms used on these pages.

To this work I have brought to bear all the expertise at my command. I am a veteran of many important naval actions in the Pacific during World War II, including major surface engagements and the great amphibious operations. This experience, coupled with years of research, allows me to portray naval life and warfare as realistically as possible. And even though technology has wrought awesome weapons systems since the Civil War, the basic concepts of warfare and the psychology of men in combat remain the same today as in warfare past. That is why many important events have been told through the eyes of contemporary observers.

MANY people contributed to the writing of this book of naval history. To name every single one would be impossible because of space limitations, but those who made substantial contributions to this work deserve a grateful nod.

First and foremost, my research assistant, Peg Coombe, who is also my life's mate, contributed immeasurably to this endeavor. Her dedicated assistance, understanding, insight, and editing skills were invaluable. Without her help, this and previous books would have been extremely long and arduous to produce.

Much appreciation is due Glenn V. Longacher, curator, National Archives, Great Lakes Division, for his advice and suggestions, and for supplying information hitherto unknown to my research assistant and myself.

Our lengthy visit to Newport News was made considerably rewarding through the cheerful assistance of Dina B. Hill and Jeffrey P. Johnston, of the National Marine Sanctuary associated with the Mariners' Museum. These helpful people allowed us to see at first hand artifacts from the *Monitor* and supplied us with the very latest information on their work on the recently discovered remains of the venerable warship. In the museum itself, a steady flow of archival material was supplied by the astute and energetic Gregory C. Cina, and valuable graphic sources were opened to us by Claudia A. Jew of the visual research and photographic archives. Mr. Edgar L. Nettles made possible our introduction to the *Monitor* National Marine Sanctuary.

Davis Jeffrey Johnson, director of the Casemate Museum at Fort Monroe, went out of his way to supply invaluable material on the history of the fort and its part in the famous *Monitor/Merrimack* battle and in subsequent military actions along the Atlantic coast.

We owe a great debt of gratitude to John V. Quarstein, director, Virginia War Museum, for taking us to a most important site of the famous battle of the ironclads and for sharing his penetrating insight and voluminous knowledge of the battle. His book *The Battle of the Ironclads* was widely used in this work.

Our most fruitful visit to Fort Fisher, North Carolina, allowed us to receive estimable assistance from Leland Smith, of the Division of Archives and History, who opened his vast archives to us and took us on a personal tour of the fort and its environs. Also, heartfelt thanks go to Richard Lawrence, Henry Warren, Tim Bottoms, and Nathan Henry of the Underwater Archaeological Unit there for allowing us to see various artifacts from wrecks of various civilian and military vessels off Cape Fear.

In Charleston, South Carolina, our appreciation extends to David O. Percy, executive director of the South Carolina Historical Society, for important information on the *H. L. Hunley* and its fascinating history. Also thanks to Katherine Sadler of the Charleston Historical Society, as well as Jackie McCall of the South Carolina Historical Society, for helping me out at the last moment with vital material.

An amazing amount of Civil War material is available at the Chicago Historical Society. We are grateful to research specialist Leslie Martin and her staff for help in locating the precise information for which we were searching.

A dear friend, historian and author John Glavin, presented me with books of substantial interest, and I am in his debt.

There is no way I can express my appreciation and heartfelt thanks to Chad Raymond and his incomparable staff at the Northbrook Public Library, with amazing resources of material, for their help in my research for this trilogy. Special thanks are due to Nancy Bishop, Hala Haddad, Spencer Hall, Thomas Morris, Joyce Nevins, Mary Kay Perrenot, and Elaine Stenzel. Our special appreciation goes to Yvonne Hutcheon and Nancy Poch and their volunteer staff in the Interlibrary Loan Department for obtaining countless important books through their services.

Finally, if anyone who has assisted me in any way has been overlooked, I extend my humblest apology. Space does not permit listing everyone, as much as I would like to do so. But you know your contribution, and you can take pride in knowing you contributed to this three-volume naval history of the Civil War.

THIS book, as with my previous works, is aimed primarily at the average reader who desires to know more about the Civil War without struggling through weighty textbooklike books. Still, I hope that scholar and student alike will benefit from this work.

To accomplish this, I have brought the chapter notes to a minimum. Experience, plus reader comments, taught me that excessive footnotes are annoying to the average reader. It should be surmised that the author knows enough about his subject, from intensive research and years of study, without interrupting the narrative with footnotes to substantiate his knowledge.

The reader will notice my frequent references to World War II naval technologies as descendants from the Civil War innovations. I am aware that these corollaries have not been pointed out by many naval historians, yet the fact remains that the earlier technology was the ancestor of techniques and weapons used today. I will discuss these innovations in detail later in the work.

ADDENDUM

Since publication and release of the hardcover edition of this book, many important events have taken place concerning the U.S.S. *Monitor* and the Confederate submarine *H.L. Hunley*. The turret of the *Monitor* has been successfully raised and at present is immersed in a conservation tank at the Mariner's Museum in Newport News, Virginia. Beside the two 11-inch Dahlgren guns, a partially complete human skeleton was found inside the 150-ton turret. The turret was raised by a "Spider," an eight-legged steel claw that clamped around the turret and was lifted by a 500-ton derrick on a barge. Earlier, one of her engines was raised and now sits in a tank alongside her propeller and other parts.

The *H.L. Hunley* was also successfully raised, placed on a barge, and brought to a conservation tank at the Charleston Navy Yard in South Carolina. Inside the vessel eight complete skeletons were discovered, including the captain of the vessel, George E. Dixon. Forensic experts have been at work reconstructing the remains, and their skulls will undergo facial reconstruction in order to reveal identities. Technological innovations discovered included a flywheel attached to the propeller that allowed the propeller to keep turning after the men temporarily stopped cranking.

NAVAL NOMENCLATURE

Throughout this book, terms will be used to describe various warships that not only were used by the Civil War navies, but by navies the world over. Below are brief descriptions of the most prominent of Civil War warships that appear most frequently on the following pages, along with some important naval terms used in this work.

NOTE: Sail rigging terms include "square-rigged" and "fore-and-aft rigged." Square-rigged means the sails are mounted on yard arms diagonally on the centerline of the ship. Fore-and-aft means sails are mounted on arms parallel to the centerline.

Frigate: Three-masted, full-rigged ships, usually carrying from 40 to 50 guns on two gun decks. But the most common and most effective frigates used in the CW were sail- and steam-propelled. These vessels carried Dahlgren smoothbore guns and were very fast. Tagged as "eyes of the fleet" by the navies, these vessels were used in a multitude of missions, including the enforcing of blockades and to partake in search-and-rescue as well as bombardment missions.

Steam Sloops: Three-masted, full-rigged sail- and steam-propelled ships, of 18 to 22 guns on a single gun deck. Sometimes they were referred to as "sloops of war." The most famous of these ships is the *Hartford,* used as a flagship by Admiral Farragut in the Gulf of Mexico campaigns.

Ironclads: There were a variety of ironclad vessels used in the Civil War. They were of two varieties: monitors and casemate vessels. Monitors were built with iron plates from the keel up, while casemate vessels had iron plates over wooden hulls. The most famous ironclad was the U.S.S. *Monitor* and the most famous casemate vessel was the U.S.S. *Galena.* The ironclad riverine fleet, built by James Eads for the Mississippi River campaigns, was built exclusively from the keel up.

Barks: Barks were three-masted sailing vessels with the first two masts square-rigged and the third fore-and-aft rigged. They could be armed with one or two guns.

Brigs: Sometimes referred to as "brigantines." These were two-masted vessels, with the first square-rigged and the second, fore-and-aft. Brigs could be armed with one or two guns.

Paddlewheel Vessels: Usually sail- and steam-propelled ships, with approximately 20 guns, using large paddlewheels, usually on the sides or, in some cases, on the sterns. The most famous of the sidewheelers was the U.S.S. *Mississippi,* of 20 guns, one of the major warships in Farragut's fleet. The most famous stern paddlewheelers were the U.S.S. *Carondelet* and the U.S.S. *Cairo,* the latter recently raised from a river and on display at Vicksburg Military Park. The stern paddlewheels were especially effective in making headway against a powerful river current and for quick maneuvering.

Acquired Ships: These vessels were of various sizes and tonnage, usually either purchased from the maritime fleets or captured from the enemy. Perhaps the most prominent of these vessels were the open-ended ferry boats because of their ability to move forward or backward without turning around, through the use of screws and rudders at both ends. Most acquired vessels were used as support vessels for the navy, assigned to carry provisions, repair supplies, troops, coal, etc. In navy parlance, a fleet of support vessels is called the "train," because it always followed the main battle fleet.

NOTE: It may be noticed that the "ship of the line" was not mentioned. This vessel, used in the heyday of sail battle fleets, was usually a heavy, ponderous vessel carrying guns on three or more decks. There is no record of ships of the line being in existence during the Civil War, except for hulks being used as receiving ships.

Collier: A specially designed vessel for carrying coal to the fleet.

Stand Out: To depart from a harbor or port and take course for seaward.

Starboard: The directional term for the right side of the ship.

Port: The directional term for the left side of the ship.

Commodore: A courtesy title for an officer below rear admiral, commanding a squadron, division, or a flotilla of two or more ships.

Flag Officer: A rank above captain, authorized to fly his personal flag.

Skipper: Slang term for a commanding officer of a ship, regardless of his rank.

Weather Deck: The main deck of a warship, or topside.

Freeboard: That distance from the weather deck to the waterline of a vessel.

General Quarters: Call to battle stations for action, as quickly as possible.

Casemate: That covering of the weather deck of ironclad warships, usually containing openings for guns and providing protection for gun crews against enemy projectiles.

CHAPTER ONE

FORT SUMTER AND THE U.S. NAVY

A strong southeast wind whipped the water into deep troughs off the bar at the mouth of Charleston Harbor, while low, angry clouds scudded across the sky. The transport steamer *Baltic* rocked in the troughs, holding its position at the edge of the swash channel.

It was April 12, 1861, and aboard the transport, Captain Gustavus Vasa Fox no doubt glanced around and frowned. In the distance he could have made out the gray outline of the two-masted side-wheel sloop *Harriet Lane,* her paddlewheels slapping at the encroaching waves. Behind her was the dim shape of the bark-rigged sloop *Pawnee,* also rocking slowly in the surf. Alarmingly, the *Powhatan* and the *Pocahontas* were missing. This must have disturbed him, because their striking power was vital to the mission.

Fox knew that those present were the only ships of an eight-vessel fleet sent by navy secretary Gideon Welles to provide a relief mission for beleaguered Fort Sumter, located at the mouth of the harbor. No doubt Fox, who was in charge of the expedition, must have deeply pondered the absence of the 3,765-ton, 11-gun side-wheel frigate *Powhatan,* which had been ordered to join the fleet. Her absence would be crucial, because her heavy guns could have provided the fleet with protection from the glowering Confederate batteries on Cummings Point and Sullivan's Island, on each side of the harbor's mouth, and also from any encroaching armed vessels the Confederates would muster against him.

Welles' order emphasized that the primary mission of the fleet was to provision Fort Sumter and that the War Department would furnish the necessary transports for the force.[1] But it was clear that those transports with 200 troops, plus three steam tugs, *Uncle Ben, Freeborn,* and *Yankee,* were also missing with no clue as to their whereabouts.

Gustavus Fox was fully qualified for the mission. A native of Massachusetts, he had been appointed midshipman in the navy in 1845 after graduating from the U.S. Naval Academy on January 12, 1838.

Fox served aboard the U.S.S. *Preble,* on which he gained experience about command at sea and the intricacies of transport duty during the Mexican War. He later resigned his lieutenant's commission and settled down as a merchant in his native state. But President Lincoln had personally contacted him to head the Fort Sumter relief mission. Fox arrived at Charleston, on March 21, to confer with Major Robert Anderson about the state of affairs at the fort. After his visit, Fox became convinced that a relief mission was possible, in spite of growing tensions around the fort in Charleston and the batteries surrounding it.

Following the rapid secession of South Carolina, Mississippi, Florida, Alabama, Georgia, Louisiana, and Texas, it became clear that war was in the offing. President Lincoln put Fox on notice to proceed with all possible speed to Charleston Harbor, with a relief mission for Anderson and the garrison at Sumter.

The task force left New York Harbor, with the *Powhatan* and the 750-ton, six-gun sloop *Pocahontas* departing on April 6, and the rest of the flotilla leaving at various times. Fox's *Uncle Ben* left on the seventh, with the rest following. Soon after reaching Sandy Hook, the force found itself in an Atlantic gale, with heavy winds that dogged the vessels all the way to Charleston.

Fox's orders stated that the flotilla was to stand off the harbor and await the arrival of the missing warships, which were believed to have been delayed by the storm. This was puzzling, considering that the warships had left one day before Fox's departure.

By April 12 it was clear that the absence of the vessels would seriously crimp the mission. The tugs, with their fast speed and low draft, would have been ideal for slipping past the enemy's gun positions, as would a small fleet of launches on board the *Powhatan*. These vessels would have carried not only provisions but a detachment of relief troops in case an opportunity allowed them to be placed in the fort under the protection of the powerful warship. None of the present ships had boats that would serve the purpose, and now there was also a shortage of personnel. Fox began to experience a feeling of frustration as the hours dragged on.

One bright spot in the picture for Fox, however, was the capture of a small ice schooner by the *Pawnee*. For a time it appeared that this fast vessel would be ideal for slipping past the batteries at night, but the idea was soon abandoned when the rumble of gunfire was heard within the harbor. As the angry clouds lifted, Fox and the crews of the vessels could witness black smoke drifting over the harbor, indicating a conflict.[2]

Their worst fears were realized: Fort Sumter was under attack! It is not difficult to comprehend the frustration and utter helplessness felt in the relief flotilla as they watched a torrent of shells reaching high and arcing down upon the hapless fort and its outgunned and outmanned occupants. For a time a heavy pall of smoke obstructed their vision, but as the wind whipped it away, the horror of it all was driven home. Meanwhile, the *Pocahontas* hove into view, delayed by the storm; alarmingly, the warship was alone, without the much-awaited *Powhatan*.

In the fort, Major Robert Anderson shared Fox's perplexity. On December 26, 1860, he had written to Col. S. Cooper, adjutant general, that he had just removed his garrison from Fort Moultrie to Sumter, except for four noncommissioned officers and seven men. He revealed that there was a year's supply of hospital stores and four months' supply of provisions. He presented the rationale for the abandonment of Moultrie and a secret move under cover of darkness.[3]

After his move from Moultrie, Anderson must have looked around the unfinished fort and wondered what was in store for the men and himself, to say nothing of his beloved country, the United States of America. But the move was necessary because of what preceded it.

The tight-lipped Anderson was well equipped for commanding Fort Moultrie. Born in Kentucky on June 4, 1805, Anderson, who was early on a very religious man, graduated 15th in his class from West Point in 1825. His combat record included the Blackhawk and Seminole Indian Wars, and he served in Mexico under General Winfield Scott, during which he was wounded. After these events, he found himself translating French military

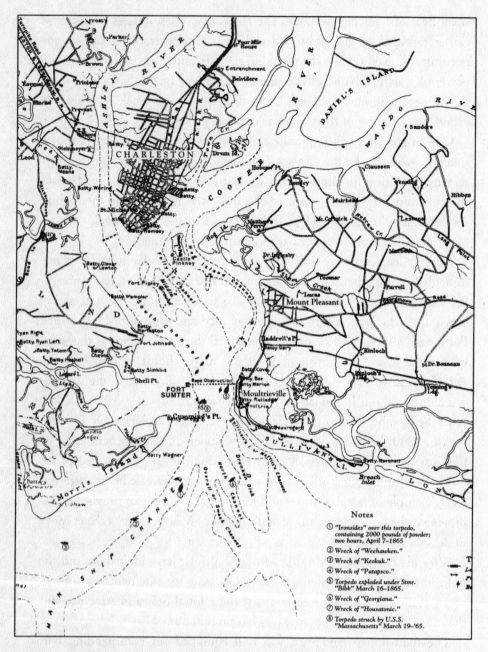

Charleston Harbor, showing the city, harbor channel, Fort Sumter, and Confederate batteries surrounding it. From *The Official Records of the Union and Confederate Navies in the War of the Rebellion.*

texts into English at the War Department. In 1845 he married Elizabeth L. Clinch, daughter of Brigadier General Duncan Clinch. He settled down to what he thought would be a quiet, peaceful life of service.

In November 1860 John B. Floyd, U.S. secretary of war, ordered him to command the garrison at Moultrie. Although Anderson was sympathetic toward slavery because of his southern origins, he remained loyal to the Union, and his devotion to duty was admirable.[4] Without question, he accepted the command. He and Elizabeth packed their bags, moved to South Carolina, and took up residence in Moultrie, which by this time had gained the reputation of being a socially agreeable place, especially because of the people of Charleston. It had become less of a military establishment and more a social club of sorts, which the upper-class residents of Charleston frequented.

The only other fortifications in Charleston Harbor were the incomplete Fort Sumter and Castle Pinckney, the latter a brick edifice on a small island a mile north off Charleston. It had a capacity of 100 men and an armament of 22 guns, but in 1860, 10 men under an ordnance sergeant occupied it. Anderson was aware that South Carolina forces, in the event of hostilities, would quickly take the Castle Pinckney site. He therefore reasoned that any hope of resistance lay in Fort Sumter, even though it was incomplete.

Anderson no doubt had recalled the impressive event of the removal of his men from Moultrie after it was painfully obvious that well-armed South Carolina militiamen could overwhelm and capture the fort. The situation became critical, so on December 26, he decided to move the garrison to Fort Sumter.

To accomplish the ruse, boats were cleverly concealed on the waterfront, a sunset parade of men was held on the grounds to present a picture of normalcy to prying eyes, and dinner was placed on the table of the officers' mess, though it was later transferred and eaten at Sumter.

The plan was so secret that even Captain Abner Doubleday, Anderson's second in command, wasn't notified until 20 minutes before the evacuation. The only personnel notified early of Anderson's plans were an engineer who supplied the rowboats, schooners, and barges to be used for transporting the families of the men, and an officer who was put in charge of three boats for them. The schooners were loaded in broad daylight with supplies for Fort Sumter, a normal procedure recognized by the

Confederates. Anderson and some of his staff stood on the ramparts of the fort, watching the schooners sailing for the fort.

At twilight, the garrison was marched through the fort and loaded on boats that had been hidden behind the seawall. Just before dark set in, the boats shoved off, headed for the fort, and managed to elude a Confederate patrol boat; the men had removed their coats and placed them over their rifles on the bottom, and Doubleday had opened his coat to hide his buttons, in order to make him look like a civilian. The Confederates concluded that this was a boatload of workers heading for the fort and let them get under way. Behind them, a detail of men spiked the guns, burned gun carriages, cut down the flagstaff, and removed needed supplies to take over. They managed to finish in time to join their comrades the next morning. It was a well-thought-out and well-crafted operation, accomplished without a hitch, with Charleston's civilians and militia never suspecting a thing.

Fort Sumter had an interesting history. It was one of a series of important coastal fortifications built by the U.S. government after the War of 1812. Constructed on a shoal in the middle of the harbor, it was named after Thomas Sumter, a general in the South Carolina militia during the Revolutionary War. It contained 10,000 tons of granite shipped from Maine and 60,000 tons of other rock, plus millions of bricks from local brickyards. Nearly completed before Anderson and his men occupied it, it was an imposing structure with 5-foot-thick, 50-foot-high walls and a parade ground of one acre. The facility was designed for 140 guns and a garrison of 650 officers and men. At the time of Anderson's occupation, the fort had only 48 guns mounted on the ramparts.

The sight that met Anderson and his men at the fort must have been jolting. The parade ground was cluttered with building materials, guns, carriages, shot and shell, derricks, timber, tackle and blocks, and coils of rope.[5] Undaunted, they went about cleaning up, mounting guns, bricking up unused embrasures, and hoisting barbette guns to the ramparts of the fort. It was an effort to prepare for any eventuality.

In Charleston, howls of protest went up as crowds collected in the streets to vent their anger at Anderson's clever move. South Carolina's governor, Francis W. Pickens, sent an envoy to the fort to demand an explanation and to order Anderson and his garrison back to Fort Moultrie. Anderson sternly refused to move, and the envoy departed in a huff, full of fuss and feathers.

Meanwhile, the Buchanan administration was doing what it could to help Fort Sumter. General Winfield Scott, now the head of the army, grew impatient and declared that Fort Sumter was to be held, provisioned, and given the help of a couple of first-class warships.[6] Gloomy, pessimistic Buchanan, worried about his political legacy, believing that the secession would never be overthrown by force of arms, stood by, wringing his hands, during those tense days at Charleston. He finally got off the fence and trudged into action. He basically agreed with Scott's assessment but was convinced that a flotilla of warships must never enter Charleston to antagonize the South Carolinians. Instead, he suggested one steamer carrying supplies, plus the screw sloop *Brooklyn* as a backup, to form a relief mission. But Scott vetoed the use of the *Brooklyn,* declaring that the huge warship, with her 17-foot draft, would be unable to cross the bar at Charleston Harbor. In its place, the 1,172-ton brigantine-rigged side-wheel merchant steamer *Star of the West* was picked to carry out the mission. She left New York's Governor's Island on January 5, loaded with supplies and 200 troops under the command of First Lieutenant Charles B. Woods of the 9th Infantry. She arrived at the mouth of Charleston Harbor on January 9 and boldly steamed into the harbor with the troops hidden below decks lest the gunners on each side of the channel, at Sullivan's Island and Cummings Point, get suspicious.

So far, so good. No shots were fired at them, prompting Captain John McGowan to stay his course. It began to look as if the mission might succeed.

Suddenly, a shot arced high from Morris Island and plunged into the water ahead of the vessel. Then a series of shots followed, one of which landed near the rudder; another skidded across the forechains. The situation became hopeless, and after Captain McGowan had conferred with Lieutenant Woods, he decided to abort the mission rather than risk losing his ship, its cargo, and possibly the troops.[7]

In Fort Sumter, the defenders, who had been eagerly and hopefully watching the progress of the ship, no doubt groaned with frustration after the ship turned around. And more than one man must have thrown down his hat in anger. But Anderson wisely refused to answer enemy guns with his own, thus forestalling war for a time.

Anderson and his troops busied themselves preparing the fort for a possible attack. They mounted 38 guns on the first tier of the casemate and along the parapets of the fort, including five heavy 11-inch artillery pieces called Columbiads, mounted on the parade ground to be used as mortars. By April 12, they had managed to mount more than 60 guns in the fort. While not nearly matching the armament of the Confederates, it was still a formidable defense. However, the specter of having supplies cut off was of real concern to the defenders.

Back at the flotilla, Fox was eagerly awaiting the arrival of the *Powhatan,* but the powerful warship never came. Unknown to him, she had been diverted to relieve Fort Pickens at Pensacola, Florida. It was later revealed that the secretary of state, William Henry Seward, had presented some papers for Lincoln to sign, and without reading them, the president signed all. One of the papers contained an order for the *Powhatan* to report to Fort Pickens, thus overriding Welles' order for the warship to accompany the Fox expedition. Fuming with anger, Welles tried to recall the *Powhatan,* but it was too late for Captain David Porter to reverse course for Pensacola, citing his orders from Lincoln. It is a military given that the president's orders always take precedence over all other orders.[8]

Soon after the Fox flotilla had arrived off Charleston Harbor, the city's newspaper, the *Charleston Mercury,* indignantly declared that "the gage is thrown down and we accept the challenge." It was clear that the new Confederacy was ready for war.

Meanwhile, General Pierre G. T. Beauregard had taken command of Confederate forces at Charleston in March. He repeatedly demanded the evacuation of Fort Sumter but eventually grew impatient and decided that the time was ripe for action. His aide-de-camp, James Chestnut Jr., wrote the following message to Colonel Anderson:

> SIR: By authority of Brigadier-General Beauregard, commanding
> the provisional forces of the Confederate states, we have the honor
> to notify you that he will open fire of his batteries on Fort Sumter
> in one hour from this time.[9]

On April 12, the gun crews at Fort Johnson, 2,450 yards to the north of Fort Sumter, breakfasted early, then prepared their weapons for action upon orders from General Beauregard. Captain George S. James, commanding the mortar artillery, stepped back after the 10-inch seacoast

Columbiad was loaded, yanked the lanyard, and sent a shot arcing high in the air, which exploded over Fort Sumter. This was the prearranged signal for all batteries to start firing.[10]

The Civil War had officially begun.

A holocaust opened up around the harbor. Shell after shell slammed into the fort, gouging out huge shards of brick; shells exploded in the parade ground, flinging deadly shrapnel. As Abner Doubleday wrote: "Shot and shell went screaming over Sumter as if an army of devils were sweeping around it."[11]

At first, for some reason, Anderson refused to fire back, but eventually he decided to answer fire with fire. Doubleday then sent an answering projectile against the floating iron battery off Moultrie; the shot bounced harmlessly off the iron plating, but Anderson had finally replied to the challenge. His eager gunners launched a barrage against the iron battery and the batteries on Cummings Point. The Confederates responded, and it quickly became a mad exchange of shot and shell. The harbor became a kaleidoscope of flashing light and billowing smoke, which at times obliterated the view of spectators at Charleston. There, citizens flocked to the wharves and waterside to view the action out in the harbor; a large number of women stood whispering fervent prayers for their kinfolk, but many viewed the bombardment as a grand spectacle, and even a heavy rainfall failed to dampen their enthusiasm.

The Confederate barrage was intense and unrelenting. Fires started around the parade ground, including in the officers' quarters. A heavy rain shower temporarily halted the bombardment and managed to put out some of the fires, but after it passed, the Confederate cannonade continued with a renewed ferocity. As an observer in Charleston, Mary Boykin Chestnut, wrote: "Fort Sumter has been on fire. Anderson has not yet silenced any of our guns. So the aides, still with swords and red sashes by way of a uniform, tell us. But the sound of those guns makes regular meals impossible. None of us goes to table. Tea trays pervade the corridors, going everywhere. Some of the anxious hearts lie on their beds and moan in solitary misery."[12]

In the fort, Major Anderson and his men were hunkered down, trying to escape injury from flying debris or a direct hit. Their uniforms were blackened by smoke and cinders from burning wood, and soon the troops began to suffer fatigue. Luckily, so far no one had been injured or killed, but as the bombardment intensified, it became obvious they could not take much more punishment.

The ferocity of the bombardment moved Doubleday to later write: "The scene at this time was really terrific. The roaring and crackling of the flames, the dense masses of swirling smoke, the bursting of the enemy shells and our own which were exploding in the burning room, the crashing of the shot, and the sound of masonry falling in every direction, made the fort a pandemonium."[13]

Meanwhile, outside the bar, the Union fleet stood by helplessly as the conflagration in the harbor grew in intensity. Fox reported that as the bombardment progressed, consideration of a possible relief mission was discussed with all the commanders. The idea was rejected because heavy seas might have swamped the boats. A sense of hopelessness and frustration set in among the fleet personnel.

"A great volume of black smoke issued from Fort Sumter," Fox wrote, "through which the flash of Major Anderson's guns still replied to the rebel fire. The quarters of the fort were on fire, and most of our military and naval officers believed the smoke to proceed from an attempt to smoke out the garrison with fire rafts."[14] This was the first time in the Civil War the fire rafts were suggested as a weapon. They were later to be used against Admiral David Glasgow Farragut in the Mississippi River campaign; twice they almost cost him his flagship, *Hartford.*[15]

In the fleet, Commander Gillis, captain of the powerful steam sloop *Pocahontas,* reported his desire to enter the harbor to relieve Sumter, but he intended to proceed without pilots, the buoys and all marking removed, which would have probably grounded his vessel.[16] It is another stark example of the utter helplessness felt by the commanders of the Union fleet outside Charleston Harbor.

In the fort, Anderson had ordered his gunners to evacuate the barbette positions and concentrate on the casemates, because he was aware that the guns on the floating battery and those newly unmasked on Sullivan's Island could sweep the ramparts with shot, making it impossible for his men to hold those positions.[17]

The situation had become close to disastrous—one-fifth of the fort was on fire, and the heavy, suffocating smoke drove the defenders into refuge in the embrasures or forced them to lie on the ground, handkerchiefs over their mouths. It was painfully obvious the fort was receiving a great deal of damage.

At one point the flagstaff was hit and knocked down, giving the Confederates the impression the fort had surrendered. Meanwhile, a boat, with white flag flying and carrying Senator Louis T. Wigfall, cautiously approached the fort with a demand for surrender.

Wigfall's demand not only called for the surrender but offered a carrot in that Anderson could salute his flag as it came down and could leave the fort unharmed, with drums beating and flags flying.

Wigfall was unable to enter through the sallyport because of fallen debris, so he was forced to crawl in through a small opening, where he was met by one of Anderson's men, Private John Thompson, who at first refused to let him enter. But after Wigfall's identity was known, he was allowed in. While Wigfall was waiting for Anderson to appear, he became aware that even though the flag was down, there was still a lot of firing from Confederate batteries. He approached Lieutenant Jefferson Davis (no relation to the Confederate president) to inquire about the situation. Davis informed him the flag had been put back on the ramparts, whereupon Wigfall put a white flag on his sword, handed it to Davis, and demanded the lieutenant wave it over the ramparts. Davis refused, and a soldier was appointed to do the waving. As he was doing so, a solid shot landed nearby, causing the soldier to jump back and exclaim, "I'm not holding this flag, for it is not respected!"[18] It was later learned that General Beauregard had not authorized Wigfall's terms; the senator was acting entirely on his own.

When Anderson learned that Beauregard's terms were similar to Wigfall's, he began to realize the futility of continued resistance, especially with a scarcity of ammunition and provisions, to say nothing of the damage to the fort and the dangerous conditions his men were in. He ordered the flag down, then fired off a dispatch to Beauregard:

> In the peculiar circumstances in which I am now placed in consequence of that message [Wigfall's] and of my reply thereto, I will now state that I am willing to evacuate this fort upon the terms and conditions offered by yourself on the 11th instant, at any hour

you may name tomorrow, as soon as I can arrange means of trans-
portation. I will not replace my flag until the return of your messenger.[19]

Beauregard informed Anderson that a steamer, the *Isabel*, would be
placed at his disposal on the morning of April 14, and as promised, the
major and his men would be allowed to salute the flag as it was lowered,
and to take it with them.[20] With great sadness, but with great dignity,
Anderson and his officers and men acquiesced to the order to board the
Isabel the next morning, to be taken to the fleet waiting off the bar.

The embarkation was to have taken place the next morning, April 15, at
11:00 A.M. However, the skipper of the *Isabel* had misjudged the tide, so
the vessel was aground until 2:00 P.M. and the surrendered garrison had to
endure the spirited ceremonies of the Confederate troops as they took over
the fort.[21] Anderson's men used the time to bury with honors Private
Daniel Hough, who was killed in an explosion while firing a salute gun
during the surrender ceremonies.

As the *Isabel* moved along on its way to the rendezvous with the *Baltic*,
Confederate gunners stood at attention, saluted the ship, and heaped curses
upon the Union fleet for their timorous action.

The damage to Fort Sumter was starkly corroborated later by Captain
Gillis of the *Pocahontas*. The Confederates permitted him to visit the facility, and he found it to be "a complete wreck, the fire not yet extin-
guished, its battlements and tottering walls presented the appearance of an
old ruin."[22]

The garrison boarded the *Isabel* and was taken out to the fleet anchorage and to the waiting *Baltic*. Then that vessel, accompanied by the *Pawnee*
and the *Pocahontas*, sailed for New York. Arriving on April 17, Anderson
and his men were feted and celebrated as heroes. Anderson never recovered
physically from the traumatic, humiliating experience at Sumter, suffering
from ill health until his death on October 26, 1871. However, he did live
long enough to participate in the raising of the Union flag over Fort
Sumter on April 15, 1865, four years to the very day he left it in surrender.

As would be expected, repercussions over the fall of Fort Sumter came
thick and heavy, with justification from the South and understandable
anger from the North. Fox was furious. He maintained that the *Powhatan*
with her heavy guns, along with those of the *Pocahontas* and the five guns

of *Harriet Lane* and eight of *Pawnee,* would have created a formidable force with which to counter Confederate batteries in the harbor. The navy itself came under unfair, stinging criticism for its seeming reluctance to act decisively during the attack, while the army received all the accolades, leaving the navy with an image of impotence when it was needed most.

But in truth only the *Pawnee* could have navigated the channel at high tide, because of her shallow draft. But then she not only would have been under the many guns lining the shores, but would have presented a prime target for the batteries at Fort Moultrie, Fort Johnson, Battery Simkins, and the floating iron battery. It would have been a risky, almost suicidal venture indeed, with the possible destruction of one of the navy's prime warships in a lost cause. In this writer's opinion, the use of the *Pawnee* would have been futile.

In retrospect, one of the saddest aspects of Anderson's dilemma at Fort Sumter is the fact that he felt abandoned by his government and the navy. He mentioned this in an undated letter to an unknown friend (possibly Senator John Crittenden):

> Cut off from all intercourse with my government, I have been compelled to act accordingly to the dictates of my own judgement; and had the contingency, referred to, arise, I should, after prayerfully appealing to God, to teach me my duty, I have cheerfully and promptly performed it. My govt. had left me too much to myself—has not given me instructions, even when I have asked for them.[23]

As early as February 1861, Crittenden recognized Anderson's situation and his well-known concern that the move from Fort Moultrie to Fort Sumter and the subsequent loss of Sumter precipitated the secession of North Carolina. Crittenden assured Anderson that his move to Fort Sumter had no effect whatsoever in escalating states to secession, or in producing civil war, if that be the result.

The fall of Fort Sumter moved the Lincoln administration into high gear, with the president drafting a proclamation:

> Now therefore, I, Abraham Lincoln, President of the United States, in virtue of the power invested in me by the Constitution and the

laws, have thought to call forth, the militia of the several States of the Union, to the aggregate number of seventy-five thousand, in order to suppress said combinations, and to cause the laws to be duly executed.[24]

According to Lincoln, the people were urged to defend the Union and popular government in order to redress wrongs already long enough endured. The war of words had now ceased, and it was time for action. In actuality, both sides were unprepared for war. Only the Union had a navy of sorts, although it suffered from a shortage of fighting ships.

That shortage was the result of almost unbelievable negligence on the part of the Buchanan administration. Prior to the Civil War, in 1849, the navy was at its peak strength: 90 fighting ships in inventory, with 42 in active service not including store, supply, and receiving ships and supporting craft. These vessels constituted six squadrons based around the world, from the Mediterranean to the Pacific Ocean. Indeed, the United States was a world naval power.

The ascent to such status had been a long, hard climb for the navy, because the genesis of the U.S. Navy was in a group of privately owned ships usually armed with one or two guns. They were called into service and given letters of marque by the Continental Congress in March 1776. Their owners, aggressive men known as privateers, attacked British commerce vessels, robbed them, and captured them or in many cases destroyed them. As a result of privateer actions, numerous British ships were accosted on the high seas.

In spite of these energetic efforts, privateering was not enough to match the mighty squadrons of Great Britain, and warships were sorely needed to counter enemy naval strength. The Colonials would have to create some sort of viable navy. The Colonials, true to their powerful, patriotic aggressiveness, were ready to meet and solve the pressing problems. A navy, albeit a small one, somehow managed to come into being.

Historians are in agreement that the first American warship was the *Hannah,* a 78-ton schooner owned by John Glover of Marblehead, Massachusetts. She was taken into the fledgling Colonial navy on August 24, 1775, and armed with four 4-pounders with an army regiment as a crew.

Following the *Hannah,* many ships were built and crewed by the states themselves after Rhode Island adopted its famous Rhode Island Resolution on August 26, 1775, which became the first public proposal for an American fleet. The Continental navy itself consisted of four armed ships, and although they captured many prizes in British commerce ships, their light armament and shallow drafts rendered them inadequate as warships on the high seas to challenge British power.

On October 13, 1775, the Continental Congress approved a plan to outfit two vessels, *Andrea Doria* and *Cabot*. Then, on October 30, they authorized construction of two larger vessels, *Alfred* and *Columbus*. According to historian Nathan Miller, their mission was to be employed "for the protection and defense of the United Colonies."[25] That made it the official birth of the Continental navy. These ships were to fulfill the obligations of a true navy and were not to be used solely for privateering purposes, as were the ships built and sponsored by the states themselves. A seven-man Naval Committee was organized to create and nurture the navy.

After the Revolutionary War, the Congress decided that a navy was no longer needed, and it sold off the remaining ships of the fleet in 1785. But a limited resurrection began as a result of the struggle with Barbary pirates off the coast of Tripoli. These cruel sea robbers preyed on American ships and either killed or imprisoned the crews. To counter this threat, Congress voted to construct 6 warships, the names of which are legendary in the annals of naval history: *Constitution, Congress, President, Constellation, Chesapeake,* and *United States*.

By 1860, the existing fleet was impressive on paper only. The inventory consisted of a fleet of 61 ships and auxiliary craft that included 12 screw sloops, 8 frigates (including 5 sail frigates), and 3 ships of the line. Most of the serviceable vessels were on stations around the world, and those immediately available to the newly elected president, Lincoln, were in pitiful shape and included 11 ships at the Gosport Navy Yard at Norfolk, Virginia.

Most of these fine ships were being overhauled and at the time were not seaworthy for blockade duty, which was announced by the president on April 19, 1861. At Gosport, the U.S.S. *Merrimack* was being overhauled and awaiting a new engine, while a ship of the line, the U.S.S. *Delaware,* was nothing more than a floating hulk. Other vessels included two sister ships of the *Merrimack, Roanoke,* and *Colorado,* and some support vessels, all out of active service for repairs or overhaul. As for manpower, the prewar roster of personnel consisted of 1,200 officers and 64,000 men. After the secession, 259 officers resigned or were dismissed, many of them join-ing the Confederate cause.

Many of the officers were graduates of the U.S. Naval Academy at Annapolis, Maryland, which was founded as a result of the inadequacy of the practice of training officers at sea. Enter George Bancroft, historian and educator, who at the time was secretary of the navy. In 1845, he real-ized the need for a naval training facility that was the equivalent of the army's West Point Academy. Bancroft obtained permission from the Naval Board of Examiners to recommend the establishment of a naval school at the abandoned Fort Severn at Annapolis, along the banks of the Severn River.

With the appointment of Gideon Welles as its secretary, the navy came out of its doldrums and began to recapture its former glory and strength. Welles created the official organization of the navy that saw the establish-ment of the Bureau of Yards and Docks, the Bureau of Medicine and Sur-gery, the Bureau of Ordnance and Hydrography, the Bureau of Provisions and Clothing, the Bureau of Order and Detail, and the Bureau of Con-struction, Equipment and Repair. An assistant secretary of the navy was also added, with Gustavus Fox named the first holder of the post. Fox's appointment, in 1861, was a wise one indeed, because he soon became the right hand of Secretary Welles and remained indispensable throughout the war.

Lincoln's controversial blockade extended from South Carolina to Galveston, Texas. Then on April 27, after North Carolina and Virginia joined the new Confederacy, the blockade was extended northward to in-clude those states. The feeble United States Navy was now faced with cov-ering 3,500 miles of coastline, with 189 harbors and navigable rivers—a formidable task indeed. This set the stage for one of the most ignominious events in the history of the U.S. Navy.

CHAPTER TWO

A NAVY YARD FALLS

Gideon Welles had much to worry about after the fall of Fort Sumter. As secretary of the navy, he became vitally concerned about his shipyards and repair facilities. No one in the government doubted that the Confederates would attempt to capture one or more of them.

In 1861, there were eight major naval yards in the country: Boston, Massachusetts; Portsmouth, New Hampshire; Brooklyn, New York; Philadelphia, Pennsylvania; Washington, D.C.; Pensacola, Florida; Mare Island, California; and Gosport Navy Yard at Norfolk, Virginia. There were also several minor facilities in California, Tennessee, Illinois, and Baltimore, mostly for quick repair or coaling.

Two of these navy yards, Gosport and Pensacola, were the ones in immediate danger. A relief expedition had been sent to Pensacola, but it had failed, and the facility fell into Confederate hands on January 12, 1861. Welles' immediate concern was to protect the Gosport yard, and his worry was compounded by President Lincoln's reticence to do anything overt that would topple Virginia into the Confederate camp.[1]

Welles' concern was justified. Of all the navy yards, Gosport was perhaps the premier naval facility in the United States. The Royal Navy had used it in the 1700s for the purposes of "careening" their vessels, that is, placing them on their sides in order to scrape, clean, and repair the bottoms.[2]

In 1790, the U.S. Navy selected the yard as a site for building warships. Named after a town in England, Gosport Navy Yard had by the time of the Civil War been expanded to 108 acres, and it was the best-equipped in the country. It contained a vast array of machine shops, foundries, ropewalks, sail lofts, ship houses, and a large, impressive granite dry dock that had become the finest of its kind. The dock featured enormous "shears," or cranes, to lift heavy guns, iron sheeting, boilers, and engines. In addition, the yard contained magazines holding tons of gunpowder, shells, and a huge inventory of guns, including standard large-caliber Dahlgren guns, commonly labeled "soda-water bottles" because of their shape, invented by Midshipman John Dahlgren in the 1850s.[3] These guns became the mainstay ordnance of the U.S. Navy.

At the time of Lincoln's blockade announcement, 10 warships were at the yard for repair or overhaul. Among these were *Cumberland,* a 24-gun sloop; *Germantown,* 22 guns; *Plymouth,* 22 guns; *Pennsylvania* and *United States,* obsolete hulks; *Dolphin,* 4 guns; *Delaware,* 74 guns; *Raritan,* frigate; and the new steam frigate *Merrimack,* 40 guns.[4] Of these vessels, the *Merrimack* was one of the finest warships in the world and was the navy's pride and joy. Displacing 4,000 tons, 257 feet long, 51 feet wide, and armed with 40 guns, she was laid down in 1854 and launched and commissioned in 1859. At present, she was at Gosport "in ordinary," that is, still commissioned, but out of active service for engine overhaul. The *Cumberland,* incidentally, was the flagship of Commodore Garrett Pendergrast of the Home Squadron, and was in for repairs and provisioning. Some of the finest warships in U.S. service were immobilized at Gosport.

The yard was presently under the command of 68-year-old Commodore Charles S. McCauley, a career navy man who served during the War of 1812 and later commanded a ship in the East India Squadron. During his tenure as the commandant of the Washington Navy Yard, Welles tapped him for the position at Gosport. In truth, he was ill and unfit for duty, but the Navy Department nevertheless sent him to command the vital navy facility, an appointment that has been a mystery to historians ever since.[5]

As tensions grew around the navy yard, Secretary Welles was aware that something had to be done to protect the yard from the Virginians, who had been making threatening overtones. His problem was a lack of trained personnel at hand, many of them having been recruited for the *Powhatan* and the Pensacola flotilla. The situation was becoming very ominous.

On April 10, Welles sent a dispatch to McCauley in which he displayed some ambiguity, stating that in his view, the country must maintain vigilance and that the *Merrimack* must be prepared for a trip to the Philadelphia Navy Yard without alarming everyone concerned.[6]

In a dispatch dated April 10, Welles ordered Chief Engineer Benjamin Franklin Isherwood to Norfolk to assist McCauley and to give instructions to the old commodore in regard to the disposition of the warship.[7] But Welles kept interjecting such remarks as "Exercise your own judgement" and "It is desirable that there should be no steps taken to give needless alarm" into his dispatches to McCauley, all the while continually emphasizing the importance of removing the *Merrimack* from harm's way. With such contradictory messages, it is little wonder that the old and feeble McCauley was torn with indecision during the entire affair.

But Welles was not alone in his conciliatory tone as far as the Virginians were concerned. President Lincoln fervently hoped that Virginians would use common sense and avoid the rash move of secession.

At Gosport, Commander James Alden, who accompanied Isherwood, took command of the *Merrimack,* while the latter scurried to get the ship's engines back together and have her ready for sailing. Isherwood then called upon the yard's chief engineer, Robert Danby, and after passing on his instructions from Welles, they boarded the *Merrimack* only to find its machinery in disarray. "The engines," Isherwood reported, "were in wretched shape."[8] Then, with help from Danby and 44 coal heavers and firemen, the engine parts were assembled and put in working order in two days. After the *Merrimack* was coaled and had gotten her steam up, Isherwood called upon McCauley to report the fact. McCauley replied that he had not yet decided to move the vessel, citing an intelligence report that the Confederates had towed empty light ship hulls down the channel to be sunk as navigation obstructions. Isherwood maintained that the *Merrimack* could easily pass such obstructions.

For a time it looked as if the old commodore would acquiesce and permit the ship to leave. But then, in defiance of all logic, the recalcitrant McCauley ordered the ship's fires to be drawn; he had decided to keep the ship in the yard, put her guns aboard, and use her as a floating battery, lest the enemy storm the yard gates. Frustrated beyond measure, Isherwood returned to Washington to report the unfortunate turn of events to Welles.

During this comedy of errors at Gosport, the Confederates were not asleep at the switch. On April 18, soon after Virginia's secession, Governor John Letcher called out his militia and promptly dispatched Major General William Booth Taliferro to Norfolk. Immediately after taking command, he asked Letcher for 5,000 men with which to take the navy yard, but was promised only four companies of around 400–500 men, plus a few six-pounder field pieces to set up opposite the navy yard. However, these pop-gunlike weapons would be totally inadequate against the *Merrimack*'s guns. It was a token move on Taliferro's part, because General Beauregard was reluctant to send any artillery pieces from his command, and those Confederates at Norfolk were literally left to their own devices.[9]

Then on April 19, in a bold and decisive move, Taliferro marched his forces to Old Fort Norfolk, near the yard, and carried off 1,300 barrels of powder and other ordnance stores.[10] McCauley never entertained the idea of removing the powder from the old fort—another indication of his helplessness in the face of adversity.

Things were moving inexorably toward a climax, with the *Merrimack* unable to leave the yard and the growing but unsubstantiated belief that Confederate forces were massing outside the yard. Actually, this belief was the result of a clever ruse by the Virginians. They loaded a large group of citizens on a railroad car, backed it up out of sight and sound, then moved it in with the people waving and shouting at the top of their lungs. This ruse must have affected the already rattled McCauley, who thought they were enemy troops.

In the meantime, Welles had had enough of McCauley's intractability and decided to replace him with Commodore Hiram Paulding, career navy officer, veteran of the Lake Erie campaign during the War of 1812, and former head of the Bureau of Order and Detail. He was, in Welles' estimation, the right man for the job, and was given instructions to take all measures to save the yard and vessels.

Paulding and his staff boarded the 1,000-ton sloop *Pawnee* and sailed for Fort Monroe on the 19th. He arrived at the fort, quickly loaded troops of the 3rd Massachusetts Regiment, and set sail for the navy yard. He passed Craney Island without being challenged, moved up the Elizabeth River past the *Cumberland,* and docked at the yard.

What he saw shocked and dumbfounded him. McCauley had gone off the deep end. Pauling's dispatch to Welles is a perfect example of his self-contained contempt for the weak McCauley and his command:

> To my amazement and chagrin, I found that all the ships had been scuttled two or three hours before, and were fast sinking and could not be saved. This had been done by the officers in command to save the ships from falling into the hands of those who threatened the yard. Armed men were reported to be in the vicinity, but I did not see any, nor did I witness any hostile demonstration, except by a flag of truce that promised we should not be molested if we desist from destruction of public property. At this time, the frigate *Cumberland* was lying with her broadside bearing on the yard.[11]

The last sentence in Paulding's report reflects his puzzlement: Why would armed men in large numbers be outside the gates, as McCauley believed, with a powerful, heavy-gunned warship facing them in the river?[12]

Thoroughly convinced that an overwhelming force was ready to move in and further unnerved by the resignation of his junior officers, McCauley had finally lost whatever nerve he had had to begin with and had ordered the scuttling of the ships, including the splendid *Merrimack*. The seacocks on all the ships were opened, and they slowly groaned and creaked as they settled into the mud. McCauley and his remaining forces moved to the *Cumberland* to await further developments.[13]

Paulding was strapped. He had been ordered there to save the yard and the warships, only to find the yard defenseless and the ships sunk alongside the docks and in the basin. At first, he decided to defend the facility with his armed troops, plus the broadsides of the *Cumberland* and the *Pawnee*, until Welles could send reinforcements. But with lack of knowledge concerning any Confederate presence, and with time pressing on, Paulding fell victim to the uncertainty surrounding the yard. After all, he did not have intelligence that there were large armed Confederate forces moving in on Norfolk, but that very lack of intelligence must have spooked him, and he drew the conclusion that holding the yard, much less saving the ships, was a hopeless situation.

As Paulding later wrote, "[I]t was apparent that to save the *Cumberland*, it was necessary to tow her out with the *Pawnee* and it was equally apparent that the only way to keep the sunken vessels, the hulks, and government property from falling into the hands of people hostile to the government of the United States was to destroy it."[14]

He maintained that it was a "sad necessity, but an imperative duty" to destroy the navy yard, and he didn't for a moment hesitate in doing it. The grim task was assigned to Commander John Rodgers, Captain H. G. Wright, Commander Alden, and Commander Benjamin Sand along with 40 men and some members from the crew of the *Pawnee*. The force was divided into four work groups, each with a specific task. The first group had the horrendous job of preparing the yard's facilities for destruction. Nothing was to be spared: administrative offices, machine shops, barracks, storehouses, and all ship houses were to be razed. Turpentine, oil, tar, cotton waste, and other combustibles were distributed in and over structures, except, of course, for the huge slanted-roof "ship barns," which were prepared from within. Then slow matches were attached to the soaked edifices, to be lit upon signals from the *Cumberland*, which by now served as a command ship.[15]

Another group tackled the unpleasant task of preparing the ships for destruction. As with the buildings, the soldiers poured turpentine, oil, and tar over the decks and riggings. Anything combustible was placed all over the decks. But all this activity did not take place until the guns had been spiked and placed aboard the ships. Then lengths of powder, or match trains, were laid from the decks to the docks.

A great deal of trouble was encountered when the demolition parties tried to batter the guns, their trunnions, and their carriages into rubbish. The carriages were destroyed, but the guns themselves refused to give up their trunnions. Instead, railroad spikes were hammered down the priming vents, a move that was to prove disadvantageous to the Confederate crews later on. Other attempts to destroy machinery in the sheds also came to naught. Try as they would, men with sledgehammers failed to smash pumps, cylinders, and flywheels, among other items—which, ironically, was an indication of their fine workmanship. They finally decided to leave them, as without buildings they were useless.

The destruction of the magnificent granite dry dock fell to the lot of Rodgers and Wright. With 40 men from the Massachusetts regiment, they carried powder to the dock, then searched for the most advantageous place to place the explosives. They noticed that the dock had a pumping gallery running along the back of one of the sidewalls, entering from the level of the bottom near the entrance and terminating in the pump house on the opposite end of the dock. It was in this area that Rodgers and Wright agreed to place explosives for the maximum amount of damage. The pump house had two feet of water in it, so a platform was constructed upon which to place the 2,000 pounds of explosives. The powder was then connected to four slow match trains.[16]

Everything was now ready; virtually all personnel were sent to the *Cumberland,* with one crew member left to watch for a rocket signal to order the lighting of the match trains. When it came, Rodgers and Wright lit the trains and then headed for the landing, where a boat was waiting. But before they could reach the dock, flames from the burning buildings blocked their way. The awaiting boat had been driven off, so the two men were stranded and left to their own devices.

For a while it appeared the two officers would be trapped, but they made their way through a burning gateway, found a boat, and attempted to make their escape via the river, hoping to evade Confederate eyes along the way. However, they were detected, captured, and held as prisoners for a time. On April 24, Rodgers and Wright were paroled and allowed to return to Washington. In the meantime, the U.S.S. *Keystone State* arrived, and with the help of a steam tug saved from the yard, it escorted the *Cumberland,* flying the flag of Commodore Paulding, over the sunken hulks and safely to Washington. Lieutenant S. D. Trenchard, skipper of the *Keystone State,* summed up the entire Gosport affair as a "sad state of things!"[17]

And indeed things were in a bad state at Gosport. The Union navy left behind its most vital and strategic navy yard, ablaze from one end to the other. The fire was seen for miles around. In Norfolk, at Confederate Camp Pickett, Commander Robert N. Northen reported seeing the navy yard on fire along with three or four large ships.

"While we were enjoying the beautiful sight," he reported, "we were informed by one of the Smart Alecks that as soon as the Yankees finished burning Portsmouth they were coming over immediately to burn Norfolk and Petersburg soldiers out of their boots."[18]

THE Gosport Navy Yard fiasco has gone into history as a most ignominious and shameful affair for the U.S. Navy. Not only did the Union's planned total destruction of the $10,000,000 navy yard fail, but the Confederates reaped a harvest of arms and supplies. On April 20, Confederate vice president Stephens wired the president, Jefferson Davis, that they had recovered 2,500 guns (including guns of large caliber), artillery, some 3,000 barrels of powder, loaded shells, and tons of stores left undamaged.[19]

Most of the burned ship hulks were useless to the Confederates, but a careful examination of the *Merrimack* revealed that she could be saved—her superstructure had been burned to the waterline, leaving her hull and keel undamaged. Later the huge recovered treasury of guns, powder, and shells was dispersed to Confederate forts and strongholds, including Port Royal, Fernandina, New Orleans, and various points along the Mississippi. This ordnance would later be used to sink or damage Union ships.

There was much blame to go around, but the bulk of it was on the star-crossed McCauley. *Leslie's Illustrated Weekly,* a contemporary magazine, called it a "treasonable act—a $10 million dirge."[20] Taliferro labeled it as a "diabolical act," even though he fell heir to an impressive amount of arms, powder, and guns. Welles, in an understatement of the year, said it was a "most lamentable mistake."[21] Even President Lincoln was not without blame. His policy of not wanting to alienate those southern states that had not yet seceded played an important part in actions not taken sooner to save the all-important naval facility.

As expected, Paulding did not escape criticism. According to historian John Niven, had he used such forces at his command—two warships, plus 1,000 troops—Paulding could "have captured Norfolk and neighboring Portsmouth and opened up communications with Fort Monroe, raised the sunken vessels and held that area of Virginia securely in Union hands. A great opportunity had been presented to him, but he failed to appreciate it. He had handed the Confederacy weapons that it could not have produced on its own."[22]

This author agrees with Niven's assessment. The entire Gosport affair was an example of bumbling ineptness on the part of both McCauley and Paulding. It is easy to understand why McCauley acted as he did; he was clearly not in the physical and mental state to command the most vital navy yard in the country at a time when war clouds seemed to be gathering on the horizon. For a time, Paulding seemed to be in full command of the situation and was making proper decisions, issuing the orders needed to rectify the confusing and difficult circumstances into which he was plunged. But he soon lost his nerve and allowed the situation in the yard to deteriorate to the inevitable disaster it eventually became.

Of course, there was not a little timidity on the part of the Lincoln administration. The overall mind-set at the time was that of not causing "needless alarm" that might goad the citizens of Virginia into taking hostile action against the yard and against other Union forces in the area and, of course, making the much-dreaded move of secession.

The Gosport event, though shameful and the object of much fussing and stuttering, soon faded into history. Meanwhile, with Lincoln's proclamation of a blockade of Confederate ports, the Civil War entered a most vital chapter that eclipsed the navy yard fiasco. The blockade was the result of a series of events that occurred soon after Lincoln's election, the fall of Sumter, and the Gosport fiasco, the impetus of which was the secession of South Carolina from the Union.

CHAPTER THREE

THE BLOCKADE AND THE BLOCKADE-RUNNERS

The streets of Charleston, South Carolina, exploded into unbridled joy and enthusiasm on December 20, 1860, when citizens who had been witness to the debate in the state legislature, convening in St. Andrew's Hall, spilled into the streets to announce the good news: South Carolina had seceded from the Union, the state had been declared an "independent Commonwealth," and not one dissenting vote had been cast by the delegates. It was now official: The people of South Carolina were determined to have their freedom from the Union at any cost.[1]

The secession of South Carolina was a foregone conclusion as soon as Abraham Lincoln was elected president of the United States in February 1860. South Carolina had pledged secession when and if the Illinois lawyer was elected, and they did not hesitate for long after Lincoln had concluded his inaugural speech with an appeal for calm and common sense in the country:

> My countrymen, one and all, think calmly and well upon this whole subject. Nothing valuable can be lost by taking time. . . . In your hands, my dissatisfied fellow countrymen, and not mine, is the momentous issue of civil war. The government will not assail

you. You can have no conflict, without yourselves being the aggressors. You have no oath registered in Heaven to destroy the government, while I have the most solemn one to preserve and protect it.[2]

This speech became a clarion call to the South and, like lightning branching across the sky, *secession began,* first with South Carolina, followed by Mississippi, Florida, Alabama, Georgia, Louisiana, Texas, Virginia, Arkansas, and North Carolina. The situation that Lincoln feared most came into being on February 4, 1861, when delegates of states seceding after the fall of Fort Sumter met in Montgomery, Alabama, and formed the Confederate States of America. Soon after, the delegates created and signed the Provisional Confederate Congress Document based on the U.S. Constitution. Jefferson Davis was elected president of the Confederacy and was inaugurated on February 18, 1861.

At first glance, Davis was an ideal choice for president of the Confederacy. Born in Kentucky in 1808, he graduated from Transylvania University in Lexington and was appointed to West Point only a year after graduation.

Davis was 23rd out of a class of 39 at the academy, and joined a dragoon regiment of horsemen before rising to the rank of first lieutenant. He resigned his commission in 1835 to take up planting in the state of Mississippi. He returned to the military briefly during the Mexican War, during which he was wounded. He then entered the world of politics and was elected to the U.S. Senate, where he served until Mississippi seceded on January 9, 1861. It was from that post he resigned to become the president of the newly formed Confederacy.[3]

Davis was quick to respond to emergencies. When Lincoln issued a call for 75,000 members of states' militias on April 15, Davis issued letters of marque that legally gave ships' owners permission to capture enemy vessels on the high seas. Under these transactions, a ship owner had to post a bond of $5,000 if he employed up to 150 hands, but would pay $10,000 if he had more hands. In turn, the Confederate government would then pay 20 percent of the value of any enemy vessel of war boarded or destroyed, then in turn offered 8 percent of the value in bonds in the Confederacy.[4]

Reacting swiftly to Davis' action, Lincoln in turn issued a proclamation calling for a blockade of the Confederacy's coastline, ending with a stark warning to Davis:

And I hereby proclaim and declare that if any person, under the
pretended authority of said States, or any other pretense, shall mo-
lest a vessel of the United States, or the persons or cargo on board
of her, such person will be held amenable to the laws of the United
States for the prevention and punishment of piracy.[5]

The gauntlet had finally been thrown down to the Confederacy, but in
the beginning, all of this activity on the part of both antagonists was
mostly on paper. The Union was in no position to enforce a blockade of
over 3,500 miles of coastline with 189 harbors and navigable rivers, extending from Virginia around Florida and to the coast of Texas. It was a
formidable task that would take a large navy with adequate personnel.

However, looking at his available navy, Lincoln must have felt pangs of
disappointment. Out of a total of 90 ships in commission, only 42 were in
active service, with most of them scattered around the world at foreign
ports of call. As for personnel, only 1,200 officers were on active duty in
1860.[6] After the secession, 259 officers resigned or were dismissed; among
those defecting to the South were 16 captains, 34 commanders, 76 lieuten-
ants, and 111 midshipmen. As for enlisted personnel, the roster amounted
to a sparse 64,000 available men.

Lincoln, with his amazing penchant for picking the right people for his
cabinet, chose a newspaperman from Connecticut, Gideon Welles, a
Jackson Democrat, as secretary of the navy in March 1860. Welles plunged
into his job with amazing energy and vigor in spite of "a crucial state of
things" that existed in Washington at the time.[7] The U.S. Capitol was reeling from a sense of crisis, sparked by the defection of some southern-born
elected officials and some naval officers who elected to resign their commissions and to join the Confederacy.[8]

But the newly elected secretary of the navy had a job to do, and that
was to resurrect a torpid navy and build a powerful fleet to enforce the
blockade—a formidable task for any man, indeed.

The inspiration for the blockade came from the aged General Winfield
Scott, general of the army. Affectionately called "Old Fuss and Feathers" by
his admirers and critics alike, he managed to maintain a magnificent presence in spite of his age and poor health. Scott had distinguished himself in
the War of 1812, negotiated the end of the Blackhawk War, and further
distinguished himself in the Mexican War. At the outbreak of the Civil

War, he was overweight and racked by infirmities. Unable to mount a horse for reviews, he had to be lifted onto the animal, but his sharp mind was a valuable source of knowledge and wisdom for President Lincoln.[9]

His Anaconda Plan was the first viable military strategy offered to Lincoln since the war started. In its first phase, the plan called for a long, snakelike blockade winding down the East Coast, around Florida, and along the rim of the Gulf of Mexico to the Texas coastline. The second phase involved a force of 60,000 well-trained troops, backed by a fleet of gunboats, that would push down the Mississippi, taking enemy fortifications, until they reached the Gulf of Mexico, thus splitting the Confederacy in two.[10] This bifurcation would cut off the Confederate armies from the vast resources of manpower, agricultural products, and industrial material from the states of Arkansas, Louisiana, and Texas. According to Scott, this intolerable position would force the Confederacy to "come to terms," thus avoiding a prolonged conflict and minimizing casualties, because the general believed that sympathy for the secession and the South was not as strong as it was portended to be. Lincoln approved the plan; curiously, the second phase was never officially adopted.

After proclaiming the blockade, Lincoln had to step warily. By its very nature and as defined by law, a blockade is an action taken against one nation by another and not necessarily because of a civil war. The military-backed action would mean recognition of the Confederacy as a "nation." This would allow the Union to seize neutral ships attempting to run or break the blockade and those carrying contraband—actions the closing of a port would never accomplish.

The enforcing of the blockade would present a real problem to the Union. With its weakened navy, it would be hard pressed to steam off the coasts of the Confederacy with its vital ports of Charleston, Savannah, and Fernandina plus the Gulf ports of Mobile, New Orleans, and Galveston. Many prominent people in the North and many in the Congress doubted the wisdom of the blockade proclamation.

Long after the war and to the end of his life, Welles insisted that the closing of ports was the proper path to follow, in spite of the fact that a blockade implies military action in wartime.[11] But, dedicated as he was, he set about converting the blockade proclamation and Scott's Anaconda Plan into actuality. It was a formidable task, because at the beginning of hostilities, he had only 90 vessels of all classes in the navy's roster. Of major fleet units, 21 were languishing in ports and navy yards; 27 vessels were in ordinary at navy yards awaiting extensive repairs and overhauling, but fortunately not out of commission. Another 28 ships were on foreign stations and had to be recalled. The rest of the units were auxiliary vessels, many of which also were laid up at ports. The Home Squadron, active ships at hand, consisted of seven screw steamers, seven sailing frigates, and the sidewheel steamer *Powhatan*.

Welles' messages flew across the seas to call vessels home from their foreign stations. These vessels, which included seven powerful screw sloops plus those on hand from the Home Squadron, were all that could be used to enforce a blockade of over 3,000 miles of shoreline.[12]

Welles sent buyers scurrying to find any vessel that floated and upon which a gun could be placed. Recruitment programs were stepped up for the training of personnel to man the growing navy, and the Naval Academy shifted into high gear to produce officers to command these vessels.

Welles was fortunate to have Gustavus Vasa Fox as his assistant secretary of the navy. Fox was an experienced and most capable navy man—the sort that Welles needed to carry out his awesome task of enforcing the blockade.

Then, as his fleet expanded, Welles was forced to consider strategy that would require detailed knowledge of the coastline, from Virginia to Texas, that was scheduled to be blockaded. To accomplish this, he called upon the very able superintendent of the Coast Survey, Alexander Dallas Bache, who was more than able to help out. Bache, a cable engineer by trade, immediately suggested a Commission of Conference to study the hydrographic and meteorological aspects of the coastline for a comprehensive strategy to carry out the blockade program. Welles appointed a group, which later became known as the Blockade Board. Besides Bache, Welles chose as other members of the board Captain Samuel Francis du Pont of the U.S. Navy; Commander Charles Davis, also of the navy; Major J. G. Bernard of the U.S. Topographical Services; and Gustavus Fox, who chaired the board. The purpose of the board was to establish the blockade's effectiveness in dealing with blockade-runners, and to establish coaling and provisioning stations for the fleets.

The board wasted no time. Plunging into action, it made five reports to Secretary Welles during July and early August, all dealing with strategy for implementing the blockade.

Of the five reports, the third and fifth were the most important. The third dealt with the "Southern Atlantic Coast to be divided into two sections, one of which would extend from Cape Henry to Cape Romaine [now Roman], about 370 miles; the other from Cape Romaine to St. Augustine, about 220 miles." The final report extended the blockade from Virginia to the coast of Texas. As a result of these reports, the Navy Department divided the Atlantic fleet into two sections: the North Atlantic Blockading Squadron, covering the coast from Virginia to Fort Fisher in North Carolina; the South Atlantic Blockading Squadron, covering Fort Sumter to Key West; the East Gulf Blockading Squadron, covering Key West to New Orleans; and the West Gulf Blockading Squadron, covering New Orleans to Galveston and Brownsville on the Texas coast.[13]

Faced with a growing Union navy, and having no navy of their own, the Confederates were forced to employ other means at hand to circumvent the expanding blockade threatening the influx of food and supplies for their armies and populace, items that they had no means to garner or manufacture. Therefore, as previously noted, the Confederacy turned to the use of privateers, who were daring adventurers willing to risk their necks for profits by seizing Union vessels of commerce on the high seas.

On May 6, 1861, the Confederate Congress supported Jefferson Davis' proclamation allowing letters of marque to shipowners. Under this proclamation, privateering flourished for a time, but as the Union navy tightened the blockade, privateering became more and more a risky business. The privateers soon found it exceedingly difficult to evade the blockading ships and to bring their cargoes safely into southern ports.[14]

One of the objectives of the Confederacy's blockade-running program was centered on its most important crop product, cotton. This objective became labeled with the slogan "Cotton is king," and it was the center of southern attention for a long time during the Civil War. The idea was to influence Great Britain, whose mills were prime customers for cotton crops, to come to the Confederacy's aid with naval power and war materiel to counter the Union blockade.

The British, of course, upon the wise counsel of the queen and her advisor Prime Minister Lord Palmerston, chose to take a neutral course; it is believed that they did not want to risk a confrontation with the growing might of the Federal navy. The energetic efforts on the part of Union diplomats, plus the Union's iron resolve to prosecute the war, all contributed to

England's reticence. Some historians maintain that bumper crops of cotton in the 1850s and early 1860s produced a glut of cotton in England and therefore doomed the South's efforts to influence that country, although it took until 1863 for such efforts to end.[15] The British never made a move to counter the Union blockade by using their naval power.

The Confederacy's ability to maintain a blockade-running program also depended on having the right vessels to do the work. At first, commercial craft were modified for the job and were moderately successful, but as time went on, the need for speedy craft became apparent. All the attributes of a successful blockade-runner involved the elements of high speed, shallow draft, seaworthiness, and low silhouette in order to evade Union ships and slip into harbors at night or up the many navigable rivers along the Atlantic and Gulf coasts.[16]

With their smaller size and limited capabilities, the blockade-runners would not be able to make transatlantic voyages, so the Confederates worked out a plan whereby these smaller vessels would use such nearby bases as the Bahamas, Bermuda, Havana, and Matamoros in Mexico. At these points, cargoes were to be loaded on oceangoing vessels to make the trips overseas to Great Britain or to the European continent. The situation would be reversed with incoming cargoes. By this method the larger oceangoing vessels would elude capture.

Unfortunately, the Confederates had no shipyards with which to build or even modify existing craft to these specifications. The recently acquired Gosport yard was still out of commission as a viable building and repair facility. Other sources had to be considered, and the Confederacy assigned this problem the highest priority.

To obtain these specialized craft, the Confederates turned to England and Scotland. Buyers were dispatched to Great Britain with specifications in hand. The vessels launched from British yards had long, slender hulls with rounded forecastles for plowing through angry seas. The masts were thin, and in some cases funnels were on hinges for lowering to deck level to maintain low silhouettes. The fuel picked for these vessels was anthracite coal, which burned with a minimum of smoke. The hulls of these remarkable craft were painted gray, making them difficult to spot in fog and cloudy weather, as well as at night.[17] Some prominent names of these fine vessels included *Hope,* 1,788 tons; *Peterhoff,* 1,000 tons; and *Beauregard,* tonnage unknown.

Besides the design of the vessels, unique sailing tricks were devised by blockade-runners to evade Union ships, such as sailing in the dark of the moon; in fog, rain, and snow squalls; and at high tide. In some cases, the runners carried the same signal rockets as the Union ships. These rockets would be fired in the air, sending Federal ships running off on another course and allowing the Confederate ship to slip away. In order to make use of all bottom space, cargo was packed as tightly as possible in the holds, and some was stored on deck. In many cases, luxury cargo was even stored in the captain's cabin. There was no crew comfort to be found on a blockade-runner, and in many cases, crew members were forced to sleep on top of tarp-covered containers on deck or in the holds.

The efforts of blockade-runners, especially during the early days of the Civil War, were rather impressive, and it is a recognized fact that were it not for these brave and resourceful men, the Confederacy would have collapsed much earlier.

Of course, blockade-running was also a profitable venture. In a case that was not unusual, the officers and crew of one blockade-runner made a profit of around $92,000 on a single voyage, with the captain taking $5,000 of this amount.

It is not easy to determine the amount of supplies, both civilian and military, brought into the Confederacy by blockade-runners through Wilmington and Charleston. However, a special report from the Confederate secretary of the treasury, Christopher G. Memminger, revealed that between October and December of 1864, 3,500,000 pounds of meat, 1,507,000 pounds of lead, 1,933,000 pounds of saltpeter, 452,000 pairs of shoes, 542,000 pounds of coffee, 69,000 rifles, 2,639 packages of medicine, 43 cannon, and a "very large quantity of other articles" came into the Confederacy this way.[18]

Of course, as the blockade tightened, the blockade-running system was forced to change tactics. Instead of one vessel making a complete run from Europe to Southern ports, she would instead enter the Bahamas and distribute her cargo to smaller vessels, which in turn would make the voyages to the ports.

As would be expected, prices soared in the South as the blockade became more effective. For example, a ton of salt was worth $6.50 in the Bahamas but would bring $1,700 in the South; coffee, selling for $249 per ton in the Bahamas, would fetch $5,500 in the South. It was indeed a

profitable venture, albeit very risky. But, unquestionably, this commerce was
what permitted the Confederacy to continue operations on the home front
and in the field—for a time, that is. By the end of the war, 1,149 blockade-
runners (210 of which were steamers) had been captured, and 355 had
been destroyed. The value of these ships and their cargoes was estimated at
$35,000,000.

At first the Confederate government refused to be directly involved with
blockade-running, but because many private ship owners refused to carry
items such as steel, copper, and munitions in their holds, government-
sponsored blockade-runners were launched. Many of these vessels, crewed
by naval officers and men, were highly successful because of their knowledge and experience.[19]

One of the most famous—or infamous—runners was the *Little Hattie,*
a fast steamer skippered by Captain H. S. Lebby. This vessel steamed in
and out of Charleston more times than any other, but *Hattie's* real claim to
fame was the way she had managed to elude the blockade and slip into
Wilmington in broad daylight in October 1864. The captain flew every
flag on board to confuse the Federals; his crew threw everything combustible, including bacon, into the boilers to raise steam pressure. In spite
of heavy shelling by the Union ships, she did manage to enter the Cape
Fear River and berth under the protection of the guns at Fort Fisher. Many
attempts were made by the vengeful Union fleet to capture the *Hattie,* but
she eluded them and brought in valuable munitions for the Confederate
armies. The *Hattie* survived the war, and after hostilities ended she was
found tied up at a pier in Nassau, as if still awaiting cargo.[20]

Perhaps the greatest blockade-runner loss to the Confederacy was *Modern Greece,* a 1,000-ton schooner-rigged propeller steamer. Loaded with
badly needed supplies for the Confederate armies, she was run aground by
Federal warships on the Cape Fear River in June 1862. Most of her cargo
of guns, powder, and clothing was not salvageable, even though the guns of
Fort Fisher kept Union ships at a distance. It was not until 1962 that divers
found the wreck and discovered her huge cargo of British rifles, cannon
projectiles, lead and tin ingots, bullets, eating utensils, Bowie knives, car-
penter tools, medical kits, and leather shoes. Her badly corroded bones still
lie off Fort Fisher, along with many other luckless blockade-runner vessels
sunk in their attempts to evade the blockade.[21]

Meanwhile, the Union navy, determined to enforce the blockade, forged ahead at full steam. Welles not only pulled in warships from their foreign stations but managed to get the many ships laid up in navy yards repaired quickly. Vessels of all sizes and descriptions were obtained and pressed into service: tugs, merchantmen, yachts, scows, and even double-ended ferry boats, whose ability to go forward or backward without turning around proved to be invaluable in narrow rivers.

Then the indefatigable navy secretary embarked on a massive shipbuilding program, which included 23 gunboats labeled as "ninety-day wonders." This shipbuilding feat remarkably foreshadowed the Liberty ship program early in World War II, during which the magnate Henry Kaiser built and launched vessels of around 10,000 tons in an average construction time of 42 days.

Welles' construction program involved small-screw vessels capable of high speeds and armed with rifled guns. They were ideally suited for operating on the bays, inlets, and rivers along the East Coast. Each of these ships cost between $80,000 and $103,000.[22] In less than six months' time, Welles and Fox had built or procured vessels for a respectable navy of over 100 steam-powered vessels, all well armed and crewed. More and more ships were added as time went on. By the end of September 1861, 264 vessels—in aggregate, 218,000 tons—were in commission in the Union navy. And by December, manpower for this fleet had risen to over 20,000.[23] This massive shipbuilding undertaking had a twofold purpose: to provide ships for the blockade squadrons, and to show European powers— especially Great Britain and France—that the blockade was not one on paper only and that the Union was prepared to meet any country contemplating naval interference with the blockade or supplying the Confederacy with vital war materiel.

In the meantime, the Confederacy was having a problem of its own— that of building a navy to counter the growing might of the North. President Davis was prepared to do something about it.

CHAPTER FOUR

A NEW NAVY IS BORN

Jefferson Davis was faced with the most momentous decisions of his life.

After the Provisional Confederate Congress, made up of delegates from six seceded states of the South, met in Montgomery, Alabama, and elected him president, he had the difficult task of picking a cabinet. These men had to be carefully chosen; each must hail from a different walk of life, and each must be a slaveholder. He wrote:

> Unencumbered by any other consideration than the public welfare, having no friends to reward or enemies to punish, it resulted that not one of those who formed my first cabinet had born to me the relation of close personal friendship, or had political claims upon me; indeed, with two of them I had no previous acquaintance.[1]

The cabinet consisted of Robert Toombs, secretary of state; Leroy Walker, secretary of war; Judah P. Benjamin, attorney general; Christopher G. Memminger, treasury secretary; John H. Reagan, postmaster general; and Stephen R. Mallory, secretary of the navy. The latter personage was a most vital choice.

Stephen Mallory's background well suited him for the all-important job of creating a navy for the young Confederacy. He was a native of British Trinidad, having been born there in 1813 and later raised in Key West, Florida. As a young man, Mallory spent his spare time studying law, and he was admitted to the bar in 1840. While serving as inspector of customs at Key West, he came to the attention of President Polk, who appointed him collector of customs.

His military experiences included service in the Seminole War, from 1835 to 1843. Then in 1851, he was elected to the U.S. Senate, where he served his state efficiently and honorably as a committee member of naval affairs.

He resigned from the Senate in 1861, after his home state seceded from the Union, and swiftly joined the Confederacy with hopes of obtaining a naval appointment because of his vast experience with the navy. Davis had similar thoughts and, fully aware of Mallory's experience in U.S. naval affairs, appointed him secretary of the Confederate navy on February 20, 1861. It was a most fortunate choice indeed, because of the Confederacy's need for a viable navy with which to oppose the Union blockade.[2]

Mallory's first job was to organize his department. Pursuant to his tenure in the United States Navy Department, he modeled his new department after it to include the Bureau of Order and Detail, the Bureau of Ordnance and Hydrography, the Bureau of Medicine and Surgery, and the Bureau of Provisions and Clothing. The only department missing from Mallory's department was a Bureau of Yards and Docks, which was a segment of the U.S. Navy Department.[3]

A career navy man, Commodore Samuel Barron, headed the important Bureau of Orders and Detail. This department handled all matters concerning the personnel of the navy, officers and men, and was responsible for filling ship complements, rank and promotions, courts-martial, and courts of inquiry, plus the recruiting service.

Following the guidelines of the Provisional Confederate Congress, the personnel of the new navy were to include 3 admirals, 3 vice admirals, 3 rear admirals, 6 commodores, 20 captains, and 20 commanders, plus 356 other ratings. Furthermore, the government conferred commissions upon officers in accordance with their relative ranks in the U.S. Navy.[4]

With that core of officers at hand, Mallory was well aware that he had no ships, and that became a priority of his office. The only vessels available at the secession were the 1,000-ton *Fulton,* a decommisioned sloop of war at Pensacola; the burned-out hulks at the Gosport Navy Yard; six revenue cutters; three coastal survey ships; and a few tugs—a pitiful lot of floating hardware, to be sure, but it was a start.[5]

Armed with his vast knowledge of naval affairs, Mallory realized that the South could not match the North in vessels of war and shipbuilding capabilities. He concentrated instead on breaking the blockade; however, he kept the option open concerning ironclad warships, an idea of which he had been aware for some time. In fact, he wrote to the Provisional Confederate Congress:

> I entered upon the duty of procuring vessels for the navy of the Confederate States. Experienced and judicious naval officers and civilians have been actively engaged in the ports of the United States, Canada, and the Confederate States in search of steamers suitable for, or which might be readily converted to, war purposes and offers to build vessels have been received from leading naval contractors. The expediency and policy of purchasing rather than building vessels at this time are obvious.[6]

He went on to estimate the cost of building ships, to compare with those of the United States Navy, to be from $850,000 to $1,200,000, which was a heavy sum of money in those days. If the funds were available, ships certainly could be constructed within the Confederate states, but delays would of necessity be encountered due to the lack of skilled workmen.

Mallory's eye was constantly on the "possession of an iron-armored ship as a matter of first necessity." To him, it was the Confederacy's only hope of countering the powerful steam frigates that were the mainstay of the U.S. Navy. The hard, cold necessities of any shipbuilding program would entail construction facilities, foundries, rolling mills, and materiel manufacturing sources, which were facilities the South sorely lacked. The resourceful Mallory cast around for foundries to roll plating and to forge cannon for his navy; however, he had only a handful of established firms with which to deal.

The largest of these foundries was the Tredegar Iron Works in Richmond. This venerable old firm was the only major foundry and rolling mill in the Confederacy. The company had produced cannon, carriages, locomotives, and boilers for the U.S. government; after Virginia's secession, it became the South's major arsenal, with a workforce of over 2,500. Tredegar had produced the major portion of the Confederacy's armor, plating, guns, and cables, as well as heavy machinery for powder mills. The company also operated a sawmill, a firebrick factory, a tannery, and even a shoe factory, plus nine canal boats along with coal mines and blast furnaces, for a secure supply of raw materials. Other large foundries were located and/or established in Tennessee, Atlanta, and New Orleans, and there were 10 smaller firms in the Confederacy. Much hinged on this lack of heavy industry with which to build Mallory's navy, as opposed to the awesome industrial strength of the North and its vast pool of skilled workmen.

At the Selma works, naval ordnance was the primary product, and the facility soon bristled with activity, providing naval guns throughout the war. Between June 1863 and April 1864, nearly 200 guns were cast, most being 6.4-inch and 7-inch Brooke rifles.[7] One of Mallory's engineers established a powder mill in Virginia, plus a few plants for making gun carriages and percussion caps.

In spite of a large core of officers, a real problem for Mallory was the availability of enlisted men. Until recruiting and training facilities were established, it was the custom to obtain crewmen from alternative sources, such as seamen from commercial vessels. But this was not enough, so the Confederate congress provided that "all persons serving in the land forces of the Confederate States who shall desire to be transferred to the naval service, and whose transfer as seamen or ordinary seamen shall be applied for by the Secretary of the Navy, shall be transferred to the naval service."[8] Therefore, the first enlisted personnel to man the new navy vessels of the Confederacy were transferred from the army, although many men were picked from various other trades, such as steamfitters, carpenters, and lumbermen.

Unlike the Union navy, the Confederate navy never had a viable training program for its enlisted men. The average pay for this rate was $283 per year. Therefore, many commands were wanting for trained seamen.

The officers, on the other hand, were plentiful, and because there were not enough billets for them, many were sent to various batteries around the states, particularly on the East Coast, which were set up to provide protection for blockade-runners and to challenge any Union ships that dared to sail near. Others held desk jobs in their states, and others were lucky enough to have billets in the fledgling navy that was slowly taking place.[9]

Confederate navy officers were of the same rank as their counterparts in the Union navy, but the uniforms had to be changed to steel gray lined with black silk serge and decorated with gold and brass buttons. There were minor variations in insignias on the uniforms; otherwise they were much the same as their adversaries'. Yearly salaries for the officers ranged from $800 for passed midshipmen to $6,000 for an admiral.

It soon became apparent that an academy for training officers had to be established. The first move was made in December 1861 when the Confederate congress passed a bill authorizing a source for the education of midshipmen. In April 1862, the training facility became a reality when 106 acting midshipmen were appointed to attend the new Confederate Naval Academy, which was a school ship established on the C.S.S. *Patrick Henry*, a 1,000-ton, brigantine-rigged gunboat that had been damaged in Hampton Roads during the *Monitor/Merrimack* battle. The ship was moored at Drewry's Bluff on the James River and remained there for almost the duration of the war.[10]

Lieutenant William H. Parker was the first superintendent of the academy. Classes began in October 1862 with only fifty midshipmen, because of the limitations of space on the school ship. The curriculum was similar to that of the U.S. Naval Academy, with the exception of one aspect: combat experience. Many times the midshipmen were called upon to man artillery at shore batteries in answer to Union fire directed at their facility. A much heavier emphasis upon seamanship was also a hallmark of the academy.[11]

Mallory was proud of this facility, so in October 1863, he was moved to write to President Davis that the officers connected with the school were "able and zealous, and the satisfactory progress already made by the several classes gives assurance that the navy may look to this school for well-instructed and skillful officers."[12] Later, he communicated to Davis that naval education and training lay at the foundation of naval success, and that the power that neglected this fact of life would, when the battle was fought, find that its ships, no matter how formidable, were "but built for a more thoroughly trained and educated navy." By 1863, there were 693 officers and 2,200 enlisted men in the Confederate navy.

But a fleet of ships comparable to the quality and efficiency of these personnel was never built. Mallory and his staff were constantly hampered by a shortage of skilled workmen, engineers, and major construction and repair facilities with dry docks, plus heavy-duty foundries for ordnance and mills for gunpowder.

With only a handful of viable fighting ships on hand, Mallory turned to Europe for warships, particularly to shipyards in England and Scotland. On May 9, 1861, he called upon one James D. Bulloch of Montgomery, Alabama, to proceed to England for the purpose of purchasing or having built six steam-propelled vessels that must be enabled to keep to the sea and to make extended cruises; ships that were fast under both steam and canvas and possessed the ability to evade blockading ships.

In addition to the ships, Bulloch was to obtain Armstrong breech-loading rifles for them, plus a vast supply of supplies from ammunition to clothing and shoes for the crews. On May 10, Bulloch left for England with an appropriation of $1,000,000 for the purchase of ships, ordnance, and ammunition.

By the end of June, Bulloch had contracted with a shipbuilder at Liverpool, Birkinhead Iron Works, owned by John Laird, to construct two vessels: one 210 feet long and displacing 1,000 tons, the other 185 feet long and 695 tons. While doing his job, Bulloch ran into continued opposition from Charles F. Adams, the U.S. minister to Britain, who had been appointed by President Lincoln in 1860 and was well respected by the British government. Adams made it clear to Britain that recognition of the Confederacy, or the building of ships for its use, would be considered a hostile act by the United States, and that it would jeopardize England's neutrality.[13] It soon became apparent that the queen and her advisors listened carefully to him.

Ignoring all this opposition, Bulloch forged ahead with his plans for building the two warships, and toiled day and night at the Liverpool shipyard while they were being built.

The astute Bulloch possessed admirable credentials from his tenure in the U.S. Navy. He became a midshipman in 1839 and was promoted to lieutenant in 1853. When his home state of Georgia seceded, he commanded several commercial mail ships for the government for a time. He joined the Confederacy on January 19, 1861, where Davis recognized his expertise and appointed him civilian purchasing agent for the Confederate navy.[14]

The two vessels, later launched and delivered to the Confederacy, were the *Florida* and the *Alabama,* both destined to become world famous, along with their remarkable commanders, and for chalking up many successful exploits, as cruisers. We shall meet up with them in a later chapter.

Not content with the British endeavors, Mallory launched a program for building a navy with whatever was at hand. At the secession, Southern states confiscated all vessels within their harbors. These makeshift vessels were equipped with guns, and this "Mosquito Fleet" was in action long before the Confederate navy was created. No complete record of them has ever been found, because a lot of them were owned by the states in which they were confiscated; consequently, they were loaned out to various causes and often changed ownership. Some managed to capture a few Yankee ships.[15]

Mallory did manage to build a respectable fleet in the Mississippi theater of action, which included ironclad men-of-war. This action was taken in order to match the Union's ironclad building program at St. Louis, Missouri, and Mound City, Illinois, during 1861 and 1862, in which seven such vessels were built in record time by the industrialist James Eads and named after cities along the Mississippi and Ohio rivers: *Carondelet, St. Louis, Pittsburgh, Cairo, Mound City, Louisville,* and *Cincinnati.* Each displaced around 500 tons and was 175 feet long with a 50-foot beam and a draft of 9 feet. Their armament usually ran around 13 guns, and their casemate consisted of 2½-inch-thick charcoal iron. In addition to these "turtles," as they were euphemistically called, three 500-ton timberclads were commissioned; these were river steamers that were fitted with five-inch-thick oak bulwarks and armed with eight guns. Later, a 633-ton ironclad gunboat, the *Benton,* constructed from a catamaran-hulled river snagboat, was commissioned and became the most powerful river gunboat afloat, bristling with 16 guns.[16]

Meanwhile, in spite of interdepartmental bickering, the Confederate River Defense Fleet began to take form, with a motley group of vessels, mostly from New Orleans shipyards and some commercial vessels. Those yards were located in the suburbs of Algiers, across the river from New Orleans, and consisted of eight dry docks with construction, docking, and adequate maintenance facilities for handling the various types of ships built in them.

The River Defense Fleet finally consisted of the following ships: *McRae,* eight guns, 297 tons, a former bark-rigged Mexican navy ship; the side-wheeler *Jackson,* 297 tons, two guns; *Governor Moore,* a 1,215-ton cotton-clad ram; and the *General Quitman,* 945 tons, two guns. In addition, a private group in no way connected to the military but with Confederate sympathies purchased a tugboat and converted her to an ironclad at the Algiers shipyard. The turtlelike craft displaced 387 tons and was 143 feet long with a 36-foot beam and a draft of 12 feet. The concave hull was plated with 1½-inch iron and projected only 2 feet 6 inches above the water. Its armament consisted of two guns, a 64-pounder and a 32-pounder. The strange vessel, commissioned the *Manassas,* had the appearance of a giant egg—its shape was designed to deflect cannon balls.[17]

The *Manassas* was later commandeered into the Confederate navy and pressed into service with the River Defense Fleet. She was used to challenge Admiral Farragut's fleet on its attempt to pass Forts Jackson and St. Philip in order to capture New Orleans in April 1862. Because of poor engines and a lack of trained crew members, the vessel suffered an ignominious fate by being crippled and forced to beach, and she was used thereafter as a floating artillery platform. She was later destroyed by the Confederates after Farragut breached the forts.[18] Her only positive act was to create a lot of apprehension in the Union navy as to her potential.

The greatest hopes of the River Defense Fleet rested on the building of two huge ironclad rams, *Mississippi* and *Louisiana,* under construction at Jefferson City, north of New Orleans, by two entrepreneurs, Asa and Nelson Tift. The *Mississippi* displaced 1,400 tons and was 260 feet long with a 58-foot beam and a 12-foot draft. Her armor was three-inch charcoal-iron plating and she was to be armed with 20 guns, including two 7-inch rifles. The ram was launched on April 19, 1862, but never completed and armed. She was later burned to prevent her being captured. The larger *Louisiana* was to have displaced 1,400 tons, with a 264-foot length and a 62-foot beam, powered by two screws and two centerline paddle-wheels working in tandem. Her armament was to have been 16 guns, including two 7-inch rifles. She was never launched, having been towed incomplete to Fort Jackson and used as a floating artillery platform, but she was destroyed later to prevent capture. No doubt if she, like her sister, had been launched and outfitted, the Confederate navy would have been able to pose a serious threat to Farragut's wooden-ship fleet.[19] But instead they were typical of the makeshift vessels that would plague the Confederacy.

At Memphis, two additional ironclads were being built: *Tennessee* and *Arkansas*. Of these two, *Arkansas,* with eight guns, was towed to a Yazoo, Mississippi, shipyard, where she was completed.[20] Her sister, *Tennessee,* was burned on the stocks when the Federal fleet approached to assault Memphis.

On the East Coast, other ironclads were under construction, the star of which was to be the *Virginia* (or *Merrimack,* as many insist on calling her, despite the name given her by the Confederacy), being rebuilt at Gosport Navy Yard. At Savannah, the 1,000-ton *Atlanta* was under construction and later launched; two *Albemarle*-class ironclads were being built at North Carolina. Six other vessels were also under construction at Charleston, Wilmington, and Savannah. There were two vessels on the stocks at Selma, Alabama, one at Columbus, Georgia, and one at Richmond. Other vessels, including two on a river north of Mobile, were either destroyed on the stocks or sunk by Union troops.[21] Some of Mallory's vessels, however, later were to blaze across the pages of naval history.

Mallory's problems with his shipbuilding program were compounded not only by shortages of skilled personnel but also by second-rate materials. There was plenty of lumber available in the vast forests of the southern states, but iron was another matter. In August 1862, Mallory wrote to President Davis: "A want of iron is severely felt throughout the Confederacy, and the means of increasing its production demand, in my judgement, the prompt concern of the congress. The government has outstanding contracts amounting to millions of dollars, but the iron is not forthcoming to increase the public demands."[22] Scrap iron was collected from streetcar tracks and old rail lines. However, first-rate engines presented another problem. Many were removed from old steamers of all descriptions, and even some from sunken wrecks, but most were too weak and sluggish to propel the heavy ironclads.

In creating his navy, Mallory copied the Union's system of dividing its fleets into geographical commands, all of which were led by the rank of captains. There were the James River Squadron, North Carolina Squadron,

Charleston Squadron, Savannah River Squadron, Mobile Bay Squadron, Mississippi River Squadron, Galveston Squadron, and Red River Squadron. These flotillas had the difficult task of guarding rivers and harbors and, whenever possible, attempting to break the Federal blockade, usually by a series of hit-and-run tactics.

Obviously, the Confederate navy's weakness lay in its inability to break the blockade, which would have been difficult even with a sizeable navy. As historian Raimondo Luraghi pointed out, Mallory quickly learned about the true, immediate, and deadly danger represented by U.S. amphibious operations, which were threatening the South.[23] From then on, the highly astute secretary concentrated on other matters, such as making the Confederacy safe from the threat of seaborne invasion by Union forces, but he was hampered by the lack of a navy strong enough to repel any amphibious incursions into Confederate space along the Atlantic seacoast, where such operations would be launched.

Meanwhile, Union seapower was growing at a staggering rate, and the task of making the Confederacy safe was getting more and more difficult as the days, weeks, and months passed. And this fact was not lost on the people in the Confederacy, even beyond those high in the military. Indeed, a clerk in the war offices of the Confederacy jotted this note in his diary: "The most gigantic naval preparations have been made by the enemy . . . they are building great numbers of gunboats, some of them iron-clad, both for the coast and for the Western rivers. If they get possession of the Mississippi River, it will be a sad day for the Confederacy."[24]

Mallory did a remarkable job considering what he had to work with. His small navy, although no match for the Union, managed to hold open some ports through which Confederate supplies flowed. It also managed to give its Union counterpart a lot of headaches; in some cases, it sank and/or damaged Union ships with ingenious methods, such as submersibles and underwater mines (called torpedoes at the time). But even these triumphs could not, in the final analysis, meet the growing naval might of the North.

Though Mallory was hampered by not having a viable navy, some critics have pointed out that whatever vessels he did manage to equip and arm were not only weakened by poor workmanship and materials but also were widely scattered, unlike the Federal navy. It is true that while Mallory did manage some successes with his ships, as a strategic whole, his efforts were fruitless. His tenure could be summed up in a statement he issued to the captains of two gunboats on the eve of Savannah's evacuation: "If fall they must, let them show neither weakness of submission nor of self-destruction, but inflict a blow that will relieve defeat from discredit."[25]

Meanwhile, the Federal navy was preparing a series of campaigns that would tax Mallory's little navy to the utmost.

CHAPTER FIVE

THE FIRST AMPHIBIOUS OPERATIONS, PART 1: CAPE HATTERAS

The fiasco at the Second Battle of Bull Run jolted the Union and made them realize that they were facing a long and bitter war. It also convinced them that they needed a spectacular victory. Welles persuaded the War Department that the first of a series of amphibious operations must be launched. The first objective was the Cape Hatteras Inlet.

Resembling a giant stringless bow, the Outer Banks of the coast of North Carolina begins at the north at the mouth of Chesapeake Bay and ends at Cape Lookout to the south. It consists of a string of windswept sand islets wide enough to sustain a few hardy folk who made their living gathering oysters and salvaging from wrecked ships driven ashore by the fierce Atlantic storms in this region. During the Civil War, it was considered an unlovely string of pearls and consequently shunned by inland residents.

But the Outer Banks were of strategic importance to the Confederacy. The Outer Banks comprised a shield protecting the important waterways of Pamlico Sound to the south and Albemarle Sound to the north. Through these waterways moved a great deal of commerce to the people of North Carolina and to the Confederate armies. Blockade raiders brought goods from Europe and other places through Hatteras Inlet, which a powerful storm had opened in 1847. But more important, the inlet allowed Confederate raiders a way to prey on Union ocean shipping. In fact, seaborne raiders popped in and out with impunity. Rumors were rampant that the Confederacy was building or preparing more raiders to be protected by the Outer Banks and, in addition, was building two forts on the cape just north of the inlet.[1]

The strategic importance of this site was emphasized in a dispatch from Welles to Flag Officer Silas Horton Stringham, on August 23, 1861: "There is no portion of the coast which you are guarding [Hatteras] that requires more vigilance or well-directed efforts and demonstrations would be more highly appreciated by the Government and country than North Carolina which has been the results of pirates and their abettors."[2]

Welles was merely echoing the opinion of the Advisory Committee (sometimes called the Blockade Strategy Board) in its report of July 16, 1861, in which the members pointed out that this region, with its numerous inlets and rivers, was "vastly important to the Rebels while they are debarred the use of the entrance to the Chesapeake but for this sterile or half-drowned shores of North Carolina might be neglected."[3]

One of the ingenious Confederate methods involved collaboration with unscrupulous New England shippers who would make a pretense of shipping goods to and from the West Indies. On the outbound voyage, the vessels were "captured" by Confederate warships and their cargoes taken as "contraband goods"; then the ships were let off and allowed to continue to their original destination. After taking on goods in the West Indies, they sailed back up the North Carolina coast, where they were once more "captured" and their cargoes confiscated. Then they were again released and allowed to return to their New England ports with impunity.[4] The confiscated goods, meanwhile, were brought in on ship bottoms to the Confederate populace and armies through the Hatteras Inlet. This way, thousands of tons of clothing, foodstuffs, shoes, and guns and ammunition were supplied to Southern fighting men. In retrospect, these seagoing supply lines are a stark reminder of the bankruptcy of Confederate agricultural and manufacturing capabilities that plagued them during the war.

Considering the early successes of these ventures, it is no puzzle as to why the Confederacy needed to protect this all-important inlet by building two forts to guard it: Hatteras and Clark. Both forts were constructed of logs and sand redoubts and were rectangular in shape, and each occupied a strategic position: Hatteras guarding the inlet and its approaches, Clark covering the seaward approaches from the north. Fort Hatteras sported 10 guns mounted, including a 10-inch Columbiad, plus 5 more in reserve. Clark, a half mile away, was the smaller of the two and had only 5 guns. Ironically, all this artillery had been brought down from the Gosport Navy Yard after it was captured from the Union. The combined garrisons of the forts consisted of 350 men, mostly North Carolina militiamen. When later it became known that the Federal fleet was approaching, more men were brought in, boosting the total to 580 effectives.

In spite of the earlier fervor to use block ships, Secretary Welles and his advisors decided that a military expedition was needed to subdue the forts and to capture this important waterway; a combined army and naval assault was in order. This suggestion came from Benjamin Butler, a lawyer turned politician turned soldier from Massachusetts. In 1861 President Buchanan had appointed him a major general as a result of his effective use of force to quell the riots in Baltimore when a regiment of Union soldiers was being transferred through the city on their way to Washington. Only a month later, his men were humiliated in a battle with Confederates at Big Bethel, Virginia, while he was commandant at Fort Monroe—a defeat that almost cost him his commission.[5] It was after this that he came up with the suggestion for a combined army-navy assault on Hatteras.

To command the naval force in this operation, Welles selected Flag Officer Stringham, a career navy man with 52 years of service. He had been appointed a midshipman at the age of 11, and brilliantly served his country in the War of 1812, the Algerian War in 1815, and the Mexican War. For a time, he commanded the Gosport Navy Yard, and later became flag officer of the Mediterranean Squadron from 1848 to 1852. At the outbreak of war, Stringham was commanding the Boston Navy Yard when Welles appointed him flag officer of the North Atlantic Blockading Squadron. The lean, sometimes irritable Stringham was a natural choice to command the war's first amphibious assault on an enemy fort.[6]

On August 25, 1861, Major General John Ellis Wool, commandant, Department of Virginia, issued a directive to the effect that General Butler would:

> prepare 860 troops for an expedition to Hatteras Inlet, North
> Carolina, to go with Commodore Stringham, commanding Home

Squadron, to capture several batteries in the area . . . troops will be as follows: 200 men from Camp Butler and 600 from Camp Hamilton [both in Newport News], plus Company B of the Second Artillery from Fort Monroe . . . they will be provided with 10 days' rations of water and 10 rounds of ammunition.[7]

Stringham picked five powerful warships for the mission: the 4,833-ton *Minnesota,* his flagship; her sister ship, *Wabash,* 4,636 tons; the screw steamer *Monticello,* 655 tons; the sloop *Pawnee,* 1,500 tons; the side-wheel gunboat *Harriet Lane,* 750 tons; and the sailing sloop *Cumberland,* 1,726 tons (this vessel was to be towed by *Wabash* because she was the only vessel not powered by steam). In addition were the chartered steamers *Adelaide* and *George Peabody* and the armed tug *Fanny.* The transports *Adelaide* and *George Peabody* were to tow schooners loaded with surfboats, while *Monticello* and *Pawnee* would tow surfboats only. This impressive fleet was led by the two most powerful warships in the world, *Minnesota,* 27 guns, along with *Pawnee,* 10 guns. *Harriet Lane* had 5 guns, and *Monticello* was armed with 3 guns. The entire armada carried 143 guns in all.[8]

With Major General Butler berthed on *Minnesota,* the fleet left Hampton Roads on August 26, in good sailing weather, but a heavy surf followed them to Cape Hatteras, where the fleet anchored the next day at the south end of the cape. The surfboats were hoisted out and preparations were made for landing the troops. Fortunately, the weather dawned clear and gave promise for a successful landing.

On Wednesday the 27th, *Minnesota's* log reported a "southerly wind and a heavy surf rolling on the beach."[9] The troops were called out at 4:00 A.M., given breakfast, and then told to stand by for disembarking.

In Fort Hatteras, the commander, Colonel William F. Martin of the 7th Carolina, studied the fleet through his telescope soon after it appeared. He had only 350 men at his command; after examining the approaching ships and their potential complement of men, he calculated that he would need at least 225 more troops to "man the guns and give necessary relief." With his present troop strength, he could not hope to counter any landing of a superior number of enemy troops. He immediately dispatched a boat to Portsmouth, Virginia, with orders to Lieutenant Colonel George W. Johnson for more troops, which would be ferried down by way of the Great Dismal Swamp Canal.[10]

At 6:45 A.M. on August 28, Stringham hoisted the flags as the signal to disembark troops, and he ordered the *Pawnee, Monticello,* and *Harriet Lane* to cover the landings. The troops then climbed down into four specially built iron-plated surfboats, while General Butler, with 100 marines from the fleet, transferred to the *Monticello* for a run at the beach. His plan was to land the troops, under the protective guns of *Harriet Lane* and *Monticello,* two miles north of Fort Clark, while *Minnesota* and *Wabash,* with *Cumberland* in tow, took positions off Fort Clark to begin shelling the facility. As the embarked troops raced for the shore, the ships unleashed their devastating broadsides at the fort.

The forts returned fire, but it was relatively ineffectual against the heavy guns of the fleet, and it soon became a one-sided show.[11] Large shells slammed into the fort's installations, flinging sand, debris, and men into the air, and the earth literally shook from the thunderous devastation.

Then Stringham adopted a maneuver that was to prove effective against shore installations from that day on. Instead of following the traditional method of laying to and bombarding, he had his ships sail in an elliptical pattern while they broadsided. This ingenious method prevented the enemy gunners from getting range on fairly stationary ships, and it allowed the ships' gunners to fling salvos from one side and then from the other as the vessels turned at each end of the elliptical pattern, keeping up a continuous broadside. This method was to contribute to the subduing of the forts, and it caused Colonel Martin to describe the salvos as a literal "flood of shells."[12] Stringham kept his ships moving, firing broadside after broadside at a rate of around 28 shells a minute, as estimated by Colonel Martin.[13] The punishment to the fort was severe, and it soon became obvious that it could not hold out much longer. Even the late arrival of Commodore Barron of the Confederate navy, who took charge of defenses, did little to change the situation; the optimistic Barron counted on relief troops arriving at any hour, but this hope proved to be empty, and he faced a vastly superior force in warships and in troops, which were expected to land at any minute to assault his installation.

Within the hulls of the Union ships, moving at relatively slow speeds under the hot August sun of the Carolinas, it must have been hellish, especially for the gunners, who were working feverishly to keep their charges going at top efficiency. The process of loading and firing muzzle-loading cannon was complicated, and it required rigid training and precise performance.

The routine consisted of from 8 to 15 men, depending on the size of the gun. At the command to run in, the gun crew would back the gun out of the port, by means of side tackles, to where the implements of firing were waiting: shell, powder, rammers, wads, and water buckets. Two men at the muzzle would swing into action, with one dropping a powder bag down, while the second rammed it home with a rammer equipped with a rawhide strip that marked the proper depth of the thrust. Then the first man would drop a roundshot, or a canister of grape, into the muzzle while the second rammed it down with a wad, lest the ball roll out when the muzzle was depressed. The gun captain would pierce the powder bag by means of a primer wire inserted through the priming vent on top of the breech; then he would insert a primer into the vent. At the command to run out, the crews would run the muzzle through the port by a system of pulleys. The gun was then aimed, and at the command to fire, the captain would yank on a lanyard connected to a flintlock type of hammer over the vent. The hammer would strike the primer and the gun would discharge, recoiling savagely against the ropes and pulleys.

The flash would illuminate the casemate around the area of the gun, while billows of acrid smoke poured in through the port, setting eyes to watering and throats to coughing. Then the gun would be run in again, and a crewman with a water-soaked sponge on a rammer swabbed out the bore, lest a lingering spark prematurely set off the next powder charge, likely ruining the weapon and endangering all those around the gun.

The ritual of loading and firing was done again and again, with crews mechanically loading, ramming, running out, firing, running in, and swabbing. After cease-fire, the crews would have "battle shock": sore eyes, rasping throats, and ringing ears. It would be some time before normalcy would set in, allowing crews to perform their other duties properly.

Then there was always the danger of return fire from the enemy. Hits on the bulwarks or the hulls of wooden ships would send lethal slivers, some as large as two-by-fours, flying in all directions, causing death and destruction all around. Heavy thuds signaled hits along the hull, sending damage control crews scurrying. There was also the danger of rigging coming down from lucky hits, crushing all those below it. In some cases, nets were strung under the masts to catch falling timbers. But there could be no escape from danger during a naval battle; all sections of the vessel were danger zones, from the keel to the mast tops, and all hands had to be alert at all times. The same situation applied to ironclad warships, lacking only the danger from falling rigging.

Meanwhile, the landings on the beaches weren't going as planned. A revived eastern wind whipped the surf into huge rollers; two of the surfboats capsized, and two flatboats were crushed in the raging surf. Troops were then transported to smaller vessels called block ships, which were attached to the warships with towlines. The block ships were then allowed to ride the rollers into the shore. However, when it appeared that the block ships were in danger of capsizing, the tug *Fanny* was sent to the rescue. After several futile attempts, the intrepid tug managed to tow them out, away from the rolling surf. But as a result of all this action, only 318 troops made it to the beach, under the command of Colonel Max Weber of the 20th New York Regiment. Most of the men were soaked to the skin, with wet ammunition and rations; worst of all, they were outnumbered two to one by the enemy troops in the forts. But led by the imperturable Weber, and covered by fire from the warships offshore, they advanced on Fort Clark.

In the fleet, Stringham noticed that some of the fleet's shots were falling short, so he ordered 15-second fuses on shells from the 10-inch guns. The result was a stunning concentration of huge shells on the shaken gunners in the fort, what Stringham described as "falling in and around the battery with good effect."[14] One of the shells exploded on land near the fort, sending a herd of wild cattle stampeding across the dunes. Another thudded near the advancing Union soldiers, wounding a private on the hand.

During the bombardment, an amusing incident occurred when one of the spongers on a gun on the flagship let his rammer slip overboard, much to his consternation. Without thinking about it, he dove overboard, retrieved the rammer, swam up to a port, and was lifted aboard by his shipmates while he triumphantly waved the rammer in a victory salute.[15] Secretary Fox later gave the young seaman a commendation and an advancement to master's mate. Stringham had made a note of the situation after the battle because of his great pride in the men. The incident was indicative of Stringham's popular leadership.

Finally, the troops in Fort Clark had had enough; they scrambled over the embrasures and ran toward Fort Hatteras as Weber's force approached. After realizing that the fort was abandoned, Colonel Weber took his troops and entered through a hole blasted in the one of the embrasures. A seaman from the *Pawnee* had the privilege of raising the Union flag over Fort Clark and also received a commendation and advancement from Secretary Fox.[16]

Colonel Martin, in his official report, stated that it was the lack of ammunition, plus the punishing bombardment and the advancement of Weber's force from the north, that prompted him to order the abandonment of Fort Clark. He ordered his skirmishers to harass the Union force while he spiked the guns, and with what supplies his men could carry, he fell back to Hatteras at 12:25, while that fort was taking a bombardment from the fleet.[17]

At the fort, Martin consulted with Major W. S. G. Andrews, commander of both facilities, and it was decided to cease fire, hoping to draw one or more of the ships near enough to hit. Their chance came when the *Monticello* rounded the spithead in order to get to the harbor of the cape to investigate some Confederate vessels that were spotted lurking in the vicinity, which included the steamer *Winslow*, carrying Commodore Barron to the fort. But the *Monticello* became grounded on the shoals, and immediately the Confederates swung into action, shelling the hapless ship. *Monticello*'s gunners returned the fire, and a brisk encounter took place while the ship's engines backed her off the shoal and to safety.

Clearly the fort could not withstand much more punishment, and a conference was held between Barron, Andrews, and Martin to discuss a surrender. Two guns had been dismounted, 4 men had been killed, and between 25 and 30 men had been badly wounded. A shell had fallen into the room next to the powder magazine, which was reported to be afire. Fearful of losing more men needlessly, without ammunition, and with no hope of receiving relief troops, the Confederate leaders decided to surrender. So at 11:00 the last gun was fired and a white flag raised over the parapet.[18] Stringham ordered a cease-fire, while cheers broke out in the fleet. Butler then sent an officer, Lieutenant Pierce Crosby, to the fort to receive a formal surrender from the fort's commanding officers.

The capitulation garnered 670 troops, 35 guns, 1,000 stand of arms, two strong forts, and, more important, entrance into Pamlico Sound. Included in the prisoners were Major Andrews, Commodore Barron, and Colonel Martin. Barron, ironically, was to have taken charge of resistance at the fort but instead officiated at the surrender for the Confederates.[19]

The surrender was signed on board the *Minnesota* by the three Confederate officers in the presence of Stringham and Butler. The terms stipulated that all munitions of war, men, and property be unconditionally surrendered to the government of the United States, in full terms of capitulation.[20] It was the first time the term "unconditional surrender" was used, thus predating General Grant at Fort Donelson six months later.

With the capture of Forts Hatteras and Clark, Union forces were able to roam freely within the sound with no resistance, because the Confederate squadron had retreated to Roanoke Island, midway between Pamlico and Albemarle Sounds, where a fort had been built that was surrounded by sunken obstructions. It was inevitable that this bastion would have to be dealt with, but that could wait for a time. First the presence of an enemy facility at Okracoke Inlet at Cape Lookout had to be dealt with. The tug *Fanny* was loaded with 61 troops, a launch was equipped with a 12-pound howitzer along with 22 sailors and 6 marines, and both were sent to Cape Lookout for an assault on the fort there.

The force arrived at Fort Okracoke on September 16 only to find it had been abandoned by the Confederates, who had left eighteen 32-pounders and four shell guns behind. At Portsmouth, a landing party found three 8-inch guns on the beach awaiting emplacement in a shore battery. The guns were destroyed, and the expedition returned to Hatteras.

Capture of Cape Hatteras was a signal victory for the Union and came at a time when Northerners were still reeling from the ignominious defeat at the Second Battle of Bull Run. It rescued a populace from the invidious atmosphere of defeatism. But more important, the victory not only gave the Union an entrance into the sounds, but provided a coaling and provisioning site for the blockading squadrons and would serve as a possible springboard for any future actions against Charleston, Savannah, and Fernandina.[21]

The victory was enthusiastically heralded throughout the North. President Lincoln congratulated Stringham and Butler, and the two victors raced north to bask in the glory of an adoring public—each with his own version of the story. As expected, the fall of the forts was mourned throughout the South. Jefferson Davis lamented that Barron, because of the strength of the Union forces and "his own comparative weakness," had capitulated to the enemy. That weakness was the reason his troops failed to capture enemy forces on the 27th.[22]

Criticism was also leveled at the Confederate navy for its inability to stop the encroaching Union warships. It is puzzling to even a casual observer that these carping critics ignored the fact that Mallory did not have a fleet of any size to match the overwhelming superiority of the Union forces. The small Confederate Mosquito Fleet in Pamlico Sound made a halfhearted attempt at resistance, but it would have been a pinprick in the sides of the great Union men-of-war. At the surrender of Fort Hatteras, the Mosquito Fleet fled up the sound under the protection of the Confederate guns at Roanoke Island.

Despite the victory, there was criticism in the North; most of it stemmed from the failure of General Butler and Flag Officer Stringham to move lighter warships into Pamlico Sound and to defeat the small Confederate naval force present. It was also conjectured that a combined naval and land assault on Roanoke Island would have secured that bastion and created a road to Norfolk and Richmond much earlier in the war.

The Hatteras campaign *did* demonstrate one important but temporary fact: Forts could be subdued by naval bombardment alone, but ground troops would be needed to occupy the facility once it had been surrendered. But it must also be remembered that Hatteras was a log and sand fortification, and not of masonry, such as Forts Sumter in South Carolina, Morgan in Alabama, and Jackson in Louisiana. Assaults against these strongholds were still to be resolved in the future.

There has been much discussion over the years about the strategic importance of the bombardment tactic used by Flag Officer Stringham at Hatteras: keeping the ships moving in elliptical patterns while bombarding. Comparisons have been made with World War II, during which American ships anchored off enemy shores unleashed devastating bombardments on installations. One must bear in mind that the enemy, in the majority of these cases, did not have artillery fire to equal that of the warships, some with huge 15-inch guns, thus creating a one-sided situation. In the Civil War, in many cases, the Confederates had guns of equal power and distance in the forts.

Stringham knew early on of the possibility that the Confederates had large-caliber guns to match those of his ships at Cape Hatteras. Were his vessels to anchor, they could be subjected to fierce bombardments from the fort gunners. Therefore, the only way to nullify that possibility was to keep the fleet in motion while launching salvos, thereby preventing landlocked artillerists from taking a proper sighting. In actuality, the mounted cannon at Forts Clark and Hatteras were not much larger than 32-pounders, as opposed to the 9-, 10-, and 11-inch guns of the fleet; while they could have wreaked havoc with any warship that dared to venture close, this does not alter the fact that the situation at Hatteras was a mismatch—and the first naval/land action of its kind. As we shall see later, during the amphibious campaigns at Port Royal and especially at Fort Fisher, the odds were close to even, although the moving-ship tactic was still effectively used in these campaigns.

The powerful and victorious Union fleet proceeded to preen its feathers over the victory at Cape Hatteras, all the while eagerly looking forward to the next campaign, whatever and wherever it might be. And that objective had yet to be picked by Federal planners.

CHAPTER SIX

THE FIRST AMPHIBIOUS OPERATIONS, PART 2: PORT ROYAL

The capture of Forts Hatteras and Clark, while a strategic victory for the Union navy, still fell short of the goal of obtaining a major naval supply depot for the fleet and, subsequently, a springboard for assaults on major ports of entry for the Confederacy: Charleston, Wilmington, and Savannah. Blockade-runners were using these entries with impunity, especially since the Federal navy was still in its growing stage. From the Union point of view, these major ports of entry had to be closed.

A quick glance at a map of the Atlantic coast from Virginia to Florida will reveal the problems facing Welles and his planners. The one major naval base on that north segment of the coast, Gosport, was lost to them, and although Hampton Roads and Fort Monroe were still in Union hands, there was no major facility from Norfolk to Florida with which to repair and replenish a fleet. It was imperative that something be done, and done soon, to create anchorages and provisioning sites to supply that fleet.

The navy brass turned to the Blockade Board's fourth report, dated July 26, 1861, which stated:

> Our second memoir [July 13] in which we discussed the Operation of Bull's Bay, St. Helena's Sound and Port Royal Bay has left

us little to say on the first of these subsections. When the three anchorages are secured, the whole of this part of the coast will be under complete control.[1]

The first two anchorages proposed, Bull's Bay and St. Helena's Sound,
were inadequate as fleet anchorages and naval support bases because of
their shallowness. However, Welles, in his October 12, 1861, instructions
to the flag officer of the South Atlantic Blockading Squadron, stated that
of these three proposed sites, at least two of them should be occupied.[2]
Port Royal would be the most obvious site. As far as Pamlico Sound was
concerned, it offered an adequate coaling and replenishment base at Cape
Hatteras, but the sound itself was inadequate, because of its shallow depth
and narrow confines, both of which changed constantly with the tides. A
fleet anchorage must of necessity be deep enough for large vessels to navigate, and it must have a wide mouth, or entrance, with depths not affected
by unpredictable tides. Port Royal had a wide mouth, a spacious harbor,
and the proper depth for an anchorage.

In fact, Port Royal Sound was considered one of the best harbors on the
East Coast. Not only was the huge expanse of water ideal for a fleet anchorage, but it also afforded space for a repair depot large enough for an
entire navy. Its position between Charleston and Savannah would allow it
to serve as a base of operations against these important Confederate harbors. In fact, as Union planners saw it, control of Port Royal Sound would
give them control of the East Coast, from the northern border of South
Carolina to as far south as Smyrna, Florida. The surrounding area was one
of the richest agricultural districts in the state, growing enormous crops of
rice and Sea Island cotton.[3] It contained 1,500 square miles, producing
50,000,000 pounds of rice and 14,000 bales of cotton annually, and it had
a population of nearly 50,000, including 30,000 slaves.

Of the two islands flanking the sound—Hilton Head Island and St. Phillips Island—the former was the larger and more important. Resembling a
large shoe, the island, roughly 12 miles long and a little less than 6 miles
across at its widest point, was the site of numerous plantations because of its
fertile earth. Landing and loading docks and wharves were located on the
southern end, and the northern end was barren, flat, and sandy—a perfect
site for a fort with both seaface and landface configurations to make it a formidable facility for any enemy to assault and an easy facility to defend.

Hilton Head was named after an English sea captain, William Hilton, who raised the British flag over it in 1663. In the 1800s, the island was settled by cotton planters on 15 large plantations, the largest of which was the Stoney-Baymond Plantation (known as Sea Pines today) on the southern end. Situated on the northern marshy end, facing the sound, was a large Confederate bastion, Fort Walker, guarding the entrance to the sound. This facility sported 20 guns of various calibers, including a 10-inch Columbiad. The seaface had no embrasures, which was a decided disadvantage, but this was offset by the many guns mounted facing the sound; it was hoped that they would challenge any incursions by the Union navy.

Anchoring the northern end of Port Royal Sound was St. Phillips Island. Although it was smaller than Hilton Head, its Bay Point location was excellent for a fort designed to enfilade any enemy vessels that would get by Fort Walker and had the audacity to challenge it. Its secondary task was to protect the Beaufort River, on its western face, which leads to the important town after which it was named. The fort contained 19 guns, including a 10-inch Columbiad, which (like Fort Walker's) was no doubt brought down from the Gosport Navy Yard after its fall. It was an embarrassing situation for the Union navy when these guns first appeared at Forts Hatteras and Clark, and later at Walker and Beauregard. That troublesome fact continued to plague the Union long into the war, as munitions and huge quantities of guns continued to turn up at Confederate forts and on warships on the Atlantic coast and in the Gulf.

Lurking in Skull Creek, on the western face of Hilton Head, was a small Confederate fleet of four vessels: *Savannah* (flagship), *Samson,* and *Resolute* (each with 32-pounder smoothbores), plus an armed tugboat.[4] The force was under the command of Commodore Josiah Tattnall, a former U.S. Navy commodore, educated in England and a hero of the Mexican War, who resigned his U.S. Navy commission on February 20, 1861, and accepted an appointment in the Georgia state navy. He was later given command of the feeble naval forces guarding the Georgia and South Carolina coasts.

The sobriquet "Mosquito Fleet" was certainly apropos, considering its size against that of the big and powerful Union squadron. Still, the crusty old commodore did not waver in his belief that he could annoy the enemy fleet or at least draw some of them to within gun range of the forts.

The Confederate officer in charge of the defenses at Port Royal was

Brigadier General Thomas Fenwick Drayton, who was a former plantation owner, an army officer, and a close friend of President Davis. The Port Royal forces were under the overall command of General Beauregard. The armament of the forts could have been stronger, and indeed Drayton asked repeatedly for additional troops, but for some reason Beauregard didn't address Drayton's requests. Some of the ordnance did arrive, but not in time to be prepared and mounted in strategic spots around the fort; consequently the fort had some strategic defensive weaknesses.

But as Secretary Welles was planning the assault on Port Royal, he was unaware of these weaknesses. He therefore decided that a considerable amount of naval strength would be needed, plus an adequate contingent of troops, to subdue this facility.[5]

Meanwhile, the Union navy had grown considerably, especially with the addition of 23 "ninety-day" gunboats, vessels built in record time in northern shipyards for the Union fleet. Union navy men used to joke about the fact that the keels of these ships had been growing in the forests of Maine just a few months before. Other vessels of all sizes and tonnage were being converted into ships of war by the simple techniques of strengthening and arming them in the North's many shipyards and from its numerous armament firms.

The Atlantic Squadron had grown too large for one man to command, so after the aging Flag Officer Stringham was relieved of command for his failures at Cape Hatteras, it was decided to follow the Blockade Board's suggestion and divide the fleet into the North Atlantic Blockading Squadron and the South Atlantic Blockading Squadron, and to appoint a flag officer to command each squadron. This directive would relieve the enormous pressure that would be incumbent upon one flag officer, and would set a precedent for times to come with the simple expediency of dividing the command of large fleets.

As the commission's plan was adopted, the North Atlantic Blockading Squadron would be responsible for Cape Henry to Cape Romain; the South Atlantic Blockading Squadron was responsible for Cape Romain to St. Augustine. The two commanding officers picked were Flag Officer Louis M. Goldsborough for the former squadron and Flag Officer Samuel Francis du Pont for the latter.[6]

Goldsborough, a burly career navy man, received his lieutenant's commission in 1825 and served on various stations, including command of a steamboat expedition in the Seminole War and command of a warship in the Mexican War. At the outbreak of war, he was superintendent of the U.S. Naval Academy. The tall, stately du Pont, a member of the prominent du Pont powder manufacturing family, was appointed a midshipman in 1815 and rose rapidly through the ranks, being appointed a captain in 1855. Both men were able commanders, but it was du Pont to whom the task of assaulting and capturing Port Royal was given on September 18, 1861.

Du Pont wasted no time preparing for the expedition. He immediately requisitioned three screw sloops of war and four screw gunboats, plus 300 marines, 500 landing craft, and several of the recently armed and commissioned open-ended ferryboats with light drafts for maneuvering in rivers and streams.[7]

Du Pont then chose for his flagship the magnificent 3,200-ton screw frigate *Wabash* with its 64 guns, and as his chief of staff he selected Flag Officer Charles Henry Davis, a Harvard graduate who had been appointed to a lieutenancy after only three years. He had a successful career in naval science, and held the important post as head of the Bureau of Detail in Washington.

After Port Royal was picked (upon the urging of President Lincoln) and after the dust had settled from the ignominious Union defeat at the first Bull Run, with Washington declared safe for now, a cloak of secrecy was to have been thrown over the project. However, the secret leaked out and was picked up by the newspapers hawked about the streets. Even Governor Pickens received a dispatch from the secretary of war, Judah Benjamin, to the effect that "the enemy's expedition is intended for Port Royal."[8] He immediately ordered reinforcements from Savannah and Wilmington to Forts Walker and Beauregard. The question arose as to who the traitor in the U.S. government was, but to nobody's knowledge was he ever uncovered.[9] Some speculated it may have been the ubiquitous Senator Wigfall again, but there is no proof to back that allegation.

At the same time that du Pont received his orders, similar orders were sent to Brigadier General Thomas West Sherman (the brother of William Tecumseh Sherman and often referred to as "the other Sherman") to the effect that he had been appointed commander of 12,000 troops for an unnamed operation.[10]

Du Pont's orders, similar to Sherman's, were careful to explain that co-operation was essential between the army and navy commanders. The command was divided. At sea the navy was in charge even when army personel were on board. But in land assaults which included navy personnel, army officers were in charge. Du Pont assembled his battle fleet with care and precision. The fleet was to be built around the frigates *Wabash* and *Sabine,* plus 15 other vessels including screw sloops, schooners, side-wheel steamers, and a tugboat, plus various ships of a supply train.[11]

Many of these vessels were initially scattered, but in record time, du Pont had assembled the largest and most powerful naval force afloat to date. The objective of Port Royal was made available to all captains through sealed orders not to be opened until under way. The navy thought it imperative to keep the objective of this expedition a complete secret; the enemy knew of the existence of the mighty fleet but was unsure as to the target of the expedition.

On October 16, du Pont hoisted the signal to get under way, and the *Wabash,* along with three gunboats and three transports, sailed out of New York Harbor, sent off by du Pont's wife and other well-wishers. It must have been a grand sight to behold, with ships steaming in formation and their bunting and flags flying in the wind.

The fleet passed Sandy Hook, turned south, and, after forming two columns, set a course for Hampton Roads. They arrived there on October 18 and dropped anchor off Fort Monroe to await the arrival of the rest of the armada, which straggled in ship by ship for ten days, until 75 vessels were at anchor in the spacious waterway.[12] One cannot resist a conjecture about the reaction of the Confederates in the Gosport Navy Yard and the encampments on Newport News when they saw the Federal armada riding at anchor in that vast body of water, not knowing why they were there or what their target was. (They later thought they had evidence, after someone retrieved a Union sailor's lost hat containing a clipping from a Boston newspaper conjecturing that the objective of the armada was Charleston.)

While waiting for the remaining ships to straggle in, du Pont and his commanders conferred on the strategy to be used in the coming assault on Forts Walker and Beauregard. He had to meet the timeworn objection that ships were at a disadvantage against a land fort, an objection still held in spite of Stringham's success against the forts on Cape Hatteras. After all, those had been but weakly defended log and sand facilities, whereas the forts in Port Royal were reported to be substantially stronger. However, du Pont's study of the Crimean War, fought from 1853 to 1856, during which the French introduced armored floating batteries that were startlingly successful against wooden Russian ships, convinced him that Stringham's elliptical pattern was the best.

Du Pont's coming strategy depended on the proven dictum that warships in motion have a tactical advantage over a land facility, because the ships' gunners can enfilade at will, while the land gunners, on the other hand, have a difficult time sighting on them. This would be especially true of steam-powered vessels, which are not subject to the vagaries of wind and tide as sail-powered vessels are.[13]

After the fleet had assembled, du Pont once again raised the flag and fired one gun as the signal to get under way in the early hours of October 28. The huge fleet slowly filed out of Hampton Roads, taking almost the entire day to exit. After rounding Cape Henry, du Pont ordered the fleet into a formation called double echelon, in which the *Wabash* led the vessels in two columns strung out, forming a sort of V formation with the flagship at the apex.[14] Earlier, the flag officer had dispatched the *Vandalia* and 25 coal vessels to a point off Savannah to distract the Confederates from the fleet's objective. Once that objective had been reached, the small flotilla would be recalled to Port Royal to join the rest of the fleet. For the first segment of the voyage, the force enjoyed fair skies and soft winds, and it looked as if all would be well. By the time the fleet reached the Outer Banks, however, a violent storm had developed, and on November 1, winds increased to near hurricane force, posing a danger to the fleet and raising havoc when it came to steaming in columns.

Du Pont conferred with his staff and decided to disperse the fleet. The vessels scattered upon du Pont's signal, and it became a case of every man for himself as the fierce Atlantic winds whipped the water into huge waves. The smaller gunboat *Isaac Smith* fell into serious trouble, so her captain ordered the entire main battery of 8-inch smoothbores to be jettisoned in order to keep the vessel from breaking up. However, she managed to keep her one 30-pound rifle.

Soon the savage storm had reached such proportions that du Pont ordered all ships to shorten sail and heave to, pointing their bows into the wind direction in order to take advantage of the most comfortable and safest heading. Meanwhile, two transports had been grounded in shoal waters.

A storm at sea is a terrible thing to behold, especially those near or at hurricane proportions. Even though the ship heads into the wind and rides the rollers straight on, it is rough on the occupants. As the ship slices through a wave, her bow rises high, then settles for a moment on the crest of a wave; in some cases the screws can be seen churning in the air for a moment before the ship plunges into the trough of the wave, her stern end pointing at the moon. Moving about the vessel is difficult and dangerous, and seasickness always overcomes the personnel who don't have their sea legs. Those who have no duties during a storm are strapped into their bunks to ride out the weather. No one can sleep, and a constant vigil is kept to determine whether there are any signs of damage to the vessel.

The most serious case of a ship in trouble was the transport *Governor,* breaking up in the raging water. The ship was carrying 300 marines and their equipment—a vital part of the amphibious aspect of the operation. All hands pitched in to bail water and save their vessel, but to no avail; the funnel snapped off and was pitched overboard, causing low boiler pressures. Then the engine broke down, and it began to appear that the main braces were going and that the ship would break in two. The vessel and its occupants were now at the mercy of the storm.

The *Isaac Smith,* now lightened of its main battery, tried passing a line to the stricken transport, but for some reason it snapped or was cast off accidentally. Meanwhile, the frigate *Sabine,* passing the fleet on her way to blockade duty, came up and rescued all but six of the marines, by using a spar and by hoving so close, the men could jump across. It was an amazing case of excellent seamanship. A few hours later, the *Governor* slipped beneath the storm-tossed waves. The steamer *Belvedere* had to turn back to Hampton Roads.

On November 2, the sun rose over a calmer ocean, revealing the *Wabash* alone, rocking in the ground swells. Gradually, more and more ships appeared and gathered around the flagship. Soon an armada of 25 ships rode at anchor outside the Port Royal bar. General Sherman lamented the loss of the transport steamers *Union, Belvedere, Osceola,* and *Peerless;* however, the main troop transports were present and safe.[15] Du Pont was pleased to see the 240-ton side-wheel coastal survey steamer *Vixen* present. On board was Captain Charles O. Boutelle of the U.S. Coast Survey. It had long been conjectured that the Confederates would remove all navigation aids and lightships from the channel, in order to thwart the Union vessels, and it was vital to bring along survey personnel.

Boutelle moved in record time to sound out the channel, and quickly placed buoys to mark the way. That opened a passage for the lighter-draft ships, including the gunboats, to enter the sound. They anchored in the roadstead, far out of range of the forts' guns.

And, as expected, Commodore Tattnall's four-ship flotilla came out from Skull Creek to challenge the Union forces.[16] But this force was easily sent scurrying back to the safety of the creek by the big ordnance of the gunboats.

Du Pont's heavier ships had to wait until high tide before crossing the bar into the harbor. The *Wabash,* with her 23-foot draft, slid over with only 10 inches under her keel. By nightfall, the entire fleet was safely anchored in the spacious harbor. But the attack, which was originally planned to first land troops and then bombard, had to be scrubbed. It was determined that there was no suitable place to land troops, so du Pont decided to subdue the fort through bombardment alone, again adopting the method of Stringham's success at Cape Hatteras. The date of attack was to be November 5, but his deep-draft ships, *Wabash* and *Susquehanna,* ran aground on Fishing Rip Shoal, and much time was consumed in getting the two vessels off and into deeper water.

November 6 dawned cloudy and stormy, with high winds sweeping in from the sea, causing an unusually high tide, so du Pont reluctantly called off the attack for that day as well. The time was profitably spent by Commander Davis studying Fort Walker's gun emplacements for weak spots. He found one on the north landface end of the facility, designed to repel attack from the land but vulnerable from the seaface.

November 7 dawned bright and calm, and early in the day all commanders were called to the flagship for instructions based on Davis' new knowledge of the fort's defenses and how this vulnerability could be exploited. The mission's strategy was to be profoundly changed to accommodate this new information.

Within the fort, Confederate colonel John A. Wagener later wrote:

> The enemy had chosen a day entirely propitious to him. The water
> was smooth as glass. The air was just sufficient to blow the smoke
> of his guns into our faces, where it would meet the column of our
> own smoke and prevent our sight, excepting by glimpses . . . no

sooner did we obtain his range when it would be changed, and time after time, rechanged, while the deep water permitted him to choose his own position and fire shot after shot and shell after shell with the precision of target practice.[17]

Wagener bemoaned the fact that his engineers failed to establish a battery on a bluff that commanded the fort's flank, a failure that had the potential of exposing the fort to raking fire, which would do considerable damage with a great deal of casualties. Lack of reinforcements also greatly concerned him.

For the attack, du Pont arranged his fleet in the following steaming order: *Wabash, Susquehanna;* sloops *Mohican, Seminole,* and *Pawnee;* gunboats *Unadilla, Ottawa, Pembina;* and the sailing sloop *Vandalia,* towed by *Isaac Smith.* The flanking squadron, consisting of gunboats *Bienville, Seneca, Curlew, Penguin,* and *Augusta,* was to enfilade Fort Beauregard and to engage Tattnall's force if he dared to sortie.[18] His plan, based on Davis' observation and suggestions, was for the main body to steam up, single file, to within two miles above Fort Beauregard, all the while bombarding that facility. Then the column would turn to port and start the downward leg of the ellipse, enfilading the northern landface of Fort Walker and the seaface at a distance of 800 yards. Then, when the column reached the southern end of the leg, it would turn to port again and start another elliptical run, this time closing to 600 yards of Fort Walker as it passed.

At 8:00 A.M., the columns got under way. The battle line moved up the sound, equidistant from both forts. At 9:26, a single 11-inch Dahlgren boomed out from Fort Walker, but the shell exploded after leaving the muzzle; another gun sounded from Fort Beauregard, but it too fell short. A lanyard was pulled on board *Wabash,* and another large weapon barked. On *Susquehanna,* two 32-pounders and an 11-inch pivot gun were activated.[19] Finally, the entire fleet opened up and the deadly fray began.

As Wagener wrote, the harbor was clouded with gunsmoke, occasionally pierced by rapid red-yellow flashes from the fleet's guns. This made spotting extremely difficult for the gunners.

Meanwhile, the flanking gunboats, having exchanged shots with Tattnall's Mosquito Fleet and chased it back to the safety of Skull Creek, turned to port and joined in the bombardment until Fort Walker was literally smothered by shells blasting away the low abutments, scattering debris, men, and guns while the earth literally shook from the impact of the heavy shells. Observers in the fleet estimated the rate of fire as 28 shells a minute.

But the ships did not escape unscathed; most of them were hit many times, though with no serious damage to any. The *Seminole* received a hit on the starboard side that passed through and lodged on the port side. The *Pawnee* received six hits, but once again no serious damage was inflicted.[20] The hits did not affect the fleet's attack capability, with the *Wabash* alone firing 880 deadly rounds.

Finally, Fort Walker had had enough. Wagener consulted with his officers, and at 1:00 P.M., he gave the order to withdraw from the fort and retreat to safety. But that retreat left behind dead and wounded men, ammunition, and supplies. Surprisingly, no white flag was raised in surrender, such as at Forts Hatteras and Clark—the order was just given to retreat.

The Confederate troops scrambled over the landface embrasures and raced across the sandy flats to the safety of the tree groves. A detachment of artillery men was left to cover the retreat, but at 2:00 P.M. they too fled in panic. The *Ottawa*, which had moved in close to the fort, signaled that the enemy was enfeebled, and the message was echoed by the *Pembina,* nearby.

Du Pont sent Commander John Rodgers and a detachment of marines into the fort to raise the Union flag at 2:45 P.M. The transports then moved up and unloaded troops for the occupation. With the Union flag now flying over Fort Walker, sailors aloft in the rigging of the ships broke into loud cheers. The personnel in Fort Beauregard, across the sound, heard the cheering and correctly assumed that Fort Walker had surrendered, so they too hauled down the flag and fled into the interior of the state. A small squad of marines was sent into Fort Walker and found it empty. Lieutenant Commander Daniel Amman had the privilege of raising the Union flag over that facility.[21]

At Fort Walker, Rodgers and his men found the place in shambles; many guns on the seaface had been either damaged or destroyed by the relentless shelling from the fleet. Debris was everywhere, covered by dirt, dust, and sand, as were the bodies of the Confederate soldiers left behind in haste. Some wounded men were half buried in the debris, including the fort's Dr. Bruist. At the western landface, the weakest point, all guns were destroyed, which substantiated Commander Davis' original findings. The

Union troops discovered that the retreating Confederates had left all their equipment and belongings behind as they desperately fled into the woods and finally to the wharf at Skull Creek, where Tattnall's gunboats and some steamers were waiting to take them inland to safety.

It was later learned from Confederate reports that Colonel Wagener had been wounded during the bombardment and had turned command over to Major Arthur M. Huger, who had the unpleasant and humiliating task of ordering the abandonment of the fort. It was surmised that he had held on longer than need be because he considered the resistance a "point of honor"; he later cynically wrote, "[W]e were defeated, except perhaps by divine interference."[22]

At Fort Beauregard, the occupying party found many guns deserted and none spiked; it had been a rout. Other guns were found to have exploded upon firing. The Confederate commander of the fort, Captain Stephen Elliot, later reported that upon hearing the cheering of ships' crews, he and Colonel R. G. M. Dunovant, who had just recently entered the fort, decided that if Fort Walker had surrendered, they would be the next subject of the naval bombardment, so they ordered abandonment.[23]

The final tally of casualties was 20 killed and 10 wounded at Fort Walker and 13 killed and 19 wounded at Fort Beauregard. The fleet suffered 6 killed and 20 wounded, and minimal fleet damage. That was a small cost for such a major victory.

On November 7, du Pont sent a contingent of warships up the Broad River to Beaufort and found it deserted, except for a few slaves looting the town and one drunken white man wandering about. All along the river, the flotilla observed the same thing—plantations deserted and liberated slaves taking over everything in sight.

The fall of Forts Walker and Beauregard reverberated throughout the South. Unlike Hatteras, this defeat was a major one for the Confederacy. The city of Charleston was in a near panic, because of its proximity to Port Royal; General Beauregard was roundly criticized for lacking a plan for Fort Walker and the fort bearing his name.[24] President Davis wrote that the capture of Port Royal gave the Union the best harbor in South Carolina and "the strategic key to all the South Atlantic Coast."[25] President Lincoln sent a message to Congress requesting that official thanks be given to the fleet for the victory.

However sweet the victory may have been, the Union army came in for its share of criticism. Some said that after Port Royal had been secured, a determined push inland might have taken Charleston or Savannah, or at least severed the all-important rail line between those two cities, thereby forcing the enemy armies to detour farther inland for communication between the cities.[26] That contingency was never a part of the overall strategy with Port Royal. However damaging that criticism might have been, General Sherman called the victory "startling" because of its negative effects on the citizens of Hilton Head, who abandoned their plantations and slaves. However, in all fairness to General Sherman, it should be pointed out that he never had any orders or intention to move inland. His job was to hold and secure Port Royal as a base for future Union operations along the coast.

Du Pont also came in for his share of the carping by critics, because he ostensibly failed to send warships to intercept Tattnall's fleeing flotilla of warships and transports on their way up the Beaufort River. But the flag officer, as did Sherman, maintained that his job was to first consolidate Port Royal as a fleet anchorage and Hilton Head as a major supply depot for the blockading squadrons, rivaling that of Hampton Roads.

Meanwhile, Union soldiers now patrolled the perimeter of Fort Walker, which had been renamed Fort Welles after the esteemed secretary. Hilton Head, turned into a coaling station and supply depot for the navy, soon became a bustling community, with a hospital, church, printing office, bakery, and theater. Life in the fort became "good duty" for the Union soldiers, although not without some distractions. "Here we are," wrote one soldier at Fort Walker, "surrounded by cotton, sweet potatoes, corn, beans, mules, oranges . . . palm peanuts." But the soldier summarily dismissed the mosquitoes that carried malaria, as well as the 110-degree summers.[27]

With Port Royal now safely within the Union camp and being converted into a major base for the blockading fleet, attention was once more turned to Cape Hatteras and Pamlico Sound as a job that needed to be finished. Suddenly, however, an unexpected event occurred with the potential to change the entire course of the war.

CHAPTER SEVEN

THE *TRENT* TRIBULATION

Soon after the Confederacy found itself embroiled in a war with the Union, it came to the realization that it was in sore need of guns, ammunition, and ships. Not having any extensive manufacturing facilities of its own, it looked to outside sources to fulfill that need, including Britain and other countries in Europe. But it was mainly Britain toward which Davis and his nation looked, because Her Majesty Queen Victoria had officially announced her country to be neutral in respect to the struggle going on in her former colonies. She fell short, however, of recognizing the Confederacy as a nation, rather acknowledging the fact that the Confederacy was a "belligerent," giving it the right to buy arms and to seize ships on the high seas. Hopes were that this method would supply most of their military needs.

When that method failed because of the growing blockade, President Davis was forced to look elsewhere. His one trump card was the South's chief product, cotton, and he intended to use it well. England's mills needed cotton, and his plan was to supply that need in exchange for vital goods. In addition, plans were to negotiate with British shipyards to build vessels in whose bottoms cotton could be carried over, and in return, ammunition, guns, clothing, foodstuffs, and other goods would be brought back not only from Britain but from other European countries as well. However, recognition was sorely needed by the Confederacy, and Davis took steps to ensure such recognition overseas. There was but one problem: The envoys he had appointed, Messrs. William Lowndes Yancey, Ambrose Dudley Mann, and Pierre A. Rost, were not proving adequate for the job, so he decided to replace them with two men who were former senators—James L. Mason and John Slidell. Both were southerners and both were loyal to the Confederate cause.

Mason, a Virginia aristocrat, was born in the District of Columbia in 1798. After graduating from the College of William and Mary, he practiced law for a time, entered politics in 1826, and in 1847 became a senator in the U.S. Congress. He was a states' rights Democrat and the architect of the Fugitive Slave Act of 1850. Later, he became a member of the powerful Senate Foreign Relations Committee. As a staunch believer in slavery, he offered his services to his friend Jefferson Davis after Virginia seceded on April 17, 1861.[1]

Slidell, a New Yorker by birth in 1793, gained prominence as a lawyer in his adopted city of New Orleans. After losing a bid for Congress in 1828, he succeeded in being elected to the House of Representatives in 1843. Like Mason, he was a states' rights Democrat. After the secession of his state, he threw in his lot with the South and his friend and former law partner, Judah Benjamin.[2]

Soon after their appointments, and because of the urgency of the situation, Mason and Slidell sent their families to Charleston to board the cruiser *Nashville* but found that vessel absent. They cast around for berths on other ships but found slim pickings because of the blockade. The men considered going overland to Mexico, where they would find a ship not affected by the blockade. Meanwhile, someone located a steamer, the 500-ton *Gordon,* a coastal packet used for runs to and from Havana, Cuba. She was generally ignored by the blockade squadron off Charleston because she was a common sight and because she was fast, with a 15-knot top speed.[3]

For the sum of $10,000, the group obtained berths on board, and on October 12, 1861, the *Gordon* cast off. True to the predictions about her, she eluded the blockaders, who essentially spotted her but chose to ignore the fast packet; she was furthermore helped by a storm. She set sail for

Nassau, which was her first objective, but the presence of Union warships there forced the captain to head for Havana, arriving there on the 16th.

The Cuban diplomats wined and dined the two men and their families and gave them excellent quarters. Arrangements were made for them to take passage on a British mail packet, *Trent,* anchored in the harbor, for a voyage to Southampton, England. It appeared all was going well for Messrs. Mason and Slidell.

In the meantime, on board the 1,567-ton screw sloop U.S.S. *San Jacinto,* Captain Charles Wilkes was in the Caribbean following his orders to find the Confederate raider *Sumter,* which was reported to be in those waters, preying on Union shipping. When his search proved fruitless, he put into Cienfuegos, Cuba, for coal and provisions. There he learned of Mason and Slidell's presence in Havana, awaiting passage to England on the royal mail packet. He quickly serviced his vessel with provisions and 60 tons of coal, then set course for Havana, with the intention of intercepting the *Trent* at sea. He entered the harbor, anchored, and cast around for information. After identifying the *Trent,* he discovered the departure date to be November 7. So as not to arouse suspicions, he quietly sailed out of the harbor. His destination was the Old Bahama Channel, 240 miles from Havana, on the northern coast of Cuba—the route the *Trent* would take on her voyage home. There, the channel was 15 miles wide, so he hove to within 90 miles of the old Paredón Grande lighthouse to await the *Trent*.[4] He didn't have long to wait, as soon a whiff of smoke was spotted on the horizon by a lookout high atop a mast. As the vessel approached, it was positively identified as the *Trent*.

At 12:55 P.M., Wilkes called all hands to general quarters. He ordered two cutters to be manned by armed men and prepared for boarding purposes. The ship's log reported the weather as having moderate breezes from the north and pleasant breezes from the east.[5] When the *Trent* came close, Wilkes ordered the ensign raised. To everyone on board, it was obvious he was going to halt the *Trent* and board her. Prior to this event, Lieutenant Donald Fairfax, his executive officer, had remonstrated with his captain about the dangers of boarding an English ship and removing the commissioners, for fear of getting Britain embroiled in the conflict, but Wilkes was determined to press ahead with his plan.[6] Fairfax, as a good naval officer, held his counsel and received his orders to board the steamer and demand the papers of the ship and her clearance from Havana, plus a list of passengers. Should Mason and Slidell be aboard, they were to be taken prisoner and brought on board the *San Jacinto*. The *Trent* moved up, and at 1:05 P.M., Wilkes ordered a shot over her bow. But the British ship defiantly continued on her way, so at 1:17 Wilkes ordered another shot over the bow. This one landed closer; the *Trent* stopped her engines and glided to a stop. Wilkes, using a speaking trumpet, hailed the vessel. The ship's captain shouted: "What do you mean by heaving my vessel to in this manner?" Fairfax ordered a ladder dropped for boarding. After instructing his men to remain alongside, he climbed up the ladder and stepped onto the quarterdeck to be confronted by an irate captain and a crowd of equally irate passengers milling about, obviously agitated over the forced halting of their ship.[7]

Fairfax demanded the passenger list, saying that he had information that Mason and Slidell were on board.[8] At the mention of their names, Slidell and Mason came forward and identified themselves. Fairfax informed Slidell of his intention to place him and his partner under arrest, but Slidell refused to surrender, announcing his intention to be taken by force. Fairfax turned and made a hand signal to the *San Jacinto,* whereupon another cutter of armed men was launched and rowed over. By this time the situation was becoming tense on the British ship.

At this juncture, one Commander Richard Williams of the Royal Navy, who was in charge of the mails, came forth and angrily excoriated Fairfax's behavior as "an illegal act . . . a violation of international law . . . an act of piracy." Then the mob of passengers became belligerent and demanded that Fairfax be thrown overboard. The marines in the boat became fearful for his safety, so they rushed up the ladder and stood with rifles and bayonets at the ready. Fairfax quickly assured them that he was safe, and ordered them back to the cutter.

With his patience running thin, Fairfax indicated the *San Jacinto* with her guns run out, and he reminded the captain and passengers of the dire consequences of a failure to comply with his mission. The sight of that formidable battery seemed to calm things down a bit, and order was restored on the quarterdeck, at least temporarily, allowing more dialogue to take place.[9]

Finally, bowing to the inevitable, the two commissioners and their secretaries allowed themselves to be escorted to the cutter, but their families refused to go. Another cutter was sent for the luggage, and the foursome was rowed to the warship, where they were cordially welcomed by Captain Wilkes and offered comfortable quarters.

Before he left the *Trent*, Fairfax informed Captain James Moir that he was free to continue his voyage to England. At 3:30 P.M., the Union and British ships parted company, and Wilkes set course for Hampton Roads. He arrived there on November 15 for coal and provisions. Wilkes' final destination was to have been New York, but Welles wired him to proceed to Boston instead and discharge his passengers at Fort Warren; Mason and Slidell were incarcerated there on November 22.

As would be expected, the North was ecstatic over what had now become known as the "Trent affair." Captain Wilkes found himself to be an overnight hero; he was feted in New York and Washington by Secretary Welles. Among the many accolades cast in his direction was one from his executive officer, Fairfax, who touted his captain as being "one of the best officers, a man of strong will power, brave and intelligent."[10] Ironically, even though Welles publicly touted Wilkes as a hero, he privately admitted that Wilkes had made a mistake in not commandeering the *Trent* and bringing her into an American port for adjudication.[11] This would have been the right thing to do.

Welles had touched upon a key issue in the affair of the *Trent*. Seizing the vessel would have rendered the entire affair a point of law instead of a political issue. Captain Moir's refusal to hand over the ship's papers made his ship liable to seizure under international law.

Fairfax gave two reasons for not commandeering the *Trent*: First, the capture of the vessel would entail the putting on board of a prize crew, thus weakening the main battery by a lack of gunners; second, the presence of a large number of women and children on board would alarm them. Fairfax also personally felt that England's sympathy with the Confederate cause might trigger a war with the Union. Meanwhile, the accolades continued for Wilkes. Congress voted to give him a bronze medal for his actions, and the mayor of New York went so far as to dedicate a Fourth of July to him.[12]

Great Britain exploded with indignation. The Royal Navy was put on alert, and 8,000 royal troops were boarded on transports to head for Canada. It was later learned that these actions were normal for the empire whenever it was faced with a crisis. The troops landed in Canada but were never deployed. The entire affair became a tempest in a teapot, and the troops were later sent home.

A rather mild-toned letter was sent from Britain to Lord Lyons, the British Minister to the U.S., to the effect that Wilkes was not acting in compliance with any authority from his government, or that he conceived himself to be so authorized, but that he greatly misunderstood the instructions he had received. Lord Lyons then proceeded to tweak the beak of the American eagle by maintaining that his government could not allow such an affront to the national honor to pass without full reparation. He then asked that the four gentlemen in question—Messrs. Mason and Slidell and their secretaries—be delivered to Lord Lyons for British protection and that an apology be offered by the U.S. government.[13]

In England, Lord Palmerston fussed and fumed and demanded war for a time, but cooler heads soon prevailed, including his own. Thanks to the prince consort and Her Majesty Queen Victoria, the war rhetoric soon died down. France poked its nose into the affair for a time, but quickly withdrew when it discovered it had no sympathetic allies. It was obvious no one wanted war over this—particularly Britain, who was having her troubles with France and Russia in Europe and consequently could not afford a war with America, especially in view of the growing might of the Union navy.

In Washington, cooler heads also prevailed, with Lincoln proclaiming that he wanted only "one war at a time," so, with the help of Welles and Seward, he began to look for a way out of the situation that had grown serious.

The astute Seward locked himself in his office for a couple of days at the end of December 1861 while he drafted a long but masterly letter to the British government in which he carefully explained that Wilkes, although acting on his own initiative, was justified in boarding the *Trent*, which was obviously carrying contraband, namely, Mason and Slidell and their papers, and that he was acting in strict observance of international law. The *Trent*, he maintained, should have been taken as a prize, and the matter, along with that of Mason and Slidell, taken to a prize court for adjudication. By taking prisoners, Wilkes had made a decision that rightfully belonged to the courts. Seward further theorized that since the Southern rebellion was obviously failing, Mason and Slidell were of little importance. He concluded his long letter by stating: "The four persons in question are now in custody in Fort Warren in the state of Massachusetts. They will be cheerfully liberated."[14] It was but an echo of Lord Lyons' letter.

That mollified the British, and the crisis passed. Tempers cooled down on both sides of the Atlantic, with the Lincoln administration heaving a sigh of relief. Everyone thought war with Britain had been averted. It was a case of national posturing on both sides, and although a fleet was alerted and troops moved about, no real overtures toward war were made on either side. It became an international standoff. The only real loser in this strange situation was the Confederacy. Their hope of dragging England into a war with the Union was destroyed in one fell swoop, and all hopes of being recognized as a nation were also dashed.

It seems that not all Northerners were happy about the outcome of the *Trent* affair. Many expressed disappointment in the releasing of the commissioners. In her diary, New Yorker Maria R. Daly, wife of a judge and a pro-Union Democrat, wrote: "Mason and Slidell are given up. It seems the law of the United States, if not their own law, is on the side of the English." Mentioning Secretary Seward, she commented that he "obliged us to thus set two traitors to the government at large in order to prevent a great point for which we have so long been contending from being endangered, namely, the inviolability of neutral vessels."[15]

The South protested vehemently. As expected, Jefferson Davis deplored the situation as piracy, as did many members of his cabinet. Southern diarist Mary Chestnut, upon hearing of the imprisonment of the commissioners, wrote: "The men had been taken from under the British flag. Oh, that we could hear a growl from the English lion." In another entry, she remarked: "I do hope England will resent the indignity to her flag in the taking off of Mason and Slidell." She further commented that the Richmond papers thought it *was* a cause for war and that the most important idea was, What does England think? Then, in a rare barb at the Confederates, Chestnut said, "Poor Confederate States—if that booby Mallory had only given us a navy."[16] Whether or not Chestnut realized it, she had put her finger on one of the most important weaknesses of the Confederacy: the lack of a viable navy with which to match the Union's squadrons and provide armed escorts.

Historian Ed Pollard maintained that "the concession was a blow to the hopes of the Southern people. The spectacle of their enemy's humiliation was but little compensation for their disappointment of a European complication in the war."[17]

The most scathing comments on the *Trent* affair came from the Confederate congress, which declared that it was

> [a]n outrage of national amity which could not escape the indignation of all maritime nations. It was perpetrated by a zealot who was too stupid to foresee its ill effect on the relations which his own country was endeavoring to maintain with Europe, and it produced a sensation which for a while seemed to threaten the total failure of coercion.[18]

One cannot help noticing the single thread that ran through the Southern protests: the failure of the British government to get involved in the Civil War on the side of the Confederacy. Nothing would have delighted Jefferson Davis and his government more. However, no one has ever conjectured on what would have happened if England had won such a war and conquered the Union. Would anything have stopped her from swallowing the considerably weakened Southern states? To our knowledge, no one dared consider this supposition in that day, because of the negative aspect cast upon the integrity of the British Empire.

Regarding the *Trent* affair, Flag Officer Samuel du Pont wrote:

> I now hope that our politicians will begin to learn, that something is necessary to be a "great universal Yankee Nation, etc." than politics and party. We should have armies and navies and have those appurtenances which enable a nation to defend itself and not be compelled to humiliation [such as releasing Mason and Slidell]. Thirty ships like the *Wabash* would have spared us this without firing a gun, with an ironclad or two.[19]

Du Pont was expressing what many naval officers were thinking, namely, that a clash with Britain would have been averted anyway, considering the Union's large and powerful navy. One thing the British Empire respected was a strong military force.

Canadian professor Geoffrey S. Smith summed up the *Trent* situation very succinctly when he wrote: "Although Wilkes provoked a situation that pushed Britain to the brink of war, that question turned on one variable; whether Washington would sanction the seizure. And that possibility, as even the most ardent Anglophile admitted, was remote." He added: "The *Trent* incident forced Britain and the United States to establish earnest diplomatic relations early in the war, and the episode produced channels of communications that proved invaluable in the coming years."[20]

CHAPTER EIGHT

MOPPING UP THE SOUNDS: ROANOKE

With the *Trent* affair seemingly over, the Lincoln administration once more turned its attention to the war—especially the struggle along the East Coast. Even though Hatteras was secure and Port Royal was in Union hands, the Confederates still controlled a large portion of the sounds, rivers, inlets, and harbors along the coast. To the south was the Cape Fear area; Charleston, South Carolina; Savannah, Georgia; and Fernandina, Florida. The populace of these regions, plus Confederate armies inland, were still receiving much needed supplies by the persistent efforts of blockade-runners. Through these waterways, leading to important rail systems, the lifeblood of the Confederacy flowed and, in too many cases, was left unchecked by the overtaxed blockaders.[1]

Nowhere was this fact more evident than at Pamlico Sound, only recently captured by Federal forces. Their failure to follow up on the fall of Forts Hatteras and Clark, with powerful naval excursions up Pamlico Sound to Albemarle Sound, allowed the Confederates to fortify Roanoke Island. This site was vital to the Confederates, because any enemy thrust into Albemarle Sound would allow them a back-door route to Norfolk and Richmond by way of the Great Dismal Swamp Canal and an inland railroad line. To the Confederacy, Albemarle Sound had to be kept out of

Union hands at all costs. In addition to control of waterways, a heavily fortified Roanoke Island would threaten the vital railroad line to Norfolk and
Richmond.

Roanoke Island, shaped like a sweet potato, is 12 miles long and 3 miles
wide, dividing Roanoke and Croatan Sounds, with Albemarle Sound to
the north, the North Carolina mainland to the west, Pamlico Sound to the
south, and the Outer Banks to the east. The historically rich island was
the site of the English colony originally established by Sir Walter Raleigh
and lost in 1587.

In December 1862, the Confederates, under the command of Colonel
Henry M. Shaw, built Fort Forrest on the mainland and three forts on
Roanoke: Fort Huger, at the north end of the island, with 12 guns; Fort
Blanchard, one mile south, with 4 guns; and Fort Bartow, with 9 guns, lo-
cated at Pork Point near the proposed Union landing site at Ashby's Point.
On the east coast of the island was a small battery protecting Shallow Bay.
Near Ashby's Point, a small three-gun battery was placed athwart the
causeway leading north in the center of the island. The personnel at these
points amounted to around 3,000 troops.

To discourage any naval incursions into Albemarle Sound, gangs of
slaves labored to pound a double line of piling into the bottom of Croatan
Sound, along with sunken hulks, a little above Fort Bartow. Behind this
line, the Confederates would station their Mosquito Fleet of seven gunboats under the command of Flag Officer William Lynch, a career naval
officer and an explorer. It was an impressive squadron, but was woefully
undermanned. The entire area, island and adjoining waters, was under the
command of Brigadier General Henry Wise, a lawyer and former governor
of Virginia. On the surface, at least, the island and surrounding environs
looked formidable enough, but the real test would come when the Federal
forces arrived.

After the disastrous Bull Run campaign and its disheartening effect on
the Union populace, great pressure was put on General George Brinton
McClellan, who, succeeding the aging and retiring General Scott, whipped
the Army of the Potomac into a powerful fighting machine. Soon after
Cape Hatteras and Port Royal were secured, he recognized the importance
of gaining control of both Pamlico and Albemarle Sounds.

McClellan commenced planning his Peninsular Campaign to take
Richmond through a seaborne and land assault by way of Newport News

and the James River. The recapture of Norfolk and the Gosport Navy Yard would benefit his campaign by denying any resistance from Confederate forces there. Therefore, when he heard of Brigadier General Ambrose Burnside's plan to take Roanoke Island, he wrote instructions to Burnside, who had recently been appointed to head the invasion force in conjunction with Flag Officer Goldsborough: "Your first point of attack, will be Roanoke Island and its dependencies." Then, keeping in mind the spectacular naval bombardments at Cape Hatteras and Port Royal, he continued: "It is presumed that the navy can reduce the batteries on the marshes and cover the landing of your troops on the main island, by which, in connection with a rapid movement of the gunboats to the northern extremity as soon as the marsh battery is reduced, it may be hoped to capture the entire garrison of the place."[2]

McClellan then went on to outline military activities after the fall of Roanoke Island: the taking of New Bern on the Neuse River; then the capture of Fort Macon, at the south end of Pamlico Sound; and finally Beaufort. A move upon Goldsboro, farther up the Neuse River, would then sever the North Carolina railroad, thereby preventing supplies from reaching Richmond and the Confederate armies inland. This, he contended, would secure the entire coastal area of North Carolina, except for Fort Fisher, the gateway to the vital Confederate port, which would require another campaign.[3]

Burnside had no resistance against raising the forces needed for what was to become known as the Burnside Expedition. A division of 15,000 army troops was specially trained and given to his command. The naval aspect was another story, however; since most of Goldsborough's warships were in action elsewhere, he assembled a mishmash fleet of vessels consisting of armed ferry boats, barges for floating batteries, schooners, tugs that he labeled "propellors," and practically anything that could float and support a gun. The fleet grew as 1861 passed into 1862, until he had a force of 80 vessels of all types. To round out this armada, Goldsborough pledged some of his gunboats, along with colliers, tugs, and transports of various tonnage.

Most of the personnel for his fleet, aside from those on the navy vessels, were recruited from the army, specially trained, and given distinctive uniforms.[4] The troops were gleaned from New Englanders and those from the mid-Atlantic states who had firsthand knowledge of the Atlantic Ocean, because it was thought that they would be best equipped for the jobs at hand. That experience was sorely tested early on, when the troops first saw the shallow draft of the flotilla, designed for maneuvering in the sounds and rivers and not equipped for the capricious, fierce gales off the Atlantic coast.[5] But the troops' seamanship and savvy would help save many of their lives during the fierce storms on the way down and off Cape Hatteras.

On January 11, 1862, the hodgepodge armada of warships, men, and transports sailed forth from Hampton Roads, headed for Cape Hatteras, to be followed by Goldsborough's powerful squadron of 19 gunboats, all scheduled to arrive at Hatteras Inlet on Monday, January 13. As expected, bad weather dogged the fleet, but it stayed together until it reached its destination. Then began the laborious task of getting the fleet over the bar into Pamlico Sound; many ran aground, and it was soon learned that original estimates of the bar's depths were greatly overestimated, as some spots reached only seven feet. Adding to the distress of the fleet was the weather, as a fierce gale came up and caused damage to the ships in this storm-ravaged area. One large transport, the *New York,* was beached, deserted, and broken up by the powerful surf. Then the army gunboat *Zouave* ran afoul of her anchor and sank.[6] A third vessel had to turn back and return to Hampton Roads.

In order to get ships over the bar, they had to be lightened by removing all moveable heavy equipment, then snaked over the shallow shoal into the sound. Some of the heavier vessels were snaked across by deliberately running into the shallow shoal, where they would stick fast. Then, with their anchors out ahead, either in the bottom or on tugs, the tide would sluice out a channel beneath the keel, allowing the ship to be towed into the inner part of the sound. Of course, the removed heavy equipment had to be replaced on board; it proved to be hard work, and was made even more difficult by the weather that dogged the fleet incessantly.

Finally, by February 5, after more storms and delays, the fleet was safely at anchor in Pamlico Sound, and preparations were under way for the assault on Roanoke Island. Now gathered in the sound were 22 transports, between 20 and 30 schooners, a number of sailing troop vessels, and 4 propeller tugs. In addition, there was the naval contingent, consisting of 20 gunboats of various tonnages, with division commander Stephen Rowan, riding in then flagship *Delaware*. Flag Officer Goldsborough raised his flag on the yardarm of the 504-ton side-wheeler *Philadelphia*.[7]

Wednesday, February 6, dawned with a heavy fog to the north, which soon dissipated in the morning sun as the ships began forming in three columns. At 10:00 A.M., the order was hoisted to get under way, and the fleet moved northward into the sound, 35 miles from their destination. As the fleet moved, scouts were sent ahead to ascertain if batteries were located on some of the earlier points, and to watch for the Mosquito Fleet, which up to this time had offered no opposition except for a very brief reconnaissance foray. Ten hours later, the slow-moving fleet arrived at Stumpy Point, within visual distance from Roanoke Island, where the order was given to anchor for the night.

The next morning, Thursday, February 7, dawned cloudy but bright. The fleet up-anchored and headed for the island, passing through the area known as the marshes and entering Croatan Sound, drawing close to the island by nightfall. A heavy rainstorm halted the fleet, causing it to anchor for the night. But, early on the seventh, the order was given to attack, and the normally quiet sound was split apart by heavy gunfire when the gunboats unleashed their broadsides on Fort Bartow. Meanwhile, Ashby's Landing, below the fort, had been scouted and pronounced free of enemy opposition, and the order was given to bring up the transports and prepare for landing troops. Then followed an innovation in the concept of amphibious landings: Some 20 surfboats were attached in long lines to the rear of a number of fast steamers. The steamers ran full steam ahead toward the shore, pulling the boats behind. As they neared the shore, the order was given to let go—the lines were cut, and the vessels veered off to starboard or port. The surfboats were thus slung with great force forward, and their momentum would thrust them far up on the shoreline, where the troops disembarked without opposition. It was a prophetic picture of future amphibious landings 81 years later, in World War II's Pacific campaign.[8]

The gunboats shelled the areas surrounding the landing site to drive away any enemy opposition. Others continued their bombardment of Fort Bartow. The thunder of guns rolled across the sound, and smoke enveloped everything on the water as shell after shell rained down on the Confederates. Still, the defenders bravely responded in kind, and some of the attacking vessels were hit, but with no serious damage.

On the island, the forces of Union generals Reno, Foster, and Park made short work of the small battery athwart the causeway leading north, where three guns and a line of infantry had been placed to protect the forts to the rear. The Union forces split into three columns: one on the west side of the causeway, a second on the right, and one, the aggressive 9th New York Zouaves, advancing on the causeway itself. The flanking columns had a tangled, almost impenetrable swamp in which to move forward, and it did not take long for the Confederates to capitulate, either surrendering or fleeing. Fort Bartow now stood open and naked.[9]

During the lull in the bombardment, while Union troops mopped up, Goldsborough ordered a penetration of the obstacles in the channel, in order for his forces to get at the Mosquito Fleet hiding behind them and under the protection of Fort Bartow's guns. Flag Officer Lynch's squadron had been sniping away at Goldsborough's ships and generally making a nuisance of itself, trying to draw some of his warships within range of the fort's guns, but they were unsuccessful in their efforts and took a beating in the process. Lynch's efforts were brave against overwhelming odds, but the price he paid was the loss of the 350-ton armed tugboat *Curlew,* which took a direct hit straight through the keel, plunging her to the bottom. Another armed steam tug, *Forrest,* was hit hard and sent to Elizabeth City for repairs.[10] The Mosquito Fleet was now down to six fighting vessels.

Nine Union gunboats, headed by the 341-ton side-wheeler *Underwriter,* were ordered to find a weak spot in the obstruction. The *Lockwood* was the lucky one to find a break in the obstruction. She slipped through, and soon the entire squadron had passed over while Lynch's fleet went scurrying up Albemarle Sound to Elizabeth City.

On the island, the Union flag went up over Fort Bartow, signifying the victory won by the attacking forces. Fleeing Confederate soldiers were trapped on the north end of the island, where they surrendered to Union troops. The island was now in Federal hands.

The victory was an impressive one: three forts, 3,000 stand of arms, cannons, and other military materiel. Also captured were the commander of the island, Colonel Shaw, and Colonel O. Jennings Wise. It was then learned that General Henry Wise was over on Nag's Head, lying ill. A contingent of troops was also on Nag's Head but never deployed to assist those on Roanoke Island. The battery on the east end of the island was also mopped up soon after. After the island was secured and the sound cleared of enemy warships, Goldsborough could wire Secretary Welles that "Roanoke Island is ours."[11] He had accomplished a most important military objective of the Union, that of closing the back door to Norfolk and Richmond. His casualties were surprisingly light: 37 dead and 214 wounded, while the Confederates suffered 23 dead and 58 wounded. His fleet escaped any serious damage, with only the gunboat *Hetzel* heavily damaged and the *Delaware* almost destroyed by a whiskey-crazed gunner's mate.

The Confederate squadron, meanwhile, having fled up the Pasquotank River to Elizabeth City, found themselves in quite a predicament. The city lay at the south end of a 22-mile-long intracoastal waterway, the Great Dismal Swamp Canal, a direct water highway to Norfolk. The Great Dismal Swamp is a 35-mile densely forested series of marshes and swamps explored by William Byrd in 1728 and by George Washington in 1763 as a member of a survey and engineering team. The canal was dug from 1790 to 1828 and quickly became an important waterway with heavy traffic. Today the Great Dismal Swamp Canal still exists but is not used for commerce anymore.

Lynch and his commanders were relying on this waterway to escape to Norfolk after the fall of Roanoke Island, but they discovered the canal's lock mechanism was broken, so they had no choice but to stand by while it was being fixed. With only 200 pounds of powder, they turned to face the superior Union fleet that was sure to come.[12]

Lynch formed a battle line across the river with what was left of his fleet: the gunboats *Seabird, Ellis, Appomattox, Beaufort,* and *Raleigh* and the tug *Fanny,* plus a schooner, *Black Warrior.* The last of these was anchored near the fort to be used as a floating battery. This was all that was left of his fleet.

At early light on February 10, Commander Stephen Rowan, in the *Delaware,* and 16 gunboats came up the river, spoiling for a fight. At the signal to make a dash for the enemy, the Union flotilla opened fire. The answer came from the enemy gunboats, the soldiers at Fort Cobb having fled. The battle was short-lived, with all Confederate vessels either captured or destroyed.[13] The *Raleigh* and the *Beaufort* took no part in the action and managed to escape through the now-repaired locks of the canal to Norfolk. The *Appomattox* tried to follow, but she was too large and jammed in the locks; she was later destroyed, along with the locks. Lynch and some of his commanders escaped to Norfolk by wagon.

The Union squadron suffered only minor damage, and soon they were anchored off Elizabeth City only to find it partially burned by the fleeing citizens, except for a large warehouse full of food and supplies. The *Forrest*, which had been damaged at Roanoke Island, was burned on the stocks along with an unfinished gunboat hull. Only a few freed slaves were roaming around.

Next, Rowan sent a detachment up the sound to the town of Edenton, where another gunboat was being built. There the Union troops were almost drawn into a trap set by the Confederate militia. A slave woman was sent to wave a handkerchief at the approaching fleet, to inform them that the town was ripe for the taking. But as the vessels approached, a lookout in the mast spotted the sunlight flashing off muskets in the hands of waiting militiamen. The squadron veered off and backed downriver. The residents of Edenton celebrated what they thought was a victory, but the festivities were cut short by the return of the gunboats. Sitting amidstream, the war vessels unleashed a bombardment on the town, pounding it into submission as punishment for the treacherous act. Then the city and its small shipyard were burned to the ground by angered Union troops.[14]

Albemarle and Pamlico Sounds were now in Union hands, and it appeared as if that part of the Confederate Atlantic coast defense system was neutralized. Only one more operation remained for the victorious Union navy.

New Bern, North Carolina, was the second largest town on the North Carolina coast. Located at the confluence of the Trent and Neuse Rivers, it was once the capital of the North Carolina Colony and was a leading port. While it had earlier been of even greater significance, it was still of relative importance to the Confederates because of its location near inland railroads and its direct connection to the Atlantic Ocean, 35 miles away.

On March 11, General Burnside and 11,000 troops, followed by Commander Rowan and 13 gunboats, left Hampton Roads and set course for Pamlico Sound, where they gathered forces at the mouth of the Neuse River. March 13 dawned bright, and the flotilla of gunboats and transports moved up the wide river to a landing point 16 miles below New Bern. Using the same tactics as those at Hatteras and Roanoke Island, the gunboats unleashed a shelling ahead of the advancing infantry.

When Confederate troops met Burnside's men head-on, the fighting continued into the next day, until finally the defenders had enough and were routed. They burned the town behind them as they fled inland. The Union troop successes were achieved by the same commanders as at Roanoke, Generals Foster, Reno, and Park, who used the same three-pronged attack. When Commander C. S. Rowan entered the town, he asked a black woman where the Confederates were. She replied, "Runnin' as fast as they can."[15] The casualties for the Union amounted to 90 killed and 380 wounded; the Confederates had 64 killed and 101 wounded, but 413 men were listed as missing.

On April 25, Federal troops, backed by a flotilla of gunboats, assaulted and took Fort Macon, at the south end of Pamlico Sound. The entire North Carolina coast was now in Union hands, and the way was now open for a drive inland.

The Union victories in the Carolina sounds were due in part to their overwhelming force and in part to the Confederacy's shortages of supplies, manpower, and armament. This was borne out in a letter sent by Confederate General Henry A. Wise to President Davis shortly after the fall of Roanoke Island: "The North Carolina troops," he complained, "had not been paid, clothed or drilled, and they had no teams or materials for constructing works of defense, and they were badly commanded and led, and, except a few companies, they did not fight."[16]

Repercussions flew thick and fast throughout the Confederacy. On February 20, 1862, the first Confederate congress issued a rebuttal to the defense department:

> Who could explain, or who dared to defend the late affair at Roanoke Island? Had the Secretary of War or the Secretary of the Navy ever been down to Roanoke Island or Norfolk, or to see *any* of our defenses on the James River? Not at all. Those affairs of our military policy were not to be discussed in secret. The Senate at Rome, which stood five hundred years, had never sat with closed doors.[17]

The Congress went on to ask where the gunboats were. "The appropriations which have been made for the purpose of building them, where was it? It had not been used. But where were the gunboats that were to effectively withstand the enemy on the waters?"[18] This is a bit puzzling, because there's no doubt the congress knew that Flag Officer Lynch's Mosquito

Fleet had been stationed above the main Union landing site, although they were hiding behind obstructions in the main channel. Perhaps their timidity was what the congress was referring to.

Also, much of the blame for the Roanoke disaster had fallen on Judah Benjamin, the newly appointed secretary of war. It appeared that a requisition for powder had been made by the commander on the island to the new secretary, but it was never filled. The congress issued a statement voicing concern over what the probable effect such shortages would have on the congress and the people in general:

> General Huger was in command of Roanoke Island and Mr. Benjamin was fulfilling the post of Secretary of War. A requisition for powder was made and not filled. This was twice reported without avail, and Roanoke fell.[19]

Benjamin had to appear before congress and explain to the session that there simply was no powder to send.

With the coastline and its rivers in Union hands, General Burnside saw the possibility now open for a military thrust inland, possibly using cavalry troops, to cut the Confederate interior lines of communication. He asked General McClellan for troops but was denied on the grounds that the Peninsular Campaign was in its final stages and that every man, horse, and gun was needed. From a modern perspective, what was lost was not only a valuable opportunity to cut those lines but also a chance to bring the war to an early end.

While all this activity was taking place in the North Carolina sounds, an event occurred in Hampton Roads that was destined to change the navies of the world forever.

CHAPTER NINE

MONITOR VS. MERRIMACK, PART 1: THE ANTAGONISTS

With the growing might of the Union navy, Secretary Mallory became increasingly concerned about countering that expanding strength. His resources were badly strained. Aware of the fact that the Confederacy could never match the Union in the number of warships, he had set out to obtain existing vessels of commerce and convert them to viable warships. Glancing at the Union navy, he saw one consisting mostly of wooden vessels: ships of the line, frigates, schooners, and side-wheelers. These, he deduced, would be vulnerable to a ship with iron plating around her hull and equipped with formidable armament.

Ironclads were not unheard of, but Mallory's problem was how to construct them from scratch for his fledgling navy. He was aware that during the Crimean War, the French constructed six armored floating batteries to be used against Russians at Fort Kinburn on the peninsula. Three of them were towed through the Black Sea and placed within 800 to 1,000 yards of the fort, where they unleashed a bombardment on the powerful fort, which mounted 51 guns and 12 mortars. The Russian shells, in return, made no impact on the sloping iron casings of the floating batteries. After 40 minutes, the Russian fort was neutralized, with no appreciable damage to the batteries. The French quickly capitalized on this innovation and began planning a fleet of iron-armored ships "upon which armor the missiles of naval warfare would fall harmlessly."[1] The first such ship planned was to be wooden with iron plating over it. Launched in 1857, the *Gloire* was 250 feet long, with a 21-foot beam and sides of iron plating 51 inches thick. She was armed with thirty-eight 50-pound rifles and was powered by a 500-horsepower engine with a top speed of 12½ knots. At the time, she was considered to be the most powerful warship in the world. The French planned to construct four vessels of this class.

In commenting on the *Gloire* class, Mallory wrote: "The power of such a fleet [that can] carry 300 rifled 50-pounders could hardly be estimated . . . there is no sea castle, fort or defensive work in the British Channel that it could not demolish with comparative immunity."[2]

Mallory then expressed his views to C. M. Conrad, chairman of the Committee on Naval Affairs, to the effect that he regarded the possession of such an armored ship as one of the utmost importance. He was of the opinion that such a vessel could traverse the East Coast of the United States and break the blockade, possibly meeting and destroying the Union navy. At first he turned to European shipbuilders, only to learn they were already engaged in a race of building battleships and had none to sell to outside buyers. The hard, cold fact was that he had to build one himself, and he was sure that, in spite of limited resources, one could be built in the Confederacy, using whatever materials and artisans were on hand, at the Gosport Navy Yard.

And, as fate would have it, an ordnance expert in the Confederate government, Lieutenant John Mercer Brooke, came forward with the answer. It happened in June 1861, when Mallory came by way of the sounds on his way to the new Confederate capital in Richmond, Virginia, where it had been moved from Montgomery, Alabama. He had traversed Pamlico and Albemarle Sounds and the Great Dismal Swamp Canal, then decided to come ashore at Norfolk, where he planned to rest before going on to Richmond to confer with President Davis.

At Norfolk, in spite of being exhausted and slightly seasick, he met with Brooke and Chief Engineer William Price Williamson. Brooke, who had been waiting for such an opportunity to present his plan for an ironclad vessel to an authority in the government, was delighted. Here was the top man himself! Brooke had been examining the raised hulk of the *Merrimack,* on the stocks of the dry dock at Gosport Navy Yard, and was struck by the good condition of her hull, to say nothing of her power plant. He asked himself, why not put a frame on this hulk and make an ironclad out of her? After all, the keel all the way up to the berthing deck was still sound, and it would be better than building a new ship from the keel up. Quickly he drew up some plans for an ironclad vessel to be built at the navy yard.

He showed Mallory a body, sheer, and deck drawing that to the secretary simulated an "iron cooking pot."[3] The most unusual feature of the model was its submerged ends. For all the world, it resembled a cake pan upside down on a raft, designed to operate in shallow water as a harbor defense craft. Although Mallory wanted a seagoing craft, he nevertheless told Brooke to go ahead and build the thing, along with Williamson and John Luke Porter, a naval engineer based at Gosport Navy Yard.

There has been a lot of controversy over the years as to who really planned the *Virginia*. Both Brooke and Porter drew models and presented them to Mallory, but historians now believe it was Brooke who first submitted the plans, soon after she was raised and placed in dry dock.

Soon after the meeting at Norfolk, an appropriation was approved by the government for the construction of the proposed ironclad, in the munificent amount of $172,523.[4]

Engines and ordnance were needed for the ironclad, so Brooke and Williamson began a search for a source. First of all, they consulted the Tredegar Iron Works at Richmond, but the firm demurred, declaring that it was putting all its effort into building ordnance for the Confederate armies. Returning to Norfolk, the duo examined the raised *Merrimack,* and Williamson came to the opinion that her engines could be cleaned, repaired, and installed in the ironclad.[5] Williamson's idea was a brilliant one, because the lower hull of the frigate was strong and salvageable. Her power plant, if restored, would solve the problem of obtaining engines from another source. The plan was submitted to Mallory, who quickly approved it, and construction began on July 11, 1861, under the overall jurisdiction of Commodore French Forrest, commandant of the navy yard. Williamson was responsible for restoring the power plant, Brooke for her armor and guns, and Porter for overall construction.

A better hull could never be found than that of the *Merrimack*. Built in Boston and commissioned on February 20, 1856, she displaced 4,636 tons, was 300 feet long with a 51-foot beam, and had a draft of 22 feet. With her formidable armament of 40 guns, she was considered to be one of the finest warships in the world. Her weakness, however, was her balky engines, and that was one reason she had been in ordinary at Gosport Navy Yard for overhauling.[6]

In July, construction of the ironclad was well under way. The *Merrimack* had been stripped down to her berth deck, which became the main deck of the *Virginia*, as it was to be later named by the Confederates. A framework over 160 feet of the hull was constructed of oak and pine wood 22 inches thick, at an inclination of 35 degrees, which formed the base for the iron plating. The plating on the casemate itself was eight inches wide and two inches thick. The first layer was bolted on longitudinally, the other horizontally. The iron plates were mounted, using 1⅜-inch bolts countersunk and secured with iron nuts and washers. Both the front and back sides of the casemate were rounded and pierced for fore and aft guns. The plating of the casemate, or citadel, projected two feet below the waterline, and was pierced for 10 guns of the broadside batteries: four Brooke rifles, a single-banded gun invented by the very same designer, and six 9-inch Dahlgren shell rifles. Two of the rifles were the bow and stern pivot guns. Each gun-port had an iron door that slammed shut after the gun was fired.

The square topside consisted of two-inch-square iron gratings, 2½ inches apart, leaving openings for three hatches, one fore and aft and one abaft the smokestack. The pilothouse, forward of the stack, was conical in shape and was plated with the same four-inch iron as on the sides. A 1,500-pound wedge-shaped ram was bolted on the prow and extended out four feet. The rudder and screw were unprotected, although the rudder chains were partially protected by a metal shield aft.

When completed, the *Merrimack* ironclad had a displacement of 3,500 tons and was 262.9 feet long, with a 51-foot beam, a draft of 19 to 22 feet, and a top speed of six knots, although she was rated at nine knots. Her five boilers were tubular, with one auxiliary, and consumed 3,400 pounds of anthracite coal per hour. Her two engines were horizontal, back-acting, two-cylinder models with a 72-inch diameter and a three-foot stroke that produced her 1,294 horsepower. The screw was a two-blade Griffiths with a diameter of 17 feet, 4 inches.[7]

Her crew of 320 officers and men was a mixed bag of personnel obtained with great difficulty, because of a lack of trained seamen. Mostly, with a few exceptions, they were volunteers from the army and landsmen, except for the naval officers and 55 marines.[8]

The progress of the *Merrimack* was dogged with difficulties along the way, especially for the iron plating from the Tredegar Iron Works. Flatcars loaded with iron plates sat on sidings for weeks on end, because of shortages of rolling stock and the priorities of matériel for the Confederate armies. Other problems stemmed from the shortage of skilled labor and lack of tools and other construction necessities.[9] In many instances, Commodore Forrest had to send officers out to scout for the delayed flatcars.

Then to add to everyone's frustration, a labor strike was called for the shipyard in January of 1862, which all but closed down the yard. However, Commodore Forrest settled the strike in short order by appealing to the patriotism of the workers.

Finally, in February, *Merrimack* was floated in her dry dock in order to test her seaworthiness. She proved to be top-heavy, so additional deck plating was put on, keel ballast was added in her hold; other modifications were made to her keel to level her off in the water. Then, on February 13, 1862, she was launched without any fanfare, five marines on board. One of the privates wrote: "There were no invitations to [the] governor and other distinguished men, no sponsor, no maid of honor, no bottle of wine . . . no brass band, no blowing of steam whistles and no great crowds to witness this memorable event."[10] She was commissioned in the Confederate navy and named C.S.S *Virginia,* in honor of her host state.

The *Virginia* needed a commanding officer, so Mallory ignored all tradition, passed over qualified officers, and picked a career navy officer, Franklin Buchanan. Nicknamed "Old Buck" by his contemporaries, he held the post of the first superintendent of the U.S. Naval School after participating in the Perry expedition to Japan; in 1855 he was appointed captain and became commandant of the Washington Navy Yard. After the secession, Buchanan joined the Confederacy and was appointed by Mallory to the post of chief of the Bureau of Orders and Detail. Now Mallory appointed him flag officer of the James River defenses, with *Virginia* as his flagship.[11] Surprisingly, there was no captain of the vessel officially appointed; she was equipped and run by the executive and ordnance officers. For all intents and purposes, Buchanan was the squadron commander and ipso facto skipper of the warship.

Mallory then ordered Lieutenant Catesby ap Roger Jones, a career navy officer who had worked closely with Lieutenant John Dahlgren at the Washington Navy Yard in the development of the Dahlgren gun, to Norfolk to take over the post of executive officer. This capable officer was to prove his mettle in the days to come because of his intimate knowledge of naval ordnance.

One of Buchanan's early actions was to convince Mallory that the *Virginia* could not make a foray up the Potomac as far as Washington. It was impossible because of her shallow draft and her limited fuel capacity, plus the fact she was top-heavy and not suited for deep-water sailing. Greatly concerned about the odds on the enemy side and the presence of General Porter's Union troops on the Newport News peninsula, he considered the idea of a joint operation with General John Bankhead Magruder—also known as "Prince John" because of his lavish parties, elegant uniforms, and courtliness with the ladies. In this operation, Confederate troops would sweep down the peninsula to rout enemy troops there while the *Virginia* engaged their ships in Hampton Roads and subsequently bombarded their artillery emplacements at Newport News. But Magruder rejected the idea because the roads would be impassable during the rainy season.

Buchanan was undaunted and dedicated himself to doing as much harm to the enemy fleet as he could. He would go it alone to destroy Union frigates first, then turn his attention to the shore batteries.[12]

Mallory was pleased with the progress of the *Virginia,* though he was impatient with the constant delays in getting the vessel ready for her sortie, and these delays were the probable reason he sent Jones to Norfolk. In his orders to Buchanan, he wrote that the vessel was a "novelty in construction, is untried, and her powers unknown . . . Her powers as a ram are regarded as being very formidable and it is hoped you will be able to test them . . . the painful reverses we have just suffered [Cape Hatteras, Port Royal, and Roanoke Island] demand our utmost exertions."[13]

Jones, with his characteristic energy and aplomb, busied himself with the many problems concerning the ironclad. He was concerned that the vessel was riding too high in the water and that "between the wind and water," her vulnerable sides would be exposed to enemy fire. He wrote:

> The ship is too light or I should say, she is not sufficiently protected below the water. Our draft will be a foot less than was first

intended, yet I was this very morning [March 5] ordered not to put any ballast in fear of the bottom. The eaves of the roof will not be more than six inches immersed, which in smooth water will not be enough; a slight ripple except the one-inch iron which extends some feet below.[14]

In spite of this, Buchanan was determined to make his sortie as soon as possible, so the sides were sloshed with grease to repel shot and shell, then coal and ammunition were brought on board and the crew assembled.

When Buchanan was satisfied that all was well, he planned an attack on the Union fleet for Thursday, March 6. However, further delays brought more frustration to Buchanan and the crew. Jones informed the flag officer that the five pilots hired to guide the ponderous vessel through the Elizabeth River were adamant that they could not pilot the ship in darkness; to guide a vessel with such a great draft would be difficult under ordinary conditions, and the channel lights and buoys with which they were familiar had long since been taken out. Buchanan wanted to leave at daybreak, but once again he was refused, as it seems that the ironclad's deep draft, 22 feet, could pass over the bar only at 2:00 P.M. Buchanan reluctantly accepted the inevitable consequences, and the attack was called off until Saturday, March 8. Once more, mechanics swarmed over her, ready to work day and night to get her ready for what everyone outside of the officers thought was to be her trial run. Buchanan, meanwhile, had ordered an escort, including the 65-ton screw steamer *Raleigh* and the 85-ton steamer *Beaufort,* both with one gun each.

That darkened night, as crews and construction personnel feverishly put on the finishing touches, Charles MacIntosh, captain of the C.S.S. *Louisiana,* came across the dock and said sadly to *Virginia's* chief engineer, H. Ashton Ramsay, "Good-bye, Ramsay. I shall never see you again. She will be your coffin."[15]

An interesting footnote to the genesis of the *Virginia* concerns an amazing stunt performed by the *New York Herald* reporter B. S. Osbon, after his managing editor sent him to Fort Monroe to obtain more information on the mysterious ironclad being built by the rebels. He secured a boat and, in spite of a heavy fog, managed to slip past the Confederate batteries on Sewell's Point. As he approached the navy yard, the fog lifted and he caught a full view of the "great ram" in the dry dock; he made notes and a rough drawing of the vessel. Then he slipped away undetected. Later, Osbon suggested leading a boarding party to destroy the ram while she was defenseless, but the commandant of Fort Monroe, General Wool, thought the proposal foolhardy and refused to sanction it. No photo of her was ever taken, but based on Osbon's drawings and those of other identified observers, plus statistical data available, a fairly accurate portrait of the famous vessel has been created by various artists over the years.

Meanwhile, in Washington, an incident occurred that caused the Navy Department to sit up and take more notice of the rumors about the "great ram" the Confederates were building at the Gosport Navy Yard. A black woman came to the Navy Department and announced that she was a resident of Norfolk and had some important information about the building of the *Virginia*. When Secretary Welles agreed to see her, she claimed that she and others had observed the building of the *Virginia* and had come through the lines to Washington, at a great risk to herself and others. Taking a letter from her bosom, she presented it to the secretary. It was written by a Union sympathizer working on the ram, stating that the ship was nearly finished and was ready to come out of dry dock to receive her armament. The news ended any plan of destroying the vessel by a boarding party, and it made Welles and his staff increasingly anxious to build a deterrent to the enemy ram.[16]

In spite of some historians who have criticized Welles for not exploring fully the concept of ironclad vessels, the facts are that the secretary was fully aware of the latest technological advances in world navies, including the advent of ironclad warships. In May 1861, he had discussed the concept with an ironmaster from New Jersey, but made no plans to build one.[17] But as more knowledge came into his department, his attention and that of Fox turned more to the ironclad concept, and they sought advice from such naval experts as Captain Joseph Smith and Captain Charles H. Davis.

Then on July 4, 1861, Welles approached Congress for an appropriation to form an ironclad board to study the feasibility of building such a craft. Congress voted an appropriation of $1,500,000 for the board, and President Lincoln signed it on August 4. The appropriation was rushed through and sent to the appropriate departments for quick deployment.

The board was composed of Welles' friends and advisors, Smith and Davis, plus Commodore Hiram Paulding. Smith was chief of the Bureau of Yards and Docks, Davis was head of the Bureau of Navigation, and Paulding was head of the Bureau of Order and Detail.

Welles asked the board for plans and bids for a ship built of iron or wood, the specifications to include 80 to 120 tons of armament and rigging with two masts and wire rope. The response was some 16 proposals, out of which he chose two designs. One was from Cornelius Bushnell, a New England businessman, for a 950-ton vessel, called the *Galena*. The 18-gun vessel was designed by Samuel Pook, and it featured iron slats placed one over the other on the sides, much like clapboards on a house. The other proposal was a 3,480-ton, 20-gun steam frigate, *New Ironsides*, under construction at Merrick and Sons shipyard in Philadelphia.[18]

When Bushnell was asked to prove the stability of the *Galena*, he turned to an engineer friend, Swedish-born John Ericsson, who had an office in New York. Ericsson quickly soothed the businessman's fears and claimed that the concept of the *Galena* was a sound one. Then he asked Bushnell if he would examine his own model for an ironclad that was impregnable to the heaviest shot or shell. When Bushnell agreed, Ericsson took down a dusty box and, to Bushnell's amazement, removed a cardboard model of a flat-bottomed, self-propelled battery with an ironclad rotating turret with two guns. According to Ericsson, the flush-decked hull would be made of iron over wood and extended over the rudder and a screw propeller of his own design. The strange object had no rigging or spars, and the only projections on the flat deck were the turret and a pilothouse forward near the bow, except for a jackstaff forward and a flagstaff on the stern, a radical new concept. Ericsson had stored the model away toward that day when he could present it to a United States official.

Now that the time had come, Bushnell was captivated by the model and its inventor, so he took the model and set out for Welles' office, knowing that the secretary, like himself, would be captivated by the new and radical concept for an ironclad vessel of war. As Bushnell expected, Welles was equally enthusiastic, and together they took it to the board. The board declared the model to be a novel one, but they admitted some apprehensions about her seaworthiness. In the end, after reassuring words from Ericsson, they approved the plan, except for Captain Davis, who told Bushnell to take it home and worship it, because it was the image of nothing in heaven above, or in the earth beneath, or in the waters under the earth. President Lincoln had another view. He declared, "All I have to say is what the girl said when she stuck her foot into the stocking, 'It strikes me there's something in it.' "[19] Now greatly encouraged, Ericsson plunged into his work with a new fervor.

Ericsson was born on July 31, 1803, in a small village in Sweden. His talents as engineer/designer came from his father, an engineer and canal designer. John was early schooled in the classical tradition, plus architectural and mechanical drawing. He worked with his father on the canal project and invented a "caloric hot air engine" that ran on heated air instead of the traditional steam. After his discharge, he traveled to England, where he invented a railroad locomotive that was highly successful, and before he left England and headed for the United States, he had already envisioned a new screw propeller as well as an ironclad vessel.

In the United States, his enthusiasm and indomitable spirit would almost cost him his career. In 1844, he developed and built a prototype screw steam vessel, called the *Princeton*, that featured two new 10-ton, 12-inch cannons designed by Ericsson himself. But during a presentation before President Polk and government officials on the Potomac River on February 29, 1844, one of the guns exploded, killing the secretaries of state and navy, plus the chief of the Bureau of Construction, Equipment and Repair, two congressmen, and a black servant, plus wounding twenty others. The result was a storm of protest and incriminations against the inventor. Disgraced, Ericsson moved to New York and worked privately as an engineer. But his inventive mind was still active and produced a flood of new ideas. It was during that time he formulated his "sub-aquatic system of warfare."[20] And it was there that the ironclad vessel he would design, the *Monitor*, was born.

Bushnell finally located Ericsson and brought him to Washington. The board was at first a bit hostile toward the inventor because of the *Princeton* incident, and facetiously referred to the *Monitor* model as "Ericsson's folly," without first examining it. But the irrepressible inventor won them over. They agreed on the building of the radical new vessel, but they gave him only 90 days in which to build it. However, with his usual indefatigable energy, he went to work on the project after raising $275,000 through a private syndicate of civilian businessmen. In fact, he let out contracts for various parts of the project, based on the ream of plans he had drawn up, before the board gave its approval.[21]

The design (and the final product) that finally took shape was ingenious, to say the least. The rectilinear iron hull was flat-bottomed, with curved sides meeting at stem and stern. This outer shell of ⅜-inch iron plate curved upward to a shelf, or upper hull, at a 35-degree angle. This upper hull was an armor belt of 5-inch iron plating and was the basis for the main decking structure, made of 10-inch-square oak beams covered by 8 inches of planking. Over this deck platform, the deck plating was laid, using two layers of ½-inch iron plate. The main feature of her topside was the 120-ton turret of eight overlapping layers of 1-inch iron plating bolted to a ½-inch layer of iron on the inside. The sides were pierced for two Dahlgren 11-inch smoothbores, and the top was covered by an iron grating with two escape hatches.

A novel feature inside the turret was a track surrounding the guns, called a "brass monkey," upon which the 180-pound solid shot was placed and then rolled to the gun positions for faster distribution by the crews.

The inside dimensions of the huge turret were 9 feet in height and 20 feet in diameter, and the entire structure rested on a brass ring recessed into the hull and supported within by railroad iron braces and beneath by a large traverse bulkhead at midship. The turret was supported by a spindle that reached down into the keel and was cog-wheeled by two steam engines capable of turning the turret a full 360 degrees. A specially designed wedge was fitted to lift the turret and also engage it to the main gear, allowing the structure to rotate.

The remainder of the topside was equipped with a four-foot-high pilothouse made of wrought-iron bars and located near the bow. Two hatches and blower ports were located on deck, and the rudder ports above the rudder and screw were protected by the overhanging deck. The nine-foot, four-bladed screw propeller was a special design by Ericsson.

The traverse bulkhead supporting the turret also separated the ship into two parts: officers' and crew's quarters forward, and the propulsion machinery aft of the bulkhead. The officers' quarters were unusually posh for a warship, with oilcloth-covered decks, tapestry, rugs, lace, brass railings, and polished walnut woodwork. The crew's quarters were fairly comfortable but were designed to contain only half of the crew at any one time, presumably with the remainder on duty stations, much like those on World War II submarines.

The Ericsson-designed vibrating-lever-type engines had 36-inch cylinders bored into a single casing geared to a single drive shaft, and were capable of 320 horsepower. Steam was supplied from two forced-air-type Martin boilers, also designed by the inventor. Special blowers supplied fresh air to below spaces throughout the vessel.[22]

On a warship, one of the primary considerations is the head, or toilet facilities. Ericsson came up with an ingenious system consisting of a pipe that was closed on the lower end. Waste was dropped into the pipe by way of a commode. The upper end was closed and the lower end opened while a force pump emptied the contents into the sea. This concept was the forerunner of the heads in World War II and later submarines.

Ericsson carefully picked the manufacturers of his vessel. In a concept ahead of its time, components were to be manufactured separately and brought together at a single shipyard. For the rivets and bar iron for the pilothouse, he chose Rensselaer Iron Works of Troy, New York; Albany Iron Works provided angle iron for the frame and some iron plating, with more plating supplied by Abbott and Sons of Baltimore. The Delameter Iron Works of New York City built the engines, and the Novelty Iron Works built the turret.

In this challenging operation, the rolled, curved plating was assembled around a wooden framework; gunports and rivet holes were then drilled. But because of the great weight of the turret, it had to be dismantled with the parts carefully marked, then reassembled on the vessel during its construction at the Continental Iron Works in Greenpoint, Brooklyn.[23]

By the end of February 1861, the vessel was nearly completed. It needed a captain, so Welles chose Lieutenant John Lorimer Worden, a career navy officer with impeccable credentials. Worden had been taken prisoner, after a secret mission to Fort Pickens in the Gulf of Mexico failed, in October 1861. Worden had been carrying a message to the senior officer of the squadron of the beleaguered Fort Pickens, to land troops and supplies.[24]

The launching date for the new ironclad was January 30, 1862. A large group of excited yard workers and officials gathered around the way upon which the nearly completed ironclad, minus her turret, rested. There was no breaking of champagne bottles on the bow, elaborate ceremonies, or long, patriotic speeches. The name *Monitor* was chosen by Ericsson, because he believed it would be a "severe monitor to the Confederacy," and that the presence of this vessel would convince the enemy that their coastal defenses and war vessels would not persevere against her presence.

As expected, skeptics abounded. Some declared that the vessel would go to the bottom of the East River and stay there. But to prove them wrong, Ericsson stood defiantly on deck as the *Monitor* slid serenely down the way and floated with ease on the water.

Shortly thereafter, while the vessel was being fitted with her turret and other equipment, Ericsson received a telegram from Fox, who urged him to hurry the *Monitor* to sea, because the *Merrimack* was nearly ready at Norfolk. However, the inventor and Captain Worden needed at least three weeks to get the ship fully equipped, armed, and manned with its crew of 58 officers and men.

When completed, the *Monitor* measured 173 feet in length and displaced 776 tons, with a beam of 41½ feet and a draft of a little over 10 feet. Her freeboard was less than a foot and was often awash on the waters. She seemed to have earned her nickname of "cheese box on a raft." Her trials revealed many defects: Her top speed was 3½ knots instead of the planned 9, and communication between the pilothouse and the turret was defective. The problems were solved, but on her trial runs she zigzagged all over the river and ended up bumping into a dock and being towed to the Brooklyn Navy Yard for repairs.

At last, however, the *Monitor* was finally ready for sea. Upon orders to report to Hampton Roads, Worden took her down New York Harbor in company with the steamers *Sachem* and *Camtuck,* until they reached Governor's Island, where the steam tug *Seth Low* came alongside and took her in tow.

The quartermaster recorded the wind as coming from the south-southwest at 5½ knots as they steered south, passing Barnegat lighthouse on the Jersey shore. Executive Officer Samuel Dana Greene reported waters as being ideal for sailing, and the officers lingered at the supper table in the wardroom as the captain reminisced about his naval experiences.

Then things changed rapidly. A typical spring Atlantic gale whipped the ocean from calm to heavy seas. By afternoon, the sea was breaking over the decks at a great rate and entering the forward hawse pipe. The sluicing washed away the hemp packing that had been placed under the jacked-up turret, in spite of Ericsson's order to leave the turret on its brass ring, because it would be efficient at keeping out seawater. The storm raged, causing the ship to rock vigorously. The two escort vessels were almost on their beam ends as they plunged into huge troughs in the raging waters. Visibility was practically nil, and the tow line was the *Monitor* crew's only link to their escort.

The water continued to pour into the hawse pipes and over and down the blower pipes and six-foot smokestacks in such quantities that there was imminent danger of the ship foundering. In fact, the water came through the narrow slits in the pilothouse with such force that it knocked the helmsman away from the wheel. The water, by wetting pulley belts, also caused the blowers to give out and fill the engine room with gases, causing many of the engineers to pass out. Greene entered the engine room and, with help from crewmen, carried the prostrate engineers to the turret for revival. They did the same when the boilers in the fireroom also gave out. Things began to get bleak for the struggling ironclad, but the towline held.

With an ill Captain Worden taken to his bunk, Greene was everywhere, doing all he could: rigging hand pumps on the berth deck, organizing bucket brigades that would throw the water out through the hatches on the top of the turret (but there just was not enough space to toss the water out without going topside). Things for a time looked desperate, and there was a possibility the ship might have to be abandoned. At one time, the water rushed into the anchor well, forcing air out through a hawse pipe, causing a noise that was described as sounding like the death throes of a thousand men.

When Greene had done all he could possibly do, he tried signaling the *Seth Low,* some 400 feet ahead, with a speaking trumpet, but there was no way anything could be heard above the roar of the wind and the crash of the waves.

Further signal complications ensued from a failure to install lights designed for night signaling, and a steam whistle had not been installed even though it had been suggested by Greene's father. With the vessel immobilized, it began to yaw from side to side, threatening to snap the towline, but fortunately the heavy line held. Greene, in one desperate measure, ran up the flag upside down, an international signal for distress. Finally, the storm abated long enough for the crews to relight the boilers and get the pumps working. The *Seth Low,* by this time alerted to the distress of the *Monitor* by the upside-down flag, came up, and Greene ordered a tow closer to the shoreline. The tug managed to bring all the convoy toward shore, and once again, they floated in calmer waters.[25]

With the weather brightened, the convoy again resumed its course toward Hampton Roads. Greene wrote that during the ordeal, he had thought that the sun would never again set on them.[26]

As the convoy neared Hampton Roads, lookouts spotted flashes of gunfire on the horizon, indicating that some action was taking place there. When they approached the mouth of the sound, a pilot boat came up and informed Captain Worden that the *Merrimack* had come out and that the *Cumberland* was sunk and the *Congress* was on fire.

Worden, Greene, and the entire crew hoped they were not too late to stop any further destruction of Union ships, and they vowed vengeance on the *Merrimack*.[27] Worden cast off from the *Seth Low* and headed up the sound, setting course for the *Minnesota*.[28]

CHAPTER TEN

MONITOR VS. MERRIMACK, PART 2: THE CONFLICT

Like some slumbering aquatic monster, the C.S.S. *Virginia* floated serenely alongside her dock at the Gosport Navy Yard in Norfolk, Virginia, on March 8, 1862. To eyes unaccustomed to strange species of warships, she resembled a barn roof resting on a raft; to others, she defied description, but all agreed that she was just plain ugly. Still, there must have been some redeeming quality of appearance as the sun beat down on her iron-plated citadel, or casemate, with her large black-painted smokestacks, two lifeboats nestled tightly in davits on her sides, two air funnels fore and aft of her stacks, a cone-shaped pilothouse with a narrow sighting slit, and the Confederate flag waving in the breeze on her flagstaff. But the black snouts of Dahlgren guns peering from her broadside gunports, as well as two fore and aft rifled guns, further enhanced her unlovely features.[1]

An observer might have seen workmen scurrying over her, putting on finishing touches, while crewmen were bringing in stores and ammunition. Hovering in the background would have been Flag Officer Buchanan tirelessly overseeing all activities. Something big was in the air, and everyone in the navy yard knew it. This "barn roof" or "floating monster" was to be the Confederacy's answer to the accursed Yankee blockade, attacking and sinking their ships anchored in Hampton Roads.

Hampton Roads was the result of subterranean upheavals of the earth's crust eons ago that left behind a natural harbor roughly 6 miles across at its widest point and 20 miles long, emptying into the Atlantic at an area called Cape Henry. In this vast anchorage, varied units of the U.S. Atlantic fleet sat at anchor, including five major men-of-war: the 50-gun screw frigates *Minnesota* and *Roanoke*, the 40-gun sailing frigates *Congress* and *St. Lawrence*, and the 24-gun sloop of war *Cumberland*. In addition, there were three gunboats, *Cambridge, Dragon,* and *Whitehall,* and two armed tugs, *Zouave* and *Young America.* This anchored fleet was present to keep an eye on the mysterious ironclad rumored to be at Gosport Navy Yard and to destroy her if she sallied forth to do battle. It was a formidable fleet of warships of around 227 heavy guns that, according to Union naval personnel, would easily "dispatch the ironclad monster."

Speculation about the fabled enemy warship flew thick and fast over the Union communication network between Fort Monroe and Washington. As early as October 12, 1861, Flag Officer Louis M. Goldsborough wrote Secretary Welles he was "quite satisfied that . . . she [*Virginia*] will, in all probability, prove to be exceedingly formidable."[2] Captain Henry Van Brunt, skipper of the *Minnesota,* in a letter to Goldsborough, maintained that "we have nothing new here; all is quiet. The *Merrimac*[k] is still invisible to us, but reports say she is ready to come out. I sincerely wish she would; I am quite tired of hearing of her."[3]

There were some Confederate doubts about the efficacy of the *Virginia*. One of her officers, Lieutenant John Taylor Wood, wrote: "From the start we saw that she was slow, not over five knots. She steered so badly that with her great length, it took from thirty to forty minutes to turn around. She was as unmanageable as a waterlogged fowl."[4] Still, even with her faults—and there were many—the Confederacy was placing its bets on this warship to break the blockade and sink those cursed Yankee ships.

Another personage who considered a stake in the premiere of the *Virginia* was General George Brinton McClellan, the commander-in-chief of the U.S. Army, who was at that time planning his campaign to capture Richmond, Virginia, the capital of the Confederacy. He was gambling that a huge army and unlimited supplies would allow him to wage a swift and victorious campaign to bring about an early end to the war, but the *Virginia* stood firmly in his way.

At first, McClellan decided on a direct thrust toward Richmond from

Washington, but when the Confederate general J. E. Johnston withdrew his army from a line around Manassas to a line around the Rappahannock River, McClellan scrapped his plan for a direct assault on Richmond and instead planned a drive up Newport News Peninsula, with supporting gunboats on the James and York Rivers. The plan called for over 100,000 troops to gather at Fort Monroe, which would be a springboard up the peninsula direct to Richmond. The presence of the *Virginia,* however, prevented the Union navy from protecting the transports in their assault up the rivers. McClellan had no choice but to await the coming struggle between the Union navy and the enemy ironclad ram, the outcome of which would determine the success of his campaign.[5] For the time being, the general known as "Little Mac" was reduced to just sulking and planning.

For these reasons, Welles had the cream of the navy crop present in Hampton Roads. Many historians have asked this puzzling question: Granted that everyone knew the *Virginia* to be a screw-propelled vessel, why were there not more Union screw frigates present, as opposed to sail vessels? One answer is that many people were of the mind that this one vessel, armored or not, could not stand a chance against the devastating broadsides of those frigates. It was a classic case of the mind-set of naval officers who were weaned in the wooden-battleship era. Any other explanation for this fallacy seems unthinkable.

March 8, 1862, dawned bright and clear. In a rallying talk to his crew, Buchanan assured them that the negative reports about their inefficiency and his were not true, that he was to be trusted in doing his duty, and the crew should do the same for themselves. At 11:00 A.M., he gave orders to cast off, even though there were some civilian workers on board. No one was concerned, because the officers and crew were under the impression that she was about to go on a shakedown or maiden cruise. Slowly and ponderously, the huge war monster moved away from the dock and into the main channel of the Elizabeth River. Then, with screws churning the water furiously, she began to inch forward, black coal smoke boiling from her huge stack. She headed upriver, course set for the main Hampton Roads channel 10 miles upriver from Gosport Navy Yard. From the banks of both Portsmouth and Norfolk, along the way, huge crowds had gotten the word. They had lined the banks, cheering and waving their hats, civilians and military alike. Artillery pieces thudded out in salute as she moved by at a sluggish five knots. According to one of *Virginia*'s engineers, E. V.

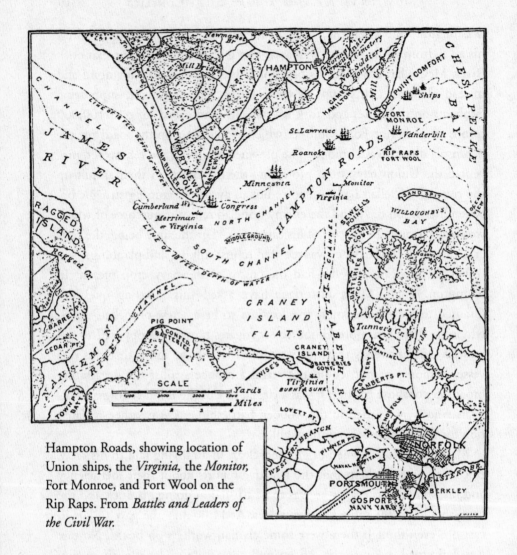

Hampton Roads, showing location of
Union ships, the *Virginia*, the *Monitor*,
Fort Monroe, and Fort Wool on the
Rip Raps. From *Battles and Leaders of
the Civil War*.

Gideon Welles, Lincoln's Secretary of the Navy
(U.S. Naval Historical Center Photograph).

The screw sloop *U.S.S. Brooklyn*, participated in action during Gulf of Mexico and East Coast campaigns (U.S. Naval Historical Center Photograph).

The screw frigate *U.S.S. Wabash* took part in the first attack on Fort Fisher.

Line drawing of *U.S.S. Monitor*, the famous ironclad that fought the Confederate ironclad *C.S.S. Virginia* to a draw (U.S. NAVAL HISTORICAL CENTER PHOTOGRAPH).

Deck view of *U.S.S. Monitor*, showing dents made in turret, during battle with *C.S.S. Virginia* at Hampton Roads (U.S. NAVAL HISTORICAL CENTER PHOTOGRAPH).

Aerial View of Hampton Roads, showing Fort Monroe in foreground, Fort Calhoun on the Rip Raps at center left, and Newport News at far right (COURTESY FORT MONROE ARCHIVES).

Screw frigate *U.S.S. Roanoke* before conversion to an ironclad
(U.S. Naval Historical Center Photograph).

U.S.S. Roanoke after conversion to an ironclad. Note three gun turrets
(U.S. Naval Historical Center Photograph).

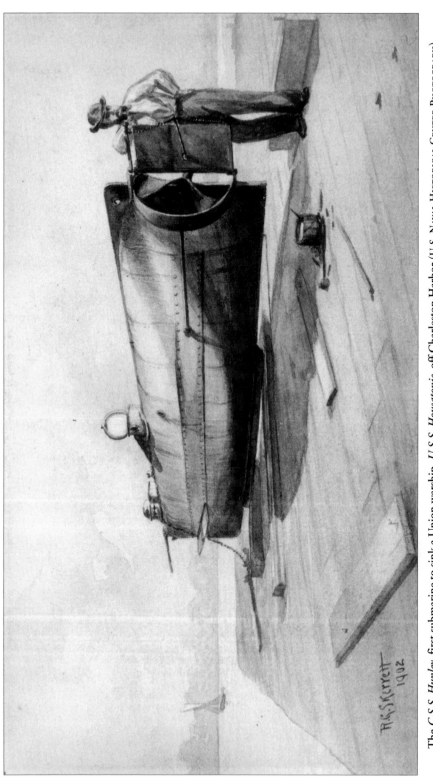

The C.S.S. *Hunley*, first submarine to sink a Union warship, *U.S.S. Housatonic*, off Charleston Harbor (U.S. Naval Historical Center Photograph).

The land face of Fort Fisher, as it looks today, still showing traverses and reconstructed log palisade. Union soldiers successfully assaulted the fort to the left of the photo (AUTHOR'S PHOTO).

View of Newport News from James River shore. The derrick barge is anchored over the spot where the *U.S.S. Congress* was sunk, during battle with *C.S.S. Virginia* (AUTHOR'S PHOTO).

Union fleet preparing for pre-invasion bombardment of Fort Fisher
(U.S. NAVAL HISTORICAL CENTER PHOTOGRAPH).

Union marines and sailors landing on beach above Fort Fisher, preparing for assault
(U.S. NAVAL HISTORICAL CENTER PHOTOGRAPH).

White, "those people on the shores were about to witness the initial engagement of this new idea war-ship the result of which was eagerly awaited by the whole world . . . for there never had been a bolder attack than what was about to be made that day."[6]

Before reaching Craney Island, the ironclad was joined by her escorts, the gunboats *Beaufort* and *Raleigh*, both veterans of the battle for Roanoke Island. As she came abreast of Craney Island, her keel scraped the bottom of the river and she failed to answer her helm. The *Beaufort* tossed a line and towed her past the island and into the deeper channel of Hampton Roads.[7]

Ahead, the *Virginia*'s crews saw the Union warships at anchor, their sides reflecting the late-morning sun. The 1,726-ton, 24-gun sailing sloop *Cumberland* sawed at her anchor in the James River 800 yards off Camp Butler, on the southwest tip of Newport News. Less than a mile away, to the northeast, lay the 1,867-ton, 44-gun sailing frigate *Congress*. Both vessels were guarding the mouth of the James River. Farther up, beyond *Congress*, was the 4,833-ton, 47-gun screw frigate *Minnesota* and her sister ship, the 46-gun *Roanoke*. Beyond that, near Fort Monroe, but almost on Chesapeake Bay, was the 1,607-ton, 47-gun sailing frigate *St. Lawrence* riding at anchor.[8] The observers on the *Virginia* were quick to notice that the peacefully anchored ships had washed clothing strung out on the rigging, with boats swinging at the lower booms. It was as if the fleet was not expecting an enemy attack. There were no visible signs of alarm anywhere.

Buchanan decided to take the north channel of the shoal, now known as the Middle Ground. For a time it appeared as if the *Virginia* was headed for the ships off Fort Monroe, but she halted for a time. Then she answered to her starboard rudder, and it was apparent she was about to enter the north channel, which was to take her into the mouth of the James River.

Off Newport News, the big frigates *Cumberland* and *Congress* were anchored. Buchanan had decided to attack the two ships in a one-on-one situation in which he could attend to each one individually. It was an ideal tactical situation for him; he decided that the ships anchored to the east could wait.[9]

Meanwhile, Union personnel were not asleep in Hampton Roads. Lookouts on the parapets of Fort Monroe spotted much activity near Craney Island and, concerned that the dreaded ironclad was appearing at last, telegraphed the lookout station on Newport News to confirm the suspicion that the *Virginia* was standing down on the Elizabeth River. They did, and the Union forces in Hampton Roads went into a condition of alert.

The quartermaster of the *Congress* spotted the activity off Craney Island at about the same time and reported to his deck officer that the dreaded enemy ironclad was at last approaching. Lookouts on the *Cumberland* were of the opinion that the big black warship poking her nose around Sewell's Point was different from any vessel ever seen before. Other lookouts reported the same thing from other ships in Hampton Roads, and commented that she resembled a large black housetop. Brigadier General Joseph K. F. Mansfield, commandant of Camp Butler, quickly wired General John E. Wool of the ironclad's appearance, and the big guns at Fort Monroe were manned and ready for action.

The armed tug *Zouave* was sent to investigate. Nervous crew members were impressed by fire and smoke belching from her big stack. Gunners on the tug's 30-pound Parrott gun fired several shots at the monstrous warship, but the shells either bounced off her sides or splashed around her. The *Virginia* ignored this small irritant and pressed on. The *Zouave* then beat it back to Newport News to report her sightings.[10]

The Union crews sprang into action; boats were hoisted on board, clothing pulled down from the rigging, and topsails shaken out. The ships were put in a state of readiness for battle.

Captain Van Brunt, on the *Minnesota,* had been alerted early. His report read:

> On Saturday, the 8th instant at 12:45 P.M., three small steamers, in appearance, were discovered rounding Sewell's Point, and as soon as they came into full broadside view, I was convinced that one was the iron-plated steam battery *Merrimack* from the large size of her smoke pipe. They were headed for Newport News, and in obedience to a signal from the senior officer present, Captain J. Marston, immediately called all hands, slipped my cables and got underway for that point to engage her.[11]

He immediately cleared his ship for action; he and all hands were eager for a confrontation with the dreaded enemy war vessel.

Unfortunately for the *Minnesota,* the tide had ebbed, and because of her 22-foot draft, the frigate ran hard aground on the Newport News bar, but not until after taking a shot from a rifled gun in a Confederate battery on Sewell's Point that crippled her mainmast.

Similar action was taking place on *Roanoke,* which, with the help of the gunboats *Dragon* and *Young America,* was attempting to get under way toward Sewell's Point, but she too ran aground on the bar, and there was frantic activity by the tugs to get her off. Meanwhile, the crew of the *St. Lawrence,* anchored outside the capes of Chesapeake Bay, received a tug whose captain informed them that the *Merrimack* had appeared and was engaging the *Congress* and the *Cumberland.* A line was passed, and the sloop was towed toward the battle arena. As they passed Sewell's Point, a Rebel shell hit the vessel's forefoot. The war sloop returned fire that was believed to be "with some effect."[12] Unfortunately, and with an almost incongruous effect, she too ran aground and was unable to take part in the action.

In the meantime, at 4:00 P.M., the *Virginia* was almost parallel to the *Congress.* The gunboat *Beaufort,* off the ironclad's bow, fired the first shot of that day, but it fell short. The *Virginia* followed up with a broadside of grape, killing many crew members on the frigate. The *Congress* responded with a full broadside that hit, but the shots flew off in all directions, much to the horror of the gunners, who were used to ships being torn apart by such broadsides as the *Congress* could deliver.

According to a soldier observing from Sewell's Point, the *Virginia,* after firing hot shot at the *Congress* and setting her on fire, moved inexorably on until she was within musket range of the frigate *Cumberland,* and the fight began between the two war vessels.[13]

The *Cumberland,* anchored 800 yards off the southwest tip of Newport News, was trying to slip her stern cable, which would allow her to swing parallel to the shore and bring her broadsides to bear. The ironclad fired a shot from her bow Brooke seven-inch rifle that slammed into the frigate, killing some marines. It was to be the first loss of life in the great carnage that day.[14]

Then a great duel began as the two antagonists exchanged furious fire, with the Union ship getting the worst of it. The Union shells bounced off the ironclad like pebbles thrown against a brick wall. The *Cumberland*'s pilot, A. B. Smith, watched apprehensively as the great monster came on, and later wrote: "As she came ploughing through the water . . . she looked like a huge half-submerged crocodile. Her sides seemed of solid iron, except where the guns pointed from narrow ports . . . at her prow I could see the iron ram projecting straight forward, somewhat above the water's edge."[15]

The massive "crocodile" plunged through a torpedo net of logs surrounding the *Cumberland,* and with a sickening crunch, the bow and iron ram, propelled by 3,000 tons of iron and wood, slammed into the hapless vessel under the fore rigging on the starboard side, opening a large hole.

The shock of this blow drove the Union sloop against her spring anchors, but surprisingly, the impact was hardly felt at first by the crew of the *Virginia.* Catesby ap Roger Jones reported that "there was no sign of the hole above water [on the sloop]. It must have been large, for the vessel began to careen. The shock to us was slight."[16]

Water rushed through the hole as the sloop began to go down by her head. But this proved to be an unexpected danger to the *Virginia* as well. The iron ram had become jammed in the sloop's heavy timbers, so Buchanan ordered full speed astern, and the ironclad's screw began to churn the water furiously, desperately trying to keep from going down with the sinking ship. During this struggle, shots from *Cumberland*'s guns kept hammering at the attacker's citadel, destroying one of her guns, ripping off the muzzle of another, and shattering the bow rifle. It was to be the only damage sustained by the Confederate vessel that day.

Finally the ram broke off the *Virginia*'s bow, and she backed away from the doomed Union ship, whose guns were still blasting futilely at her tormentor. It has long been a mystery to historians that no one on the *Cumberland* thought of dropping her anchor on the *Virginia*'s bow, which would have most assuredly brought her down with her adversary. The only answer is that the furious battle, with its extensive carnage and damage, completely occupied the attention of *Cumberland*'s personnel, especially given that so many key officers had been wounded and taken out of action.

The battle was not over yet, however. A deadly duel of guns began between the ironclad's broadsides and the dying ship's remaining gunners on the spar deck. Someone described the carnage on the Union sloop as consisting of "streams of scarlet gore running from the *Cumberland*'s scuppers."[17]

The doomed Union ship finally plunged to the bottom in nine fathoms of water with her colors still flying from her masts. Confederate gunners stood and saluted her, with all hands aware that the enemy ship was well handled and that her crew had fought bravely. (It is not unusual for a victorious crew to salute their vanquished foe in a gesture of appreciation for a battle well fought, even in recent times. Imperial Japanese sailors stood at attention and saluted the destroyer U.S.S. *Johnston* as she went down in the battle off Samar Island in the Philippines on October 25, 1944.)

The *Virginia's* attention was now diverted to the *Congress,* which had gone aground and was licking her wounds from the earlier encounter. But it took the ironclad an hour to turn around in the James River, while down from the north came the Confederate James River Squadron gunboats *Patrick Henry, Jamestown,* and *Teaser* to join the fray, under the command of Lieutenant John R. Tucker. They, along with *Virginia,* came under heavy fire from Union shore batteries, with the *Patrick Henry* receiving a shot through her boiler that put her out of action for a time.[18] The gunboats stood off, awaiting the ironclad's agonizing turnaround.

While turning, the *Virginia* exchanged fire with the shore batteries of Camp Butler at Newport News. Both sides suffered some damage and casualties during this short encounter.

Meanwhile, the crew of the *Congress* was attempting to pull her off the shoal, assisted by the tug *Zouave,* all the while coming under fire from *Raleigh* and *Beaufort.* It was a futile attempt; the *Congress* was too deeply grounded. With her rear end out, she could only man her stern guns as the ponderous *Virginia* came up. Because her draft was too deep, the *Virginia* could not use her ram, so she took a position some 150 yards off and opened broadside after broadside into the ill-fated frigate.

It was the *Cumberland* all over. The ship was pounded mercilessly and reduced to shambles. Again, onlookers observed that "her scuppers ran red" as she lost a quarter of her crew.[19] The ship's commander, Lieutenant Joseph B. Smith, was decapitated. Finally, it was too much, and the acting commander took down the colors and ran up white flags on her fore- and mainmasts. Buchanan ordered the *Beaufort* and *Raleigh* to stand in and send over boats to receive articles of surrender and to make arrangements for removal of the dead and wounded and to take the remaining officers prisoners. Union gunners on shore, infuriated at the surrender, opened fire on the *Congress* and *Virginia.*

Buchanan, who had a reputation for being hot-tempered and easily excitable, thought the *Congress* was doing the firing and became infuriated. He ordered Catesby Jones to burn the enemy ship, because she was firing upon *Virginia's* boats under flags of surrender. Hot shot was poured into the *Congress* until she was afire from stem to stern. He was so aggrieved that he picked up a musket himself and fired back at the shore batteries until a Union sharpshooter put a musket ball through his thigh. He turned command over to Catesby Jones and was carried below.[20]

The new Confederate commander took a hard look eastward, where the *Minnesota, Roanoke,* and *St. Lawrence* were still aground. They appeared to be easy targets—especially the stricken *Minnesota,* the nearest. By now it was 6:00 P.M., and darkness was setting in; it was time to retire to Sewell's Point to anchor for the night. Why worry? The Union ships were helpless and could be dealt with on the morrow. After firing a few shots at *Minnesota,* he set course for Newport, and the huge ironclad lumbered off, leaving behind an awesome amount of damage, human death, and suffering. The toll that day was two major Federal ships destroyed and one damaged. Union casualties came to 250 dead and 75 wounded. The Confederates did not escape punishment. The *Virginia* took over 100 hits and lost her boats and davits, railings, and flagstaffs; there was also some plating damage. Her stack was riddled with holes, and she lost two crewmen, with eight wounded—all within less than five hours of fighting. It was time to retire and lick her wounds. She returned to Newport and the navy yard to a hero's welcome.[21]

On Sunday morning, March 9, panic took over in Washington, when the news of *Virginia's* victories came pouring in over the telegraphs. Lincoln hastily called a cabinet meeting to discuss the situation, and it didn't take long for fear and trepidation to take over. The secretary of war, Edwin Stanton, in particular was greatly agitated. He was convinced that the entire East Coast was in mortal danger, and he declared that the "monster" herself might throw a shell into that very room before they left. Many precautions were discussed, including sinking a fleet of stone-filled hulks in the Potomac and even evacuating some key cities. When it was revealed that their only hope lay in the *Monitor,* with but two guns, more depression set in, except for Secretary Welles, who had some inkling that the Confederate "monster," because of her deep draft, could not even leave Hampton Roads. He declared that the *Merrimack* could not come to Washington and go to New York at the same time.[22] Only President Lincoln remained calm; instead, he wanted to know more about the ironclad, her guns, her crew, and her potential to inflict damage. They concluded that all had better wait and see what that strange ironclad warship they had sent to Hampton Roads could accomplish.

However, if Lincoln and the cabinet had been present at Hampton Roads, their anxieties would have been greatly substantiated. The *Virginia* was at anchor off Sewell's Point waiting like some great beast, licking its chops over a coming meal, while in the Roads, the *Congress* was burning furiously, with *Minnesota, Roanoke,* and *St. Lawrence* struggling to get free of their imprisonment in the shoals. It looked like a great stage tragedy about to take place. All Union personnel knew what daylight would bring, and consequently there was little or no sleep that night.

Then the *Monitor* made her entrance.

Earlier, as she had approached Fort Monroe, her personnel could see the dim flashes and hear the sullen thud of guns in Hampton Roads. Captain Worden ordered the ship stripped of her sea rig, the turret keyed up, and the vessel otherwise prepared for action.[23] He set a course for the *Roanoke* to report to Captain John Marston, the senior officer present. As they proceeded, all hands had an opportunity to see the fire from the *Congress* lighting up the night. To a man, they vowed vengeance on the Confederate ram.

When the *Monitor* had tied up alongside the *Roanoke,* and after Worden had reported to Marston, it was learned that the flag officer had received a wire from Welles ordering him to send the *Monitor* back to Washington to protect the capital, a sad residual effect from the earlier panic in the administration. But Marston took upon himself the responsibility of preempting that order and of having the *Monitor* stay in Hampton Roads, where she was needed.

The Union ironclad was sorely needed at Hampton Roads, rather than in the Potomac River awaiting an enemy vessel that would never appear. Even though technically it was a disobedience of orders, his decision was the right one, and it showed a commendable spirit.[24] Next, he ordered the *Monitor* to the side of the *Minnesota* to protect her from the dawn attack that was sure to come.

Worden prepared to cast off, but the lack of a pilot presented a problem, one that threatened to delay his trip to the *Minnesota.* Then the *Roanoke's* acting master, Samuel Howard, came forward and volunteered to pilot him over to the stricken frigate.[25] The *Monitor* arrived alongside at 11:00 A.M., and Worden and Greene immediately reported to Captain Van Brunt, who informed them he would attempt to get his ship clear of the shoal at 2:00 A.M. high water. The stranded ship was taking on nine hundred 9-inch solid shot from Fort Monroe. Many of the ship's personnel, including the captain, cast a dubious eye on the smallish warship alongside, in silent doubt that she could best the larger and more powerful Confederate ram in a battle.

At midnight, Sunday, March 9, the *Congress* blew up after fire reached her ammunition bunkers and powder tanks. The explosion electrified the entire area. Lieutenant Greene was moved to comment that certainly a grander sight was never seen, each shower of sparks rivaling the other in height, until they appeared to reach the zenith in the sky.[26]

Another observer, H. Ashton Ramsay, described the sight as "a huge column of firebrands hundreds of feet in the air, and then the burning hulk burst asunder and melted into the waters while the calm night spread her sable mantle over Hampton Roads."[27] Other observers described the sound being as widely spread as the light of her fires.

The *Monitor's* captain and crew settled down to await the return of the Confederate ironclad ram. There was no rest for the crew. They had been at station for 48 hours during the stormy trip down, with very little sleep and food, and were close to exhaustion. According to Greene, breakfast consisted of hard bread and water. He himself had been on his feet for 51 hours.[28]

At daylight, Sunday, March 9, Catesby Jones gave the order to cast off the lines holding *Virginia* to the dock at Gosport. The huge ram once again stood out into the Elizabeth River channel and, accompanied by her two consorts *Beaufort* and *Raleigh*, headed out into Hampton Roads, her officers and crew confident of victory over the remaining wooden ships of the Federal navy. As she moved into the main channel of Hampton Roads, the crew observed the *Minnesota* still hard aground, but the *Roanoke* and *St. Lawrence* had been freed and were at anchor off Fort Monroe. Jones was determined to finish off the stranded frigate; he would deal with the others later. But off the Middle Ground shoals, the *Virginia* shuddered to a halt, herself aground for a time, though she was soon pulled free by her consorts.

Inexorably, Jones continued on his determined course toward *Minnesota*, which seemed to be abandoned at the moment. It was then that a strange object was sighted alongside the frigate. Many of the crew wondered about it. Was it a water tank on a raft? Or was it some way they were evacuating men and matériel off the ship? Suddenly, the strange object cast off and headed out into the channel toward them. Even more puzzled, the crew saw that there were no sails, no smokestack—not even masts and spars. The crew must have shrugged, no doubt thinking it was some strange but harmless object from who knew where.

However, Jones and some of his officers knew. They looked at each other and said, "The Ericsson battery!" It was the vessel that had been rumored for some time and was purportedly on its way to Hampton Roads. It was then they knew that the long-rumored battle between the ironclads was about to take place.[29]

On the *Monitor,* Captain Worden gave the order for full speed ahead. His course was set for the *Virginia,* which in turn was headed for the *Minnesota* with the obvious intention of delivering the coup de grâce. When she was around a mile from the frigate, a puff of smoke issued from her bow, followed by a dull thud that echoed across the still body of water. The *Virginia* had fired her bow rifle, and it was clear it had been repaired after the *Cumberland* guns had heavily damaged its carriage the night before.

Virginia's rifle shot hit the *Minnesota* and caused some damage, but nothing serious. Shoal water kept Jones from getting nearer the stranded vessel. As the *Monitor* approached the *Virginia,* her consorts stood out and fled. In the turret, Greene had the two Dahlgrens loaded and primed. When Worden gave the order to commence firing, Greene personally sighted a gun and pulled the lanyard.[30] The big gun belched fire, and the 108-pound solid ball slammed squarely into the citadel of the *Virginia.* It bounced off, but the impact reverberated throughout the ram and surprised many of the crew. Then the *Virginia,* in turn, gave a rolling broadside that they expected would blow the little ironclad to pieces. But the shots all thudded into the iron plating of the turret and then showered off in all directions. The crew of the *Virginia* were stunned, but those in the *Monitor* were relieved that the turret was undamaged and still able to turn, in spite of the devastating broadside.

The battle of Hampton Roads was on.

What a sight it would have been to the many observers both afloat and ashore, with the huge ironclad monster sided by this diminutive vessel half her size. Captain Van Brunt, on the *Minnesota,* described the meeting of the combatants as that of a "pygmy to a giant." The broadside from *Virginia* rebounded from the *Monitor* with "no more effect than so many pebble stones thrown by a child."[31] *Virginia's* paymaster, William Keeler, boasted that his ship would end the war in spite of that "tin can on a shingle." Furthermore, what could she do against his impregnable vessel?[32]

Another crew member of the *Virginia,* a grizzled gunner, glanced at the *Monitor,* grunted, and exclaimed, "She's a blasted toy!" But all that confidence was soon shattered when the solid shot from the Dahlgren slammed into the ironclad's side, denting her armor and forcing back some of her timber backings.

Like a prizefighter, Worden conned his vessel around the *Virginia,* pounding her while looking for a vulnerable spot. But the *Monitor* had become handicapped a bit by internal troubles. Her speaking tube arrangement had become incapacitated by the revolving turret, so a chain of personnel was set up whereby orders could be passed by word of mouth from Worden in the pilothouse to Greene in the turret.

The answering salvos from *Virginia* sprayed shot, shell, canister, and grape around *Monitor* in all directions but did minimal damage. At one time, Worden spotted the *Virginia's* screw churning a little above water, obviously caused by a lightening of her ammunition and fuel. He headed for her to ram that spot but missed by a few feet.[33]

To a balloonist high above the Roads, it would have been a fascinating sight, what with the antagonists, resembling two fighters in a ring, circling each other, throwing jabs and punches in the form of shot and shell, many times enveloped and obscured by white gunpowder smoke, and accompanied by the heavy *thut thut thut* of gunfire echoing across the big body of water. Once the *Virginia* attempted to ram her opponent but managed to produce only a glancing blow that did little damage.

In *Monitor's* turret, Greene was having sighting problems with the big Dahlgrens. The turret was acting erratically because of rust from seawater received on the way down. In addition, the heavy shutters that dropped over the gunports after each shot were making sighting extremely difficult. He solved the problem by lashing them up during the battle. He had also placed chalk marks on the deck to help in sighting, but they became obliterated and therefore affected the sighting process of the guns; they had to be fired on the fly, as it were. Also, a problem arose over the positioning of the pilothouse on the bow and blower pipes and smokestack openings on the stern, which made firing in those directions impossible.

Another difficulty was the amount of gunpowder allowed for the Dahlgrens. Instead of 30 pounds, the amount had been cut in half because of the disaster on the *Princeton* in 1844. It was later learned that had the 30-pound charge been used, the *Virginia*'s sides would have been penetrated many times, possibly sinking her.

Meanwhile, on the *Virginia*, Jones made a quick turn of his vessel, only to find one gun crew at ease. Jones addressed its division officer, Lieutenant John R. Eggleston, asking why they were not firing. "Why, our powder is very precious," came the reply. "After two hours' incessant firing, I find I can do about as much damage by snapping my fingers at her every two minutes."[34]

In the meantime, the *Monitor* retired to shoal water in order to bring up more ammunition. The *Virginia* ran aground again, but Jones took advantage of the time while being pulled loose to lob some shells at *Minnesota* from his bow rifle. The shots caused some damage, including exploding the boiler of the gunboat *Dragon* alongside.

At noon, when the *Monitor* stood up to renew the battle, *Virginia* got in a lucky shot. A shell from her stern pivot gun hit the *Monitor*'s pilothouse a little above the sighting slit through which Worden was peering. One of the iron logs was shattered, sending particles of iron and unburned powder into his face. He staggered back, clawing at his face and shouting, "My eyes! I am blind!" Greene was called from the turret to take over command. He immediately had the ironclad steered into shoal water while he attended to the situation. As the wounded captain was carried below, he pleaded with Greene to save the *Minnesota* if he could.[35]

After Greene had guided the *Monitor* off the shoal and brought her up to renew the fray, he was surprised to see the *Virginia* breaking off the engagement and heading back toward Craney Island. For his part, Catesby Jones was under the impression the *Monitor* was retreating from the fight and therefore must have been severely damaged. He decided that it was time to retire from the arena, receive more ammunition, and have his ship's damage repaired. Besides, the *Minnesota* was probably badly damaged and soundly stuck in the shoal water. Perhaps he would have another go at her.

Captain Van Brunt, observing from *Minnesota*, concluded that the Union monitor had moved off because of damage sustained or a lack of ammunition. He then prepared for the destruction of his ship rather than have her fall into enemy hands in the event the *Monitor* had failed in her mission to save the Union ships and possibly destroy the Confederate ironclad.[36]

Actually, the main reason Jones was breaking off the fight was because his pilots informed him that they could get no nearer the *Minnesota*. Believing the enemy ironclad routed and disabled, he ordered a cease-fire and then set course for Sewell's Point. His vessel, however, had not escaped unharmed. He reported 2 killed and 19 wounded, with damage to his ship: "The stern twisted and the ship leaks. We have lost the prow, starboard anchor and all the boats; the steam pipe and smokestack riddled; the muzzles of two guns shot away. It was not easy to keep a flag flying. The flagstaffs were repeatedly shot away. The colors were hoisted to the smokestack and several times were repeatedly cut down from it."[37] He also declared that had the *Monitor* showed a willingness to renew the contest, he would have remained to fight again.

As far as Greene was concerned, the enemy was breaking off the fight, and he had already set course for the *Minnesota* to assist her in getting off the shoal and to protect her and the other Union ships should the *Virginia* venture out again. He had no doubt this was his primary mission, and he intended to keep at it.

After the battle, Worden wrote that Greene's decision showed good judgment, as all Union vessels in Hampton Roads were entirely dependent on the *Monitor*. In addition, her pilothouse had been damaged, and any further engagements with the enemy could have possibly disabled his ship. "The fight was over and we were victorious," Worden proclaimed. But an officer, John Webber on the *Monitor,* was of a different opinion. He wrote: "If it had not been for Captain Worden's injury and the short withdrawal, we might have sunk her [*Virginia*] outright."[38]

When Captain Worden heard that the battle was over and the *Minnesota* was safe, he leaned back in his bunk, sighed, and declared that he could die happy. Later, he was transferred to a fast coastal vessel for a trip to Baltimore, where he was treated for his wounds (he would regain the sight in one eye, but his face would be slightly disfigured). He was hailed as a hero throughout the North. After being transferred to Washington to recuperate, he was visited by President Lincoln, who congratulated him. "You do me a great honor, Mr. President," Worden said; "I am sorry I can't see you." Lincoln replied: "You have done me more honor, sir, than I can ever do for you."[39] It was a compliment to Worden never to be equaled.

Further examination of both vessels would reveal that neither the *Virginia* nor the *Monitor* had suffered any serious damage. The Union ironclad had fired 41 shells at *Virginia*, of which 20 hit their mark, and *Monitor* received 23 hits. Casualties on both sides were minimal, and both vessels would be repaired in short order. Many historians agreed that the *Monitor* had won the battle in that the *Virginia* would be unable to further threaten the Union fleet.

At Fort Monroe, one of the witnesses to the battle was Gustavus Fox, assistant secretary of the navy. Elated over the apparent victory, he came aboard the *Monitor* and congratulated the crew. At lunch with the officers in the wardroom, he told them: "Well, gentlemen, you don't look like you were just through one of the greatest naval conflicts on record." To which Greene replied, with a touch of bravado: "No, sir. We haven't done much fighting, merely drilling the men at guns a little."[40]

CHAPTER ELEVEN

MONITOR VS. MERRIMACK, PART 3: THE AFTERMATH

Outside of the battle of Gettysburg, perhaps no battle has had more written about it than the naval struggle that took place in Hampton Roads on March 9, 1862. In retrospect, it was more than just combat between two ironclad vessels, or even a David-and-Goliath type of struggle between mismatched foes. Until then, wooden warships ruled the world's navies. Granted, some of these vessels with wooden structures—especially the giant ships of the line, with their preponderance of guns—were extremely formidable. But those structures could be shattered when exposed to a foe with equal or greater firepower and were especially vulnerable to hot shot, which could burn them to the waterline in an amazingly short period of time.

The French and British navies featured such ironclad vessels as the *Gloire* and the *Warrior*, but they had never been tested in combat with each other or with another vessel of similar type. Only the *Monitor* and the *Virginia* (or *Merrimack*) accomplished that, and it was these two similar but mismatched vessels that slugged it out—one bristling with guns, the other with only two, albeit big 15-inchers. For four hours these new innovations in ship design slammed away at each other, sometimes at point-blank range, and neither was crippled or sunk. This was a feat not equaled until November 1942, when American and Japanese destroyers also fought at times at point-blank range in the Solomon Islands campaign.

Over the fierce roaring of guns that morning in the Roads, only a few could hear the death knell of the wooden-warship era. After that day, naval architects went to work designing warships protected by iron plating and much later by steel. When one looks at a modern steel warship in today's U.S. Navy, one can give a nod of appreciation to those early pioneers in naval evolution. In fact, many of their innovations were the prototypes of designs used in the world's navies today.

Secretary Welles took a long and hard look at the new direction of naval evolution and realized, as few did, that ironclads were to be the navy of the future, so he ordered a fleet of ironclad warships for the Union navy. He called attention to the success of the *Monitor* in a letter to John Hale, chairman of naval affairs, in May 1864:

> The turreted vessels are unequalled and, although briefly in service, their great strength, wonderful capability of endurance, power of resistance and efficiency, have been abundantly proven. The first of this description of vessels, the *Monitor,* won for herself a reputation that is since born[e] by vessels of her class.[1]

The flood of turreted ironclad vessels that poured from Union shipyards were forerunners of today's navies, especially the 10 vessels of the *Passaic* class, followed by the *Canonicus* class, which in turn was followed by the *Kalamazoo* class with two turrets and by those vessels that were classed as seagoing instead of only for coastal defense. By 1864, as the war was drawing to a close, there was an entirely new Union navy of iron ships, although many wooden ships remained in service.

After the battle, the *Virginia* was not through as a fighting entity. True, she had been bested and damaged in her struggle with the *Monitor,* but she was still afloat and able to fight again. Jones put her in dry dock to patch her wounds and repair some of the problems—especially the faulty shutters for the gunports, her leaking bow from the loss of the ram, her riddled stack, and the boat davits—and, he hoped, to do something about her sluggish engines. She was still a redoubtable foe and eager for a possible rematch. The uniqueness of the *Virginia* was well chronicled by President Davis:

> It will be remembered that the *Virginia* was a novelty in naval architecture; wholly unlike any ship that ever floated; that her heaviest guns were equal novelties in ordnance; that her motive power and her obedience to her helm were untried, and her officers and crew strangers comparatively to the ship and to each other; and yet, under all these disadvantages, the dashing courage and consummate professional ability of Flag Officer Buchanan and his associates achieved the most remarkable victory which naval annals record.[2]

Soon after the battle, Jones was relieved of command of the *Virginia* because he was considered too young and inexperienced. Replacing him was Commodore Josiah Tattnall, given the sobriquet "Old Tat" by his contemporaries. A seasoned navy officer, Tattnall enjoyed a long and illustrious career. Born near Savannah, Georgia, on November 9, 1795, he received his education in England and became a midshipman in the U.S. Navy, in 1812. Tattnall saw action in the War of 1812, the Algierian War, 1815, and the Mexican War. When his home state seceded, he resigned his commission on February 20, 1861, and was appointed senior flag officer in the Georgia navy. Later, Tattnall was appointed a captain in the Confederate navy and became the commander of the famed Mosquito Fleet, which later opposed the Union Navy at Port Royal in November 1861.[3] He was a logical choice for the command of *Virginia* because of his long and distinguished career.

Tattnall found himself in an unusual situation. The *Virginia* still suffered from sluggish engines, and her deep draft prevented her from going up the James or York River to oppose waterborne support for General McClellan's thrust up the peninsula to assault Richmond. Conversely, she was ill-equipped for a sea voyage to Washington or New York, Port Royal or Savannah. After conferring with Commodore Buchanan, he came to the conclusion that *Virginia* was unseaworthy—that she was "not sufficiently buoyant, and that at sea she would founder."[4]

So instead of the long-range venture that Tattnall initially had wanted, he was ordered to remain in the area to protect Norfolk and Richmond and to break the blockade if he could. With that in mind, he decided to venture out into Hampton Roads in an attempt to lure the *Monitor* out for another fight. On April 11 at 6:00 A.M., Tattnall conned the lumbering ironclad out into the main channel of the Elizabeth River, accompanied by two gunboats. The weather was ideal, with the sun shining in a clear sky. As the little flotilla came in sight of Fort Monroe, they viewed the Roads lined with a large fleet of transports at anchor, as if there had never been a naval battle there—or as if the enemy ironclad had been vanquished.

At the appearance of *Virginia*, each vessel slipped its cable and, "like a flock of wild fowl in the act of flight, spread her sails in the race for safety."[5] Steaming up to within two miles of the fort, Tattnall spotted the *Monitor* and the six-gun, two-screw iron battery *Naugatuck*, which had been built and loaned to the U.S. Navy by ship designer John Stevens. Other vessels nearby were the iron-plated *Galena* and three visiting foreign warships.

Tattnall conned the *Virginia* in circles, hoping to draw out the ironclads for battle, but to no avail. Then, in a "spirit of bravado and provocation to them," Tattnall sent the *Jamestown* and *Raleigh* to cut out three transports that had not moved out of the Roads. Still no response. At nightfall, disappointed and contemptuous of the apparent timidity of the Union warships, he returned his little flotilla to Sewell's Point to anchor for the night.[6]

In spite of this humiliating display of bravado and daring on the part of *Virginia*, the *Monitor* was held steady by her captain, William Nicholson Jeffers, a career navy man and veteran of the Mexican War. On March 12, he had replaced Lieutenant Thomas Oliver Selfridge, who held command of the ironclad for four days after relieving Lieutenant Greene because of the latter's youth and inexperience. Thus, in a short time, *Monitor* had four skippers—Worden, Greene, Selfridge, and Jeffers.[7]

Jeffers, a New Jersey native, was a descendant of a line of seafaring men. He entered the navy in 1840, graduated from the academy in 1864, and fought in the Mexican War. He served on the steam sloop *Brooklyn*, and later commanded the four-gun side-wheeler *Underwriter*. The author of four books, he was also considered an authority on ordnance.

Jeffers and his crew had to stand by helplessly while the *Virginia* provoked them, because he was following orders to protect the transports that were supporting McClellan's 100,000 troops in his intended assault on

Richmond. The one thorn still in McClellan's side was the presence of the *Virginia,* which blocked access to the James River for his transports, gunboats, and supply vessels. In addition to that, President Lincoln had sent a wire to Captain Gustavus Fox, who was at Fort Monroe, instructing that "the *Monitor* be not too much exposed, and that in no event shall any attempt be made to proceed with her unattended to Norfolk."[8]

In spite of his disappointment over losing command of the vessel, Greene was well aware of all these ramifications when Selfridge relieved him. He said he had been taken aback at first, but one must recall the immense responsibility resting on this vessel. He wrote: "We literally hold all property, ashore and afloat, in these regions, as the wooden ships are useless against the *Merrimac[k]*."[9] So the *Monitor* remained under the guns of Fort Monroe for the time being, keeping an eye out for any reappearance of the *Virginia.* She did come out briefly again, but no fight with the *Monitor* was to occur, because wily old Tat knew that some Union warships had been equipped with rams, including the *Vanderbilt,* a 1,700-ton sidewheeler built by multimillionaire Cornelius Vanderbilt and loaned to the Union navy.

Old Tat was not about to get into the deep-water channel and be the target of these enemy ships. According to an officer on the Confederate ram, a plan had been devised to capture the *Monitor.* Four small gunboats were to be used in attacking the Union ironclad simultaneously; when the vessel was boarded by a commandolike crew, wedges would be used to stop the turret; blankets would be placed over the smokestack; and chloroform would be broken on the turret, which would then be covered by a tarpaulin, forcing the crew to come scrambling out. Of course, all this would depend on the gunboats closing on the *Monitor* without being blown out of the water.[10] Once again, Tattnall returned to Sewell's Point without a fight.

Meanwhile, Secretary Mallory and General Benjamin Huger were getting impatient. Huger wanted the *Virginia* to slip by Fort Monroe at night and sortie up the York River to support General Johnston's besieged army at Yorktown. Tattnall did sortie out at one point but turned back at the last minute because Mallory wanted to wait for a second ironclad, the *Richmond,* now under construction, along with another gunboat, at Gosport Navy Yard. The former was designed to counter the *Monitor,* while the *Virginia* would ascend the York River and attack the Union fleet there.

But, as usual, it was a case of the best-laid plans of mice and men going awry. Time had run out for the Confederates at Norfolk. On May 3, 1862, General Johnston evacuated his Warwick-Yorktown line and moved his army up to Richmond.

Norfolk was now undefended and at the mercy of the Union. Mallory visited Norfolk and the navy yard and ordered an immediate evacuation. Towed by two gunboats, the unfinished *Richmond* and *Hampton* were brought up the James River, along with guns and ordnance supplies. The *Virginia* was left behind to guard the approaches to the James.

Meanwhile, a bustle of activity was occurring at Fort Monroe. President Lincoln had arrived on the U.S. revenue cutter *Miami,* accompanied by Salmon Chase, secretary of the treasury; Edwin Stanton, secretary of war; and Brigadier General Egbert L. Viele. They conferred with General Wool, commander of the Union Department of Virginia, and the result of the conference was a planned attack on Sewell's Point and an expedition of ships up the James River to support McClellan's advance on Richmond. But when they learned that the Confederates were evacuating Norfolk, they ordered the *Monitor, Naugatuck, Susquehanna,* and *San Jacinto,* plus other warships, to shell the battery on Sewell's Point to cover an amphibious landing.[11] When Tattnall heard the bombardment, he got under way and stood out into the Roads, spoiling again for a fight, but once more was disappointed. The *Monitor* was to remain with her charges.

Swallowing his disappointment at not tangling with the *Virginia* again, Goldsborough had issued orders that the warships were to return to the protection of the fort. The Confederates were enraged and declared that the Union forces were a bunch of cowards. Tat took his charges back to Craney Island.

Blocked from Sewell's Point, the troops moved down, landed at Ocean View, and started a march toward Norfolk. That sealed the fate of the *Virginia* if she remained at Craney Island. Tattnall decided to take her up the James River to Richmond to use her armament as a floating battery, that is, if she could reduce her draft to 18 feet. But because such a reduction in draft would mean instability, the plan was dropped. She managed to be lightened to 20 feet, but the prevailing opinion was that she could not navigate the shallow waters of the Jamestown Flats. A Confederate soldier, Jasper Goldman, assigned to guard the *Virginia,* maintained that an obstruction, a sunken ship, was the reason she could not ascend the river. "We wanted to run her up the James River," he wrote, "but there was a ship sunk in the way. So we could not run up there."[12]

Tattnall grudgingly made an agonizing decision: The *Virginia* must be destroyed. He beached her on Craney Island and took the crew off. At 3:00 A.M. on May 11, Catesby Jones and John Taylor Wood spread combustible material around the ship; a slow match was applied, and the two evacuated the doomed vessel. The crew, meanwhile, was shipped north to Suffolk, to later man the guns at Drewry's Bluff upstream.

The once-dreaded naval juggernaut of Hampton Roads burned for the next two hours, until her powder magazine was reached and she blew up with a tremendous explosion. Many people, soldiers and civilians alike, witnessed the destruction of the fabled ironclad. A Union naval officer described it as "a beautiful sight . . . she had been a thorn in our side for a long time and we will be glad to have her well out of the way."[13]

With Norfolk captured and *Virginia* destroyed, Richmond lay open to attack. Orders went out to the *Monitor* and *Naugatuck* up the James River to join Commander John Rodgers' squadron of the *Galena,* the *Aroostook,* and the side-wheel gunboat *Port Royal.* The flotilla steamed up to a heavy Confederate fortification at Drewry's Bluff, armed with three big guns, two 8-inch Columbiads and one 10-inch Columbiad. The former crew of the *Virginia* manned the facility. The channel near the bluff had been filled with sunken ships and obstructions of all kinds. The squadron stood up to the 90-foot cliff and opened up on the fortification. The battle raged for three and a half hours, during which the *Galena* was heavily damaged and holed. The *Monitor* was prevented from joining the bombardment because her guns could not be elevated high enough to reach the crest of the bluff. She moved downriver a bit and opened fire, but her shots overreached the fort. Finally the squadron retreated downriver.[14] As history would show many times in similar cases, it would have to be done with ground troops.

For the remainder of the summer of 1862, the *Monitor* remained in the Roads, with her crew enduring the hot summer in the most difficult conditions, in spite of the blowers designed to change air within the vessel and, theoretically, to keep it cool for the occupants.

On September 10, Lieutenant John Payne Bankhead came on board to relieve Lieutenant Thomas Holdup Stevens II, who had earlier relieved

Jeffers. Then on September 30, Bankhead received orders to take *Monitor* to the Washington Navy Yard for overhaul. With the help of a navy tug, she was towed up Chesapeake Bay to the Potomac River and thence to the navy yard. There she was scraped and repainted and had her boilers and engines overhauled. She was opened up to the public, and huge crowds came to see the fabled warship, including President Lincoln, who participated in a special ceremony. The *Washington Post* proudly proclaimed: "Bully for the *Monitor*."[15]

Acting Master Louis Stodder wrote that souvenir hunters "went through the ship, like a flock of magpies, prying loose as souvenirs anything removable. When we came up at night there was not a key, doorknob, escutcheon . . . there wasn't a thing that wasn't carried away."[16]

But her day in the sun was not too long, for in early November *Monitor* was once again back in Hampton Roads. Then in December, after the disastrous battle of Fredericksburg, during which Burnside's army was routed and suffered 12,000 casualties, the administration wanted a victory, no matter how small, to offset the ignominy of Burnside's defeat. Plans were pushed ahead for an assault on Charleston, South Carolina. It was decided that *Monitor* would take part in the action, and she was ordered to report to Beaufort, North Carolina, to join the gathering fleet.[17]

On December 29, at 2:30 P.M., the *Monitor* left Hampton Roads, towed by the powerful, 1,510-ton side-wheel supply ship *Rhode Island,* commanded by Stephen Decatur Trenchard. At the same time, the 1,000-ton side-wheel gunboat *State of Georgia* towed the newly arrived 1,335-ton monitor *Passaic* out to the same destination.

By 6:00 P.M., the *Monitor* and her escort had cleared Cape Henry and were out at sea with "a light southwest wind, clear, pleasant weather, and everything working well."[18] The fine weather continued until 5:00 A.M. on Tuesday morning, when a swell came from the south and the sea became rough, as was and is still typical of Atlantic Ocean weather off the East Coast. (It is puzzling to historians to this day as to why the *Monitor,* with her low freeboard and near disastrous trip down from New York in March of 1862, was taken to sea at a time of year when the weather had historically proven unpredictable.)

By the afternoon of the 30th, it appeared as if the *Monitor* would ride out the storm, but by evening, when the little flotilla was 15 miles south of

Cape Hatteras, the wind shifted more to the south, increased, and caused the seas to rise. Soon the waves began to crash over the pilothouse and turret, and the ship began to leak heavily. The huge troughs caused the ironclad to yaw, or seesaw, on the towlines. Bankhead, after unsuccessfully trying to signal the *Rhode Island,* ordered the powerful Worthington and centrifugal pumps into action, but it was too late. By this time, the *Monitor* was yawing and pitching irregularly, and seawater began to pour through the blower pipes and smokestacks into the engine room. The vessel rode the crests of the waves, then plunged downward to hit the bottom of the troughs with such force that the joint between the deck and iron hull loosened. The shock of the plunges would force some of the crew members off their feet.[19]

With the engine room filling with water and the threat of the boiler fires being put out, Bankhead raised the signal of distress, a red lantern placed next to the ship's white running light. He then had the remaining towing cable cut and, with what engine power he had left, ran her under the lee of the *Rhode Island* to take off the crew. At one point, the *Monitor* came close to being pushed under the stern of the side-wheeler, which would have been disastrous to both vessels. At another, a towline became tangled in the paddlewheel of *Rhode Island,* and she veered off, almost colliding with the *Monitor.* Boats had been lowered from the *Rhode Island* to rescue the ironclad's crew, but heavy seas made the operation most difficult and dangerous, the boats almost being swamped many times. Some of the men were swept overboard, but most were quickly rescued.

In order to help the abandon-ship operation, Bankhead had the ironclad's anchor dropped, which brought her head to sea and stabilized her a bit. All crewmen had been ordered to leave the vessel, but some were washed away, and others were too terrified to leave the safety of the turret and stayed on the doomed ship. One man, an engineer, was too sick to leave his bunk and presumably perished with those in the turret.

With most of the crew safe on board the *Rhode Island,* they stood silently on the stern, watching the red lantern appear and disappear as the *Monitor* slowly foundered. Finally, the lantern disappeared for the last time at 1:30 A.M. Paymaster Keeler wrote: "The *Monitor* was no more. What the fire of the enemy failed to do, the elements have accomplished."[20]

The *Monitor* was lost, along with twelve good men, but her legacy lives on. Her radical design, her revolving turret, and her ventilating system would find their way into the great vessels of the United States Navy, starting with the Great White Fleet and leading to the battleships of World Wars I and II. The age of wood and sail had passed; man discovered that, amazingly, iron could float—something that seemingly defied the laws of nature.

The *Monitor* remained undisturbed on the bottom of the ocean off Cape Hatteras, until her bones were discovered 16 miles from the cape by a team of underwater research scientists under the auspices of Duke University's Marine Laboratory in April 1979. She was upside down on her turret in 230 feet of water and badly deteriorated, not only by elements but as the result of depth charging during World War II, when at times the U.S. Navy considered the hulk to be a Nazi submarine hiding on the bottom. Scientists brought some of her artifacts to the surface, but for the most part, it would be impossible to resurrect her hull.[21]

In 1979, it was determined that the interior iron stoppers of the turret were intact, thereby preventing a look inside the turret, where the Dahlgrens probably still are. The red lantern, posted as a distress signal, was found intact and is on display at the Mariners' Museum in Newport News, Virginia, as was the anchor, also in good condition. Much information about the ironclad, her design, her crew, and her construction has been gleaned from the wreck.[22]

Today, efforts are being made to bring one of her engines to the surface, but beyond that, not much more can be retrieved. The site of the deteriorated hulk was officially declared a marine sanctuary, and she will remain a national underwater treasure for all time.

CHAPTER TWELVE

FORT PULASKI FALLS

While the *Monitor* and the *Virginia* were clashing head-on at Hampton Roads and capturing the attention of the world, other events important to the conduct of the war were taking place. In the Mississippi River theater, General Grant and the Eads gunboats were blazing a path of victories over the Confederates that would result in the splitting of the Confederacy and opening the Father of Waters all the way to the Gulf. The Union army and navy captured Forts Henry and Donelson, respectively, on the Tennessee and Cumberland Rivers in February 1862. Earlier, in January, Flag Officer David Glasgow Farragut had been appointed to command the Western Gulf Blockading Squadron, and the way was being paved for the assaults on New Orleans and Mobile Bay. All of these actions were vital to the final conduct of the war and resulted in the collapse of the Confederacy.[1]

Of course, these actions were within the province of the Union navy, but there were a few important actions carried out in conjunction with land forces. Such was the case of Fort Pulaski at the mouth of the Savannah River, guarding the approaches to the city of Savannah. While that city was not a major blockade-runner port, it was, nevertheless, one of the destinations of incoming goods from Europe. As an example, one Confederate runner, the *Fingal,* supplied arms and ammunition to the Confederate army that almost defeated Union forces at Shiloh in April 1862.

Fort Pulaski, fifteen miles downstream from Savannah, was not a new installation. It was located on Cockspur Island and was built on the ruins of two earlier forts, the older of which was Fort George, a palisade log fort built in 1761. Later, in 1794, a facility named Fort Greene occupied the site. After the War of 1812, President James Madison convinced Congress to appropriate funds for a fort to be constructed on Cockspur Island that was to be called Fort Pulaski, after the Polish hero Count Casimir Pulaski, who distinguished himself in the Revolutionary War and who was killed in October 1779, during the battle of Savannah. The fort took 18 years to build and contained over 25 million bricks in its 7½-inch-thick walls. Construction of the facility was under the direction of a U.S. Army engineer, Robert E. Lee, fresh from West Point in 1829. The immense thickness of the walls was due to the island's nearness to Tybee Island, one mile to the south, and the structure was believed to be impervious to shot and shell from that island.[2]

After the capture of Cape Hatteras and Roanoke Island, Federal planners put Fort Pulaski on the priority list in their efforts to secure the Atlantic coast from Virginia to Florida and to tighten the blockade, upon recommendation of the Commission of Conference of the Blockade Board in June of 1861.

In November 1861, after the fall of Port Royal, Admiral Samuel Francis du Pont dispatched three gunboats to the vicinity of Tybee Island for reconnaissance purposes. After a couple of days of reconnoitering, the gunboats *Seneca* and *Pocahontas* crossed the bar and opened fire on the works of a small masonry Spanish fort built in 1562. The vessels received no response; it was deduced that no one occupied the island, so landing parties were dispatched ashore, and Tybee (the Euchee Indian word for "salt") Island became an artillery base for future Union operations.[3]

Meanwhile, Fort Pulaski had been strengthened to contain 400 men of the Savannah Regiment, and armed with five 10-inch Columbiads, three 42-pound smoothbores, three 10-inch mortars, one 12-inch mortar, one 24-pound smoothbore, two 12-pound howitzers, twenty 32-pounders, and two Blakely rifles.[4] The fort was under the command of Colonel Charles H. Olmstead.

The year of 1862 had barely opened before the Federal navy made a reconnaissance of the area surrounding Fort Pulaski, to the north and south of the Savannah River. A fleet of transports, containing 2,400 troops, accompanied by the gunboats *Seneca, Isaac Smith, Potomska, Ellen,* and *Western World,* had left Hilton Head to anchor at the mouth of Warsaw Sound.

A reconnaissance was made up of the body of water known as the Wilmington Narrows, as far as an obstruction of sunken hulks. Their objective was to reach the Savannah River to the north of the fort and to cut it off from any help from upriver, but the Confederates had already surmised such a move and had sunk the objects in order to impede Union progress up the sound.

Then, on the 28th, Commodore Tattnall, who was in charge of the Confederate Savannah River flotilla, came down to reinforce Fort Pulaski with provisions and supplies. An exchange of gunfire between Old Tat's squadron and the Union squadron took place, with no appreciable damage reported on either side. Later the Federals sank a hulk in Warsaw Sound and stationed a small force there for further reconnaisance.[5] Meanwhile, General Alfred Howe Terry, with the 46th New York Regiment, was quietly building on the north side of Tybee Island batteries of artillery brought in by du Pont's supply ships. The Tybee artillery force was planned and established by Chief Engineer Brigadier General Quincy Adams Gillmore, a top graduate of the U.S. Military Academy in 1849. He became convinced that the 25-foot-high thick masonry walls of the fort could be pierced by mortars and rifled guns instead of traditional smoothbores. The Confederate leaders had predicted that these walls would never be holed, so Gillmore set out to prove them wrong. Rifled guns had yet to prove themselves against masonry fortifications, especially those as thick as Fort Pulaski's.[6]

On April 8, 1862, Major General David Hunter, of Terry's Tybee Island contingent, sent a message to Admiral du Pont that he was considering an attack on Fort Pulaski at sunrise the next day. He asked for du Pont's assistance, but for some reason he delayed his attack for another day and opened some gunfire on Fort Pulaski on April 10 at 8:15 A.M. The fort replied in kind, but its fire was relatively ineffective.

Why the navy was not called in to use its bigger guns against the fort is still a mystery. A bombardment from the sea would have contributed greatly to the capitulation of the fort. But the navy did contribute in a small way: The frigate *Wabash* assigned a contingent of gunners to a battery of rifled guns. There they manned three 30-pound Parrotts and one 14-pound James rifle.[7] During the night, the Union gunners kept up the pressure, with 13-inch mortar shells plopping into the fort every few minutes, but it was later learned that many of the shells overshot their mark and accomplished nothing.

The next morning, the bombardment began in earnest, with the heavy rifled projectiles beginning to have an effect, creating breaches in the eastern walls. The Union gunners unerringly concentrated their fire on those breaches, with a storm of shells that widened them and through which more shells poured through, causing significant damage. The officers' quarters were destroyed, timbers were scattered all over the parade ground, the parapet walls were shattered on the southeast side, and the powder magazine was penetrated.

It soon became apparent that the fort was in danger of exploding from its own powder supply. Colonel Olmstead called a meeting of his commanders and it was decided to capitulate, rather than having the entire fort blown to pieces with all of its personnel. A white flag was raised at 2:00 P.M.[8] Gillmore and a contingent of officers were rowed over to receive the surrender from Colonel Olmstead in person. Gillmore described the surrender conference in the fort as being very cordial, with "many a jest and repartee passing between them [the opposing commanders]."[9]

A Union military thrust up the Savannah River to capture Savannah was not contemplated. That city would soon be captured by Union ground troops anyway. However, the fall of the fort did close the river to blockade-runners and the valuable cargoes they carried for the Confederate war effort. In addition to that, du Pont's ships were now free to be employed elsewhere.

Fort Pulaski also confirmed Gillmore's theory of the superiority of rifled guns over masonry fortifications, no matter how thick the walls. Gillmore was considered Admiral John Dahlgren's counterpart in the army and had proven his reputation as the Union army's most prominent artillery and engineering officer. He was twice breveted for gallantry and meritorious service and promoted to brigadier general of volunteers.[10] He was later promoted to major general and was assigned to the Department of the South and the newly created X Corps.

The fall of Fort Pulaski gave the victorious Federal forces 47 guns (the entire armament), a fixed supply of ammunition, 40,000 pounds of gunpowder, and a great deal of commissary stores, along with 360 prisoners, according to Major General Hunter. After extending kudos to General Gillmore for his "admirable energy and perseverance in the construction of the earthworks on Tybee Island," Hunter reported, "I am happy to state our loss was one man killed, the earthworks of our batteries affording secure protection against the heavy fire of the enemy."[11]

In retrospect, lessons can be learned from any military confrontation, no matter how major or minor, and the short assault on Fort Pulaski was no exception. After the surrender, Quincy Gillmore issued a report with some observations: "Mortars are unreliable for the reduction of works of small area, like Fort Pulaski," he wrote. "They cannot be fired with sufficient accuracy to crush the casemate arches." He praised the rifled guns that proved so efficient in the bombardment, maintaining that they could breach at 1,650 yards. However, he concluded by praising the 42-pound James rifle, merely noting that its grooves must always be kept clean for efficient firing.[12]

Gillmore's legendary egotism was greatly enhanced by this victory. Historian Robert Schneller wrote that he paraded around proudly, followed by a band playing loudly.[13]

Although it didn't take part in the assault on Fort Pulaski, the Union navy had been busy, especially along the Florida coast. On March 2, a fleet of warships stood off Cumberland Sound, and troops were sent in to take Fort Clinch, followed by the occupation of Fernandina. Then, on March 11, Federal troops occupied St. Augustine; the next day, Jacksonville was occupied. The Anaconda Plan was squeezing with more energy now, but there were many struggles, victories, and defeats yet to come.

CHAPTER THIRTEEN

FORT SUMTER REVISITED

The year 1863 held the promise of several momentous events that were to affect the final disposition of the Civil War: The squadrons of Admirals Farragut and Porter joined forces on the Mississippi River for the final thrust against Vicksburg; General Grant began his siege of the city in May; the gunboat *Carondelet* was sunk in the Yazoo River by one of the earliest Confederate mines; and Galveston was retaken by the Confederates after a fierce struggle between Confederate and Union gunboats and the Confederate raider *Alabama* sank the U.S.S. *Hatteras* off the harbor.[1]

On the East Coast, most Confederate ports were closed, with the exception of Charleston, Savannah, and Wilmington. Union plans were being drawn to assault and capture these important points of access to the outside world.

Of these, the vital port of Charleston had been the ever-present thorn in Union flesh since the Confederate capture of Fort Sumter in April 1861. If the city was important to the Union, it was even more important to the South. The city, with its nine-mile riverfront, was known as the "Cradle of the Rebellion," because it was the scene of the first shots of the Civil War. The South was determined to keep it as long as they could, because it was a major portal for blockade-runners. For its part, the Union chafed at the bit to reclaim Fort Sumter, a standing symbol of their ignominious defeat.

Charleston lay on a peninsula flanked by the Ashley River to the west and the Cooper River to the east. The city was founded at a point on the western bank of the Ashley River by English settlers in 1670, and named after Charles II. In 1788, Fort Lee, an outpost, occupied the site. Settlers came—mostly French Huguenots, Irishmen, and Germans. It soon became a shipping center for such crops as rice and indigo and, later, cotton. The site grew to a city and became the state capital in 1790. Three major fortifications were established in its spacious harbor: Fort Sumter, Castle Pinckney, and Fort Moultrie on Sullivan's Island. That harbor, 12 miles from the city to the ocean, was one of the most popular harbors in the world, with blockade-runners roaming freely through its three channels.

Those three channels, separated by shoals, prevented the Union from totally blockading the harbor. Because of this natural protection, blockade-runners were able to use the harbor to bring in 60 percent of Confederate arms, one-third of its bullet lead, ingredients for three-quarters of its gunpowder supply, and most of the army's cloth and leather for uniforms.[2]

General Pierre G. T. Beauregard, who had gallantly served the Confederacy at Bull Run and later at Shiloh in Tennessee, assumed command on September 24, 1862. He immediately strengthened Forts Sumter and Moultrie and established batteries on Cummings Point and Sullivan's Island. He was aware that the Union planned a sea assault, but he was determined that Charleston would never surrender to the Union, and so he oversaw the building of more than 64 fortifications in and around Charleston.[3] Fort Sumter alone had been fortified with 79 guns of various calibers, including 8-inch Columbiads; Moultrie had been strengthened with 38 guns. Plans were even drawn up for the protection of the civilian population against Union bombardment.

Then, at the end of January 1863, Beauregard played a trump card—two ironclads, to which the Confederacy had devoted its meager shipbuilding facilities soon after the stunning Union naval successes ending at the capture of Port Royal. The South Carolina Executive Council had allocated $300,000 for the construction of two ironclad vessels, and the women of the city, after a suggestion that appeared in a local newspaper, had raised funds by contributing personal items such as diamonds, bracelets, rings, paintings, and many other items that could be sold. One

11-year-old girl had given five dollars, which was a lot of money in those days, and some slaves, oddly enough, had contributed from their meager resources.[4] Interestingly, this was the beginning of a trend in the Confederacy that would soon be labeled as "ladies' gunboats."

One of the new ironclads, *Chicora,* had been constructed at the James M. Eason shipyard; the other, *Palmetto State,* had been built at the Cameron and Company yard. The two vessels were two of a planned *Richmond* class of six ironclads. They were 150 feet long, with a 34-foot beam. They were armored with 4-inch iron plates over 22 inches of wood backing. *Chicora's* battery consisted of two 9-inch smoothbores and four 32-pound Brooke rifles, while *Palmetto State's* armament was ten 7-inch rifles. Both vessels had a 14-inch draft, could cruise at nine knots, and carried a complement of 180 officers and men.[5]

Chicora had been launched on August 23, 1862, and *Palmetto State* on October 11. Both vessels were under the overall command of Captain Duncan N. Ingraham, in charge of all naval forces in South Carolina. Captain Rutledge commanded the *Palmetto State,* while the *Chicora* was skippered by Captain John R. Tucker. The former was to be the flagship of Flag Officer Ingraham.

These vessels of war were on hand in late January 1863, when Beauregard decided to launch an attack in an attempt to break the growing Union blockade, and after increasing criticism from Charleston citizens who daily viewed the ironclads languishing at a wharf. On duty at the entrance to Charleston Harbor were the Union warships *Mercedita,* a three-masted schooner; *Keystone State,* a 1,000-ton converted merchantman; *Memphis,* a captured and converted blockade-runner; *Quaker City,* a 1,000-ton converted merchant steamer; a side-wheeler gunboat, *Augusta;* and the screw sloop *Housatonic;* along with support vessels—nine in all.[6]

On the night of January 30, 1863, *Chicora* and *Palmetto State* cast off from their wharves and slipped down the harbor toward the unsuspecting Union fleet. The two ironclads crossed the bar at 4:30 A.M. on the morning of the 31st, after waiting for high tide. The *Palmetto State* made straight for the sleeping *Mercedita* with the intention of ramming her.

As she approached the Federal ship, she was hailed from the watch deck: "Steamer, ahoy! . . . stand clear . . . what steamer is that?" But the ram did not answer, instead tearing into the schooner's starboard side, passing through the outside planking and partially through her timbers. Captain

Rutledge fired his 7-inch rifle, and the shell passed through the starboard side and through the steam chimney of the port boiler, bursting before exiting the port side. Scalding steam filled the vessel, driving many crewmen out of the bowels of the ship. *Palmetto State* backed away and demanded a surrender, which came quickly. But, not having enough men for a prize crew, Rutledge convinced Captain Henry S. Stellwagon to promise that he and his crew would not act against the Confederacy until they were exchanged for Confederate prisoners of war. The *Mercedita* was then towed to Port Royal, out of the war for good.

Flushed with victory, Rutledge stood off to find more game, but the Federal ships, alarmed by the gunfire and realizing they were facing enemy ironclads, took off and soon outran the lumbering ram.

Meanwhile, *Chicora* moved on *Keystone State* and severely damaged her with gunfire. The Union vessel caught fire after her port steam chimney was pierced and the boiler ruptured, killing 20 men, with an equal number scalded or wounded. She struck her colors, but before she could be boarded as a prize, her starboard paddlewheel was activated, and she moved off to escape from her would-be captor. Captain William E. LeRoy of the *Keystone State* reported that he had run up his flag again because *Chicora* refused to respect his surrender and continued firing.[7]

After exchanging fire with the *Quaker City*, Tucker noted that the *Housatonic* was now headed toward the rams to engage. Daylight was fast approaching, so the commander called off the engagement. With only minimal damage, the rams headed back toward Charleston to anchor under the protection of the guns of Fort Sumter.[8]

General Beauregard crowed loudly about the alleged breaking of the blockade, but the truth of the matter was that only two ships, *Mercedita* and *Keystone State*, were damaged, and no Union vessels left their blockade stations for any appreciable length of time. His officially issued proclamation that the blockade had been broken was widely circulated, but his ardor was soon put down by his commanders, who assured him that it hadn't happened. In fact, the blockade was soon to be strengthened.[9] In Washington, a brief flurry of excitement prevailed when it was falsely reported that the ships had left their stations, but that was soon put down as pure nonsense.

Meanwhile, Admiral du Pont was chafing at the bit. He had planned to assault and subdue Fort Sumter and, he hoped, force Charleston's surrender. His hope lay in the ten monitors of the *Passaic* class under construction, but in the meantime, he sent the *New Ironsides* down to Charleston to deal with the enemy ironclads.

In Washington, undaunted by the enemy success at Charleston, Welles continued to plan the operation against Fort Sumter, and once again Union hopes were pinned on the 10 planned new monitors, which would bear the names *Comanche, Catskill, Lehigh, Montauk, Nahant, Nantucket, Passaic, Patapsco, Sangamon,* and *Weehawken,* vessels that were destined to go down in history. All of these formidable ships would be armed with one 15-inch and one 11-inch Dahlgren.[10]

The first of these vessels, the *Montauk,* was commissioned on December 17, 1862, fitted out, crewed, commanded by Captain John Worden, and then sent to du Pont at Port Royal. The admiral, still bothered by his skepticism, decided to test her. On January 27, 1863, he sent her, along with four gunboats and a mortar vessel, down to the mouth of the Ogeechee River, south of the Savannah River, to bombard Fort McAllister, a small enemy facility. The idea, of course, was a rehearsal for Fort Sumter.

When Worden arrived at the mouth of the Ogeechee, he was surprised to see the Confederate ram *Nashville* aground in shoal water behind the fort. He bombarded her, but with no appreciable results. Then, on January 27, the flotilla exchanged fire with the fort for four hours without diminishing the facility. The *Montauk* had been hit thirteen times but suffered no damage—although she later sustained some damage from a mine and had to beach for a time for repairs. The lesson drawn from this was that even the heavy guns of a monitor could not prevail against a masonry land fortification.

In regard to the coming engagement, du Pont expressed some doubts as to how nine vessels were going to take on the 147 guns in Charleston Harbor. He was of the opinion that monitors alone could never subdue a fort. It must be a coordinated operation between army and navy.

Still wavering, du Pont decided to send the monitors *Passaic, Patapsco,* and *Nahant,* recent arrivals from the shipyards, back to the Ogeechee to bombard Fort McAllister again. This time he became more comfortable with the "resisting power" of the monitors, but the two operations forced him to believe that the monitors had been grossly overrated by the navy and that he would need "as many as the department could give him" for the Fort Sumter operation.

The admiral got his wish. By March of 1863, he had received the remaining vessels along with the experimental *Keokuk* and the *New Ironsides*. The latter was a broadside ironclad, along regular ship lines, of 4,683 tons' displacement, with fourteen 11-inch Dahlgrens, two 150-pound rifles, and two 50-pound rifles. It was one of the most powerful warships afloat and was chosen as du Pont's flagship. The *Keokuk* was an anomaly in warships and not a true monitor, although she resembled one. She was a 4-inch-thick iron-armored vessel with two 11-inch smoothbores mounted in two stationary cylindrical turrets with three gunports. The guns inside were pivot Dahlgrens and were moved between gunports instead of having the turrets move.[11]

On April 6, the armada assembled at North Edisto Island, south of Charleston, moved up and crossed the bar of Charleston Harbor, but had to anchor because of inclement weather. The weather was reported as being cloudy and hazy, so the attack was called off until the next day. The 7th dawned bright and clear, and at 3:30 P.M., the signal was given to up-anchor and get under way. The squadron was to steam in a column, with the *Weehawken* in the lead because she had been equipped with a specially built raft, designed by Ericsson, to sweep any mines in the channel planted by the Confederates in anticipation of a naval attack. Admiral du Pont on his flagship, *New Ironsides,* occupied the center of the column, in order for signals to be understood by all vessels. The weakest vessel, the *Keokuk,* was last in the column.[12]

Suddenly, the *Weehawken*'s anchor chain became entangled with a grappling hook on the raft; the procession was halted for an hour.[13] After the column got under way again, it passed the batteries on Morris Island, but strangely, no shots were fired at the column. At 2:10, the *Weehawken* reported an obstruction in the vicinity.[14] These proved to be casks strung together in several lines, which possibly contained mines. Unable to cross the obstruction, *Weehawken* came to a halt again, turned, and threw the rest of the column into confusion until they too came to a halt. This was all the waiting Confederates needed, and a torrent of shells soon rained down from batteries at Fort Sumter, Fort Moultrie, Sullivan's Island, and Morris Island.

The bombardment was described by observers as being a tremendous concentration of fire. The monitors, ignoring the obstructions, moved up to the forts and responded in kind, while receiving many hits: *Passaic* received 35, *New Ironsides* 93, and *Weehawken* 53. The other ships received hits, but none were lethal except for those suffered by the *Keokuk,* which came within 500 yards of Fort Sumter and received a fatal beating, taking 90 hits, many below the waterline. At one point, the *New Ironsides* was forced to anchor because of her deep draft. Unknown to the crew, she was sitting directly over a mine operated by a magneto at Morris Island. The Confederates tried desperately to detonate the mine but were unsuccessful. It was later discovered that a wagon had passed over the wire, cutting it in two. This was fortunate for the Union vessel, because she most certainly would have been lost, and possibly du Pont with it.[15] For years the Confederates submitted that the wire had been deliberately cut by a Union sympathizer; no one will ever know for sure.

Aware of the beating his ships were taking, and seeing an apparent lack of damage to the fort, du Pont called for a withdrawal at 4:30 P.M. He reported to Welles that he had withdrawn his vessels because he deemed it too late in the day to attempt to force passage through the obstructions.

At the anchorage that night, du Pont called for a conference of his commanders in his cabin on the flagship. When he learned from them that his vessels had been severely damaged, he became "convinced of the utter impracticability of taking the City of Charleston by the forces under my command."[16]

Meanwhile, the poor *Keokuk,* riddled with holes and severely mauled, was moved down to an anchorage safe from the guns of Confederate forts. Her crew valiantly tried to save her, but she was too severely damaged and sank the next day, her stack and turret barely visible above water. Then during the next few days, the Confederates ingeniously, but with great difficulty, managed to remove the Dahlgrens, much to the chagrin of the Union forces.[17]

Du Pont's failure to subdue Fort Sumter was roundly criticized in the North. Secretary Welles felt depressed and concerned over what he called "the defeat," and President Lincoln shared in the gloom. He and his cabinet were having doubts about the latest campaigns against the Confederates—especially McClellan's star-crossed Peninsula Campaign—which were exacerbated by this disaster at Charleston.[18] Even some of the admiral's captains were highly critical of him and the apparent weakness of the monitors. As a result of all this contretemps, it was increasingly obvious that du Pont's command was in jeopardy.

In fairness to du Pont, it should be remembered that the admiral did have reservations about the assault on Fort Sumter, but he had been pressed into a campaign that was doomed to failure from the start—the 34 guns of his squadron against the 69 of the enemy forts on and around Fort Sumter.[19]

But while arguments swirled around Washington, the South Atlantic Blockading Squadron was racking up a naval victory of sorts. After the evacuation of the Gosport Navy Yard, and the destruction of the *Virginia,* Flag Officer Tattnall had received an order on May 19, 1862, from Secretary Mallory instructing him to take command of the naval defenses of the state of Georgia.[20] Under his command was a small squadron of vessels consisting of the ironclads *Atlanta* and *Savannah,* the floating battery *Georgia,* the gunboat *Isondiga,* a receiving ship, the old gunboat *Savannah,* plus six transports. Of the ironclads, the *Atlanta* had the greatest potential. She had been converted from the hull of the old screw steamer *Fingal,* a blockade-runner built in Scotland. She displaced 1,000 tons and was 204 feet long, with a 41-foot beam, a casemate of 4-inch iron, 5-inch decking, and a draft of 15 feet. Her armament consisted of two 7-inch and two 6-inch Brooke rifles, plus a spar mine. Her complement was 145 officers, men, and marines.[21] Commander William A. Webb was her skipper. *Atlanta* had been commissioned in November 1862 and remained in the Savannah River, protecting the city and waiting for a chance to break the blockade. According to her builder, Nelson Fix, she was "strongly and quickly built."[22]

In contrast to earlier Confederate ironclads, the *Atlanta* had a relatively new engine, and she was capable of six knots in spite of her 1,000-ton displacement, but her livability left much to be desired. According to a letter later written by the ram's master, H. B. Littlepage, to his friend Catesby ap Roger Jones, who was an officer on the ill-fated *Virginia,* the *Atlanta's* quarters were deplorable. "I think she was the most miserable I ever saw," Littlepage wrote. "There is no ventilation below at all, and I think it would be impossible for us to live on her in the summer. I would defy anyone in the world to tell when it is day or when night if he is confined below." Littlepage went on to complain about the thinness of the iron cladding (⅝ inch). "I would venture to say," he concluded, "that if a person were blindfolded and carried below and then turned loose he would imagine himself in a swamp, for the water is trickling in all the time and everything is so damp."[23] Because of a lack of skilled labor and shortages of materials, this was the norm for Confederate ironclads in the Gulf and on the East Coast.

In June 1863, Captain Webb was determined to use his ram to raise the blockade between the river and Charleston, attack Port Royal, and then blockade Union-held Fort Pulaski. But first he had to go by two Union monitors: the repaired *Weehawken* and the *Nahant,* sent to the mouth of the river to pounce on the ironclad once she made her appearance. The appearance of the ironclad had been rumored for some time, and the Union squadron was ready for it.

On the night of June 10, Webb got under way to "challenge" the monitors by ramming one and engaging the other with gunfire. He had loaded his ship with coal, weighed anchor, and headed downstream, followed by an armed steamer. The *Atlanta* was first spotted by *Weehawken's* lookout at 4:10 A.M. Captain John Rodgers ordered the crew beat to quarters in his squadron, slipped his cable, and stood upstream toward the ironclad. The *Nahant,* under command of Commander John Downes, not having a pilot, followed in the flagship's wake. At 4:55 A.M., as the combatants closed, it appeared as if *Atlanta* had stopped and was lying athwart the channel, awaiting the oncoming enemy warships. But in actuality, she had run hard aground in shoal water. Webb fired a shot at *Weehawken* that missed her but came close to *Nahant's* pilothouse.

Rodgers approached to within 300 yards of the ironclad and commenced firing his 11- and 15-inch Dahlgrens. The ram answered in kind, but her shots missed their mark. Rodgers fired only four rounds at *Atlanta,* but that did the job. At 5:30 A.M., Webb hauled down his colors and raised the white flag, in what was one of the shortest naval engagements in the war.[24]

Then at 5:45 A.M., a boat came alongside with a Lieutenant Alexander to surrender *Atlanta*. Shortly after, Captain William A. Webb came aboard and presented his sword to Rodgers, who then sent a prize crew to the ram. For some inexplicable reason, *Nahant* managed to collide with *Weehawken,* but fortunately inflicted minimal damage to her sister.

The prize crew discovered that *Atlanta* had been struck four times, but the damage was devastating. A 15-inch cored shot had struck the starboard side, sending fragments of iron and wood into the casemate, wounding 40 to 50 men. The second shot struck the knuckle but did little damage;

however, a third had taken off the roof of the pilothouse and wounded three men. The fourth shot struck a port stopper, breaking it in two. In return, Webb managed to get off seven shots, but not one found its mark. Eighteen Confederate crewmen were wounded in the short fight. The armed steamer had retreated upstream without firing a shot.

This action had a debilitating effect on the Confederacy. Davis curtly wrote that the *Atlanta* was aground at the time and "in this situation, she was attacked and, though hopeless, was bravely defended, but was forced to surrender."[25] Either he was not aware of the facts at the time, or he was opting for a propaganda coup through the press.

Welles, on the other hand, wrote a long letter of congratulations to Rodgers and his crew, lauding Rodgers' past endeavors, after he had prevailed upon President Lincoln and Congress to promote Rodgers to the rank of commodore.[26] The brave ship captain was feted and acclaimed as a hero in the northern press.

Savannah was now cut off from the ocean, along with the remaining ships in Tattnall's squadron. The *Savannah* was now relegated to being a floating battery, much like the *Georgia,* ostensibly to protect her namesake city from any Union incursion up the river. The *Savannah,* one of six vessels of the *Richmond* class, was designed by John L. Porter to be like *Atlanta,* a formidable fighting man-of-war. She was 172 feet long with a 34-foot beam. Her casemate was constructed of 4-inch iron plating over 22 inches of solid wood, and her armament consisted of one 7-inch and one 6-inch Brooke rifle. She would have been a tough opponent had she, like her sister, been able to scrap it out with Union vessels.

Those Union incursions never came. Instead, as Sherman's army approached in December 1864, it was necessary to move the squadron upstream. The lighter vessels made it, but *Savannah*'s 15-foot draft kept her from following. So she was blown up to prevent capture, along with other ships of the squadron.[27]

Savannah, like Charleston, was destined not to be subjugated by naval forces alone. Both citadels were to be taken by ground troops, supported by the navy's powerful guns, as had been proven some months before at Cape Hatteras and Port Royal. Efforts along those lines were soon to come. Meanwhile, du Pont's star had set; he was relieved of command of the South Atlantic Blockading Squadron on June 24, 1863, and the post was offered to Rear Admiral Andrew Foote. But the hero of the Mississippi River campaigns declined because of poor health; he died a short time later. The appointment was then offered to Rear Admiral John Dahlgren, who readily accepted. He took command on July 6 and lost no time plunging into the task at hand: first the subjugation of Forts Sumter and Moultrie and then the eventual occupation of Charleston.[28]

Dahlgren was aware that the enemy batteries on the perimeter of Charleston Harbor had to be either neutralized or seized. The big, tempting target was Battery Wagner on Morris Island, defended by 1,000 troops and several big guns. Major General Quincy A. Gillmore—who had proposed an assault on the battery using 5,000 troops, supported by Dahlgren's squadron—shared his view. When taken, this bastion was to be the base from which to launch either troop landings or bombardments of Forts Sumter and Moultrie and even Charleston itself. To accomplish this, he would need a flotilla of heavy guns to cover the landings. The answer, of course, lay in his vaunted monitors with their big-bored Dahlgrens. On July 6, 1863, the assault was launched. Gillmore's troops landed on Folly Island southwest of the battery, covered by a heavy bombardment from Dahlgren's monitors *Catskill, Montauk, Nahant,* and *Weehawken.* The squadron threw over 500 shot and shells into the facility but failed to keep Confederate heads down. The Union assault was repulsed with losses of over 100 men.[29]

Then it was Dahlgren's turn to receive punishment. Battery Wagner's gunners poured a heavy fire at the squadron, hitting the monitors. The *Catskill,* for some reason, was the focal point of the torrent of shells, receiving over 60 hits. The others received punishment, but none was seriously damaged. The next morning, the monitors were back, flinging a deluge of shots into the fort.

Gillmore decided on siege tactics. He sent for big siege guns and long-range rifles, and then his troops dug in around the fort. On the 18th, he launched another attack on the battery, which had been reinforced with fresh troops, but he was again repulsed with heavy losses. A third attack also failed, so Gillmore settled down and bombarded the fort for the next seven weeks with his guns and those of the fleet's big Dahlgrens.

On September 6th, the Confederates had had enough and slipped away quietly in the night. Gillmore's men were able to march into the battery uncontested. The cost to the Union for the occupation of Battery Wagner was high—over 1,500 men, including 111 officers. Confederate losses were 188 killed and wounded.[30]

Although the cost to the Union for taking Battery Wagner was high, the long-term advantages were many. Gillmore now had a base from which to launch future invasions. In the ensuing months, Union guns from Battery Wagner and other captured locations up the peninsula, supported by the monitors, managed to pound Fort Sumter into a pile of rubble.

Charleston itself came under bombardment a few times, including a night attack by Dahlgren's ironclads on August 23, 1863, that resulted in heavy damage to Fort Sumter. The monitors in turn received only six shots from Sumter, but Fort Moultrie, with its extensive earthworks, struck the monitors many times. After one of the ships ran aground for a short time, and with his crews becoming exhausted, Dahlgren ordered a withdrawal.[31]

Meanwhile, on Morris Island, a union battery, the "Swamp Angel" or "Marsh Battery," as the Confederates called it, was shelling the city on August 22. Around 15 rounds were fired by the 8-inch Parrott rifle mounted in the battery. The 16,000-pound gun had been transported through the marsh by engineers and artillerymen, a feat that was looked upon as a masterly achievement. However, on the 23rd, the gun burst; it was replaced with mortars.[32]

The bombardment came as a surprise to the citizens of Charleston, and a great deal of damage was done to the city, which was already half ruined by the fire of 1861. It was believed that the Federals were taking out their frustrations over their failure to capture Fort Sumter. Much criticism was heaped on General Gillmore for allowing the bombardment. General Beauregard wrote a scathing denunciation of Gillmore, calling the bombardment "an act of inexcusable barbarity."[33]

Few citizens were unmoved by the bombardment; a Confederate officer's wife wrote to him, describing the damage done to a neighbor's house by two shells, "ripping up the floor and tearing the planking to pieces." She wrote that one shell tore up the dining room, and that it was lucky that no one was hurt or killed.[34] The same Confederate officer, in responding to his wife's letter, lamented that his government "ought to have learned by now the folly of exposing men on islands where, in case of as disaster, there is no retreat."[35]

The Union focus, of course, was on capturing the forts in the harbor, although the garrison on Fort Sumter refused to surrender even as the walls crumbled around them. It was a perfect example of the South's resolve not to surrender, and it became painfully obvious that Charleston and the forts could not be pounded into submission nor be conquered. That task would require a large and powerful army.

CHAPTER FOURTEEN

THE *HUNLEY* AND UNDERWATER WARFARE

One of the most intriguing aspects of the history of naval actions in the Civil War is the amazing resiliency of the Confederate navy and its ability to counter the overwhelming might of the Federal fleets. Not having a major industrial base and shipyards with which to build warships, the Confederacy's resourceful leaders dipped into the fairly new technology of underwater warfare to achieve some semblance of parity with the Union. Two major devices were torpedoes (known as mines today) and self-propelled underwater craft that came to be known as submarines. Much research, study, and experimentation went into the creation of these weapons, as the Confederacy's long coastline featured a plethora of navigable rivers, bays, and harbors that needed to be protected.[1]

The program was set in motion during October 1861, at which time the Confederate congress formalized a Torpedo Bureau and a Naval Submarine Battery Service, based on the pioneering efforts of Commodore Matthew Fontaine Maury. This brilliant scientist from Virginia entered the navy in 1825 and was promoted to lieutenant in 1836 because of his exceptional intelligence and ingenuity. After an accident crippled him for life, he was assigned shore duty with the navy's Hydrographical Office. He became a renowned scholar in meteorological and oceanographic studies and wrote extensively on the subjects. When war broke out, he joined the Confederacy and was appointed to the Office of Orders and Detail at Richmond, where he pioneered the science of torpedoes for his government. He designed a prototype and arranged for a demonstration on the James River in the presence of Secretary Mallory and assorted dignitaries, during which he destroyed and sank a barge using a torpedo device. His genius was recognized overseas, and Mallory sent him to Europe to continue his research and to obtain ships and naval supplies for the Confederacy. He served out the war in England, returned to the United States, settled in New Mexico, then moved back to England, only to return to his native country again to become a professor at the Virginia Military Institute in 1868.[2]

The torpedo (which hereafter will be referred to by the modern term *mine,* except in period documents) was named after a marine species of ray *(Torpedo nobiliana)* that grows to a length of six feet and can deliver a strong electrical shock of 200 volts to its victim. The mine itself is not a new invention in history. During the Revolutionary War an American hydrographer, David Bushnell, unsuccessfully tried to destroy an anchored British ship with a keg of powder to be attached to the ship's bottom, using a small submersible boat, called the *Turtle,* that he invented. The mine failed to go off and ice floes prevented the device from reaching its target, but the resulting panic among British sailors caused the incident to be labeled "Battle of the Kegs." Incidentally, the *Turtle* came close to sinking three British ships. Thus, Bushnell can be considered the true father of the submarine, as well as the first one to invent the mine.

Then in the 1800s, a mine device invented by Robert Fulton managed to sink some old hulks. He also invented a submarine contraption called the *Nautilus,* which caused little or no stir except for a young author named Jules Verne, who used the sub's name in his famous book *Twenty Thousand Leagues Under the Sea.* Crude mines had also been used with little or no success during the Crimean War. The mines used by the Confederacy were also crude, but they were on occasion devastatingly effective, and paved the way for the much more sophisticated mine programs of World Wars I and II.

The Confederacy also experimented with the use of mines on land. During the evacuation of Yorktown and Williamsburg, Confederate general Gabriel J. Rains used pressure land mines to stop attacks by Union cavalrymen. The Union labeled this method of warfare as barbaric and, as an act of reprisal, forced Southern prisoners of war to remove the mines at their own risk, which in itself could be considered a barbaric action.

There were several types of mines invented by the Confederate navy: the Rains keg mine, the Fretwell-Singer mine, the current mine, the friction mine, the horological (timing) mine, the floating tin mine, and the copper swaying mine.[3] Of these, the most popular and widely used mine device, and the prototype for modern mines, was the Fretwell-Singer, a pear-shaped device filled with around 75 pounds of powder. It was detonated by a springlike plunger on the top that, when released, hit a percussion cap. It was usually anchored on the bottom by a large piece of railroad iron. The current mine featured a propeller that, when turned by a current, moved it against the side of a ship. The friction mine was anchored to the bottom and floated just below the surface; when a vessel passed over it, an operator pulled a lanyard on the shore, detonating the mine. Other, cruder mine devices were also used; for example, a demijohn filled with powder and activated by a magneto device on shore sank the Union ironclad gunboat *Cairo* in the Yazoo River in December 1862. Later, on July 31, 1863, another device took out the gunboat *Baron de Kalb* in the same river.[4] Jefferson Davis wrote that there were "three essentials to success [with mines] viz., the sensitive fuze primer, a charge of sixty pounds of gunpowder and actual contact between the torpedo and the bottom of the vessel."[5]

After Maury was sent to Europe, his assistant Hunter Davidson took over his work. He made improvements on the devices and contributed to their successes by destroying enemy vessels with them. He stated that "the results of this system were that the *first vessels* ever *injured or destroyed by war* by electrical torpedoes were by the torpedo department operating under my immediate command, and I might add the *only* ones that I am aware of."[6] Davidson wrote this treatise in the wake of abundant criticism about the moral implications concerning the use of mines during and after the Civil War (and which still stimulates debate today).

The thesis of General Rains, chief of the Confederate Torpedo Service, was that most weapons of destruction "were denounced as illegal and barbarous, yet each took its place according to its efficacy in human slaughter by the unanimous consent of nations." He cited instruments of war from the simple club to percussion weapons. "There is no fixed rule in deterring the ethics of war," he wrote. "That the legalizing murder of our fellow men, for even mining is admitted with its wholesale destruction."[7]

Davidson declared that mines sank around 20 Union vessels, although that figure has been debated. Jefferson Davis declared 58, and historians state the number as being either 29 or 30, but no one knows for sure. Most of these sinkings occurred on rivers, and a few in harbors or bays, such as the sinking of the *Tecumseh* in Mobile Bay on August 5, 1864, and the famous event of the destruction of the ironclad *Cairo* on December 12, 1862. Perhaps there would have been more victims were it not for the constant bickering between Confederate leaders, whether political versus industrial, or army versus navy, that shackled the efforts to perfect and deploy more mines.

But a major evolution did take place. The mine concept was adapted to moving water vehicles—namely, the submarine—because of the invention of the spar mine by a Confederate genius, Captain Francis B. Lee, who made the mine an offensive weapon instead of a defensive one. The early spar mine was fastened from a piece of boiler tube closed at both ends and filled with powder. It was detonated by percussion nipple primers filled with fulminate of mercury that were activated by contact with a ship's bottom. The device was called a spar mine because it was mounted on one end of a 10- or 12-foot pole with the other end attached to a moving vessel, either submerged or on the surface. The powder-filled explosive device was buoyant and therefore had to be forcibly lowered beneath the surface by a specially designed sleeve device when the vehicle was in motion and headed toward its target.

The vehicle to carry the spar would have to be of the submersible type, and this led to the early development of a submarine type of vessel called the *David* by the Confederates. It was a cigar-shaped boat 50 feet long and 5 feet in width, and it was propelled by a single screw turned by a hand crank on the inside of the craft. The *David* was an improvement on an earlier experimental vessel developed in New Orleans, called the *Pioneer,* which was a cone-shaped iron-plated vessel 34 feet long, 4 feet in breadth, and 6 feet in depth, displacing 4 tons and carrying a crew of three men. Like the later *David,* the *Pioneer* was propelled by a single screw activated by a crank.[8] During a demonstration, this prototype managed to sink a barge in Lake Pontchartrain, but it never saw action. It was scuttled in the lake when Farragut's fleet approached; it was later raised and is on display today in New Orleans.

The improved *David*, on the other hand, was powered by a small, powerful steam engine and had a crew of four men. She could admit water in her ballast tanks to lower her to water level—she was never fully submerged. Her explosive device was mounted on the end of a 14-foot spar. The craft was so named because of its small size compared to a warship, in a nod toward the biblical account of the struggle between David and Goliath.

During the night of October 5, 1863, the *David*, commanded by Lieutenant William T. Glassell, slipped into Charleston Harbor and made for the anchored Union flagship *New Ironsides*. At around 10:00 P.M., she approached to within 50 yards of the vessel undetected. When lookouts finally spotted the oncoming craft, she was hailed from the quarterdeck. In response, someone on the *David* fired a shot that mortally wounded the officer on the deck. Then the spar mine was thrust into the hull on the starboard quarter. A geyser of water from the consequent explosion shot up and fell over the *David*, dousing her boiler. She drifted away, meanwhile taking a beating from small-arms fire from the ship (its big guns could not be depressed sufficiently). Glassell and his crew, mindful that the craft was doomed, jumped overboard. Later, her engineer swam up, climbed aboard, relit the boiler, and steered the craft back to Charleston. Meanwhile, a boat from *New Ironsides* captured Glassell and his swimming men. The ship suffered some damage—not fatal, but she had to be towed back to Port Royal and thence to the Philadelphia Navy Yard for repairs.[9] The *David* sortied out once more, on May 5, 1864, and attacked the U.S.S. *Memphis*, a 1,000-ton blockade-runner. The spar mine failed to explode this time, even after two thrusts at the hull, and the Union ship managed to get away.

In the Confederacy, the *David* program managed to produce several other vessels along the same lines, but they were never used and were abandoned when Charleston was evacuated as the Union armies drew near. (One is believed to be buried beneath a waterfront street paved over after the war. Currently, efforts are under way to uncover this craft. When this is accomplished, it will be a major find, to be placed alongside extant mines and other weapons of the Civil War that are displayed today at museums.) Much to their credit, however, Confederate planners persisted, and finally managed to build a more sophisticated craft that was destined to sail into the halls of history: the *H. L. Hunley*.

The *Hunley* was the product of industrialist James R. McClintock, who was in partnership with Baxter Watson in a machine shop. The project to build the submarine was financed by Horace L. Hunley, a wealthy plantation owner and designer. Earlier, McClintock and Watson had built the aforementioned *Pioneer* and another unsuccessful craft at New Orleans. They now decided on a more advanced vessel that would improve on the weaknesses of the *Pioneer*. But when blockading Yankee naval forces were stationed off Charleston, they moved operations to Mobile, where they took over a machine shop on Water Street. At first they dabbled with a magnetic engine run by a series of batteries, a concept way ahead of its time. There were too many obstacles in the way of the magnetic motor, so it was abandoned in favor of the more common and productive method, that of hand propulsion. Their first model was towed to the area of Fort Morgan to attack any Union ships there, but she foundered in rough seas and the crew had to be rescued.[10] It was obvious that much more research and planning needed to go into producing a viable submarine vessel that would be safe for its occupants.

Undaunted, the tireless duo went to work on another model. This time they concentrated on producing the best boat they could. According to W. A. Alexander, they procured a riverboat boiler 25 feet long and 48 inches in diameter. The boiler was cut in two longitudinally, with boiler iron strips placed in her sides and on top, and holes cut for two hatches. When bow castings were added, the sub was lengthened to 30 feet, with a 4-foot beam and 5-foot depth. Bulkheads were added at both ends to hold water for raising and sinking the craft. A force pump was installed to control the input and output of water in the ballast tanks, and a mercury depth gauge was added. A detachable iron keel, weighing 4,000 pounds, was riveted to the bottom of the boat. A hand crank with handles for eight men ran the full length of the sub and provided motive power for a single screw located behind the rudder. A diving rudder was installed to both starboard and port sides, and glass view ports were placed on the forward hatch. She would accommodate, albeit in terribly cramped conditions, a crew of nine men, plus two officers, one serving as navigator, the other attending the after pump and tank. For illumination, a single candle doubled as a source of light and as a warning of dwindling air supply; the crew could exist for two hours with the air already in the sub, but surfacing to replenish the air supply was a necessity.

In August 1863, after a series of tests in Mobile Bay, Mallory ordered the sub transported to Charleston, where it was believed that she would be a potent weapon against the Union fleet off Charleston Harbor. The *Hunley* was disassembled and shipped to Charleston on two flatcars, then reassembled there.[11]

The *Hunley's* weapon was a copper cylinder filled with 90 pounds of explosives, equipped with percussion and friction primers. It was tied to a board and connected to the stern by a 200-foot line. Theoretically, it would be towed to the target; once there, the sub would submerge and run under it, and the explosive device would be detonated upon contact with the ship's bottom, while the sub would be a safe distance from the explosion. It was a nice theory and was successful in one test run, but a second almost destroyed the sub when a heavy surf pushed the mine toward it and the crew narrowly escaped destruction.

Tragedy plagued the early endeavors of the sub. While moored at a wharf, with crew on board and hatches open, a passing vessel swamped her, sending her to the bottom and drowning the crew; other sinkings and losses of crews occurred in following days. Historians are in disagreement as to how many times the *Hunley* sank—some say three times, others say as many as five, but some reports of sinkings or swampings at wharves may refer not to the *Hunley* but to the *Davids*.[12]

It began to appear that the *Hunley* was doomed to failure. Horace Hunley and a team of men who had experience with early trials at Mobile Bay came to Charleston to take over the project, but tragically, Hunley and the crew perished in still another swamping of the boat.

The man next chosen to command the *Hunley* was Second Lieutenant George Dixon, who was loaned from the Confederate army to the navy for the *Hunley* project. Dixon tried to recruit a crew from the receiving ship *Indian Chief* but failed, because the *Hunley* had sunk while alongside that ship, and the sailors had witnessed the loss of the sub's crew. Eventually, though, a crew was found and mustered, and the *Hunley* was ready for game. But the system of carrying the mine behind once again plagued them, until a Confederate engineer and skipper of the *David* suggested another tack, that of mounting the explosive device on an unusually long spar and attaching it ramlike to the bow. The concept was for the sub to run at hatch depth and then ram the mine against the enemy vessel; the length of the spar would protect the sub and crew against the blast.

After a lengthy training session at the very first submarine training school, established in a small bay at Mount Pleasant on Sullivan's Island, the *Hunley* was ready for its baptism of fire. At nightfall on February 17, 1864, the *Hunley,* with Dixon and a well-trained crew on board, slipped out of Breach Inlet and into the Atlantic waters, where the U.S.S. *Housatonic* was anchored. This magnificent vessel was a screw sloop—2,000 tons, plus a 23-gun armament and a crew of 160 officers and men. Truly, she was a warship inspiring great pride in the Union navy.

It was a quiet, starlit night with a gentle breeze as Dixon conned his strange vessel through the water toward the warship. On board the frigate, Acting Master J. K. Crosby had the quarterdeck watch. Gazing out over the calm water, as he had done so many times while on duty, he spotted an object resembling a "porpoise" coming toward his ship. When it came close, he became suspicious and ordered the chain slipped, engines backed, and all hands beat to quarters.[13] Deckhands fired small arms at the object, which appeared larger now, and pivot guns were swung out, but they couldn't be depressed sufficiently because of the closeness of the object. Finally, the strange vessel struck the ship's starboard side between the mainmast and mizzenmast; the powerful explosion that followed that doomed the *Housatonic.* She was lifted slightly out of the water and rolled to port while water gushed uncontrollably through a large hole torn in her side. Crewmen scrambled to safety, some in boats, others climbing the rigging, because the ship was sinking stern first in relatively shallow water. The *Canandaigua,* anchored nearby, rescued most of the crew, with the exception of five, from the doomed ship. An examination of the wreck on February 20 revealed that the screw sloop was a complete wreck, "with her spar deck 15 feet below the surface of the water. The after part of the spar deck appears to have been entirely blown off."[14]

What happened to the *Hunley?* For a long time, no one knew for sure. A few days after the sinking, a diver exploring the wreck of the *Housatonic* failed to find her. Subsequent inquiries failed to substantiate her whereabouts. Many, including some Confederates, thought *Hunley* had returned to her base on Morris Island and was being hidden away from Union forces.

A few years later, a diver exploring not far from the wreck of the frigate found the *Hunley*. Various theories were advanced to explain her fate. One theory, put forward by a Confederate officer, had her literally being sucked into the hole she had blasted in the sinking frigate, because she failed to have the power to back out.[15] Another theory held that the ship backed over the sub and took it down under her weight. But the ship had been heeled over on the port side by the explosion and went down stern first, so logic tells us that most of the ship's bulk would not have been over the *Hunley*. Still another theory has it that sharpshooters on the frigate may have aimed at the glass ports on the sub's forward hatch and shot them out, thereby allowing water to gush in.

A recent issue of a national magazine featured a story on the finding of the *Hunley* by novelist-explorer Clive Cussler. The story submitted a theory that the *Hunley*, a thousand yards from the frigate, surfaced with hatches open to receive fresh air and was swamped when the *Canandaigua* rushed past the sub to assist the stricken *Housatonic*.[16]

Historian Mark Ragan has found evidence to support the theory that the *Hunley* was on the surface some distance from the frigate with her hatches open, preparing to head home. A lookout on the sinking frigate spotted a blue light on the water a distance from the *Housatonic* and off the starboard quarter of the *Canandaigua*. The blue light was reported to have been seen by Lieutenant Colonel O. M. Dantzler, commander of a battery on shore near the bay entrance through which the sub went out and would be expected to return.[17] Dantzler thought she had returned earlier.

Reactions to the sinking came from many quarters. On the Union side, Admiral Dahlgren wrote about the dangers of Confederate submersible craft: "The whole line of blockade will be infested with these cheap, convenient, and formidable defenses." He had hoped that the U.S. commanders would take the whole subject of underwater warfare seriously. He wrote: "Torpedoes have been laughed at, but this disaster ends that."[18] In another letter to Welles he expressed the opinion that torpedoes were the most formidable difficulties in the path to Charleston.

The Charleston *Daily Courier* reported the sinking of the *Housatonic* as a "glorious victory" but failed to report that the sub and her crew had not returned home. But the Charleston papers also pointed out that the "blockade goes on and nothing had been changed by the *Hunley*—except history."[19]

In the North, Professor Hortsford, a submarine designer, wrote Welles that he would design a vessel that would destroy all Confederate floating batteries and torpedoes "without serious difficulty," but nothing apparently came of this claim.[20] A navy magazine current at the time lamented the fact that the Confederates "had anticipated us in the practical application of engines of submarine warfare."[21] This article accurately echoed the sentiments prevalent in the Union navy at the time.

The fate of the *Hunley* aside, the fact remains that she was the first submarine in history to successfully sink a warship. This feat would not be repeated until the beginning of World War I, when a submarine torpedoed the S.S. *Lusitania,* an incident that started America's plunge into the war. Perhaps the best comment on the impact of the *Hunley* came from historian Brayton Harris, who asked this question: "Was *Hunley* a failure because she sank so many times and lost so many crews? The full record reveals that she was a submarine that made repeated successful dives, and within the technical limits of the day, had an impact on the disposition of an entire fleet—and set a precedent on the entire maritime world."[22]

The story of the *Hunley,* which began in the mid-nineteenth century, continues into the twenty-first century. Clive Cussler and his associates brought the *Hunley* to the surface on August 9, 2000, and placed it in a special tank built for it at the old Charleston Navy Yard. At this writing, the remains of two crew members had been removed from the vessel. Accouterments found indicate that at least one member of the crew was a member of the Confederate army. The remains of the entire crew will be buried with honors at Magnolia Cemetery in Charleston.[23]

Back in the 1860s, however, a Confederate war vessel of another kind was giving the Union navy a severe headache.

CHAPTER FIFTEEN

THE *ALBEMARLE* SAGA

After the capture of Cape Hatteras, followed by Roanoke Island, during the winter of 1862, the Union held undisputed sway over the Carolina sounds. Federal warships patrolled the waters of these sounds and occasionally made forays up some of the important rivers to ferret out Confederate gunboats lurking there, as well as any wildcat batteries along the banks that the enemy might have established in order to impede such Union probes. But the warships could go only so far up the rivers because of shoal waters and because of the constant threat of ironclads that the Confederates were reported to be building.

The Confederates still controlled the rivers in the southern end of Pamlico Sound, namely, the Neuse, Pamlico, and Tar. But on March 12, 1862, a Federal squadron steamed up the Neuse to attack and occupy New Bern, using amphibious landings under cover of warship guns. The town's defenders were driven upriver, where enemy warships dared not venture; there they concentrated on building ironclad vessels to counter the formidable Union navy during the winter of 1863–64.[1] In the meantime, they managed to stage occasional raids on Union ships and shore positions, usually annoying rather than hurting the enemy—especially at Federally occupied New Bern.

All that was to change in February 1864, when the Confederate brigadier general George Edward Pickett planned to assault and recapture New Bern, with the help of whatever ships he could muster. His plan was fraught with danger, because heavy units of the Union fleet were usually anchored off or in deeper waters below the town. The task of neutralizing any enemy vessels at or near New Bern fell to the lot of Lieutenant John Taylor Wood, a young career naval officer and an expert on gunnery. Wood had resigned from the U.S. Navy after war was declared, and promptly offered his services to Mallory. He was on board the *Virginia* during its epochal battle with the U.S.S. *Monitor* in March of 1862. Using his close relationship with President Davis, Wood prevailed upon Secretary Mallory to authorize a series of midnight raids on enemy warships, using 15 to 20 well-trained men in shallow-draft boats light enough to be transported across country, if need be, and dropped in rivers or streams. He proved his theory on October 7 when he and his crew successfully attacked and sank a transport schooner, *Francis Elmore*. To the Confederate military, such raids would be a perfect adjunct to General Robert F. Hoke's assault on New Bern. The young lieutenant was given the green light and the necessary means and equipment with which to launch the raids.

Wood sized up the Union naval presence at New Bern and targeted a large side-wheel gunboat, the *Underwriter*, of 341 tons and four guns, moored to a dock. This would be his first objective. Orders went out to the captains of Confederate ships at Drewry's Bluff on the James River for each to fit out a cutter for a secret mission. The boats were taken downriver to Petersburg, where they were loaded on waiting railroad flatcars and then shipped to the town of Kinston, on the Neuse River, where the boats were loaded and manned by waiting crews.

At 4:00 P.M. on February 1, 1864, Wood and his small flotilla proceeded 40 miles downriver to within 2 miles of New Bern. A reconnaissance revealed no ships at the city, so the raiding parties retired upstream for the night. The following morning, before sunrise, the flotilla cautiously moved down to the same spot. To their delight, they spotted the *Underwriter* tied up at a dock. But daylight was no time to pull off a surprise raid, so they returned to their hiding place upstream to await the coming darkness.

At midnight, Wood and his boats and crews sortied downriver once again, only this time they headed directly for the sleeping warship. As they drew near, a sentry spotted the oncoming craft and the cry went up, "Boat ahoy!" Wood answered with a rallying cry, "Give way, boys!" The well-trained oarsmen bent to their task and brought their boats up to the ship's lowest point, abaft the wheelhouse, where they prepared to board her. Strangely, those on the *Underwriter* still seemed to be unconcerned about the strange boat alongside.

Upon command, the attacking Confederates, cutlasses and revolvers in hand, swarmed over the bulwarks and overwhelmed a surprised Union crew, who surrendered after a brief but furious fight. Acting engineer G. Edgar Allen of the *Lockwood,* who went to assist the *Underwriter* with 18 to 20 of his ship's crew, reported that the Union crews were no match for the 40 or 50 well-trained boarders on the ship at one time. Nearby Fort Stevens opened fire on the ship, "regardless of their own people," and one of the shots tore through the port wheelhouse, wounding several of the ship's crew.[2]

The Confederate raiders set fire to the *Underwriter,* then boarded their boats and went off upstream, suffering only 28 casualties—6 dead and 22 wounded. The Federal casualties were 9 dead, 18 wounded, and 19 taken prisoner. Wood's raid was a coup for the Confederacy, because the 341-ton Union warship was a complete loss to the Union.

Spectacular as that raid was, it was not enough. The blockade was still in effect, and more warships were being added to the roster. Confederate hopes then shifted to those ironclads being built on the Roanoke and Neuse Rivers: the *Albemarle,* the *Neuse,* and an unnamed vessel uncompleted on the stocks. Both vessels were rumored to be formidable warships and had to be dealt with. The Confederates, on the other hand, were having trouble procuring enough iron to sheath the casemate. The countryside was being scoured for bolts, bars, rails—anything that could be melted down for use.

The three vessels were of the same configuration as the *Virginia*—an armored citadel on a hull—but unlike *Virginia* with its 22-foot draft, these vessels were designed with shallow drafts for use on the inland rivers. Of the three, only *Albemarle* was to write a page of naval history, because the *Neuse* ran aground off Kinston in May 1864 and remained there until she was destroyed to prevent capture.

In many respects, the *Albemarle* was a remarkable vessel. She was built on a cleared cornfield at Edward's Ferry on the Roanoke River. Her citadel was protected by two-inch iron plating, and the tapered prow featured a solid oak ram, also plated with two-inch iron. She was smaller than the traditional ironclad, being only 139 feet long with a beam of 34 feet and a flat hull with a draft of only 9 feet. She sported two boilers and two 200-horsepower horizontal engines geared to two screws, capable of producing four knots. Her armament consisted of six gunports served by two 6.4-inch Brooke rifles on swivels that enabled them to be fired from any of the gunports, and her complement consisted of 150 officers and men.[3]

The *Neuse,* of the same configuration as the *Albemarle,* was constructed at Whitehall, North Carolina, on the river after which she was named. Her unnamed sister was never completed and was later burned on the stocks as Grant's army approached in April 1865. The vessels were the brainchild of Commander James W. Cooke, who became captain of the *Albemarle* and was the one who led her into battle during her short but illustrious career.

The makeshift yards at which they built these ironclads were shining examples of Confederate ingenuity in the face of the lack of major shipbuilding facilities. The construction of *Albemarle,* as with the earlier Confederate *Arkansas,* built on the Mississippi, required only a cleared field with a small mill, a blacksmith shop, and some forges. Cranes for lifting iron plates and heavy guns were mounted on a steamer or a barge. When the hull was to be launched, it was usually done sideways, depending on the width of the river; a larger river required a stern-first launching.[4]

The *Albemarle* was launched on July 1, 1863, and after being fitted out, she was commissioned on April 17, 1864, and was ready for action against the Yankees. Her opportunity came when the Confederate combat veteran Brigadier General Robert Frederick Hoke was ordered to assault and capture Federal-held Plymouth, at the head of the Roanoke River. On April 17, the day *Albemarle* was commissioned, the assault was launched. Union gunboats quickly came to the rescue of the beleaguered garrison and promptly shelled the Confederate lines around the city. Unfortunately, during the exchange of fire with the enemy gunners, the Union army transport *Bombshell* was sunk. Lieutenant Commander Charles W. Flusser, who was in command of the flotilla, which consisted of gunboats *Southfield* and *Miami,* kept a wary eye open for the expected appearance of the enemy ironclad reported to have been launched up the river. "The ram," he was reported to have predicted, "will be down tonight or tomorrow."[5]

Flusser was correct. On the night of the 17th, Cooke got the *Albemarle* under way, even though she was still incomplete. She towed a raft upon which was a blacksmith shop, allowing workmen to bolt on plating while the ram moved downstream. The last of her plating was placed about at the same time she reached Plymouth, and the raft had to be cast off. However, three miles above, Cooke came upon some obstructions sunk by the Federals to stop the ram. He launched a boat containing three men with long poles to probe the site for water depth. They returned and reported 10 feet of water over the obstructions, the result of a freshet caused by rain the night before. Cooke, however, decided to risk going over, so he ordered full speed ahead; the *Albemarle* moved safely over the obstructions and once again headed downriver. As she passed a Union fort at Warren's Bend, she came under fire, but the shots bounced harmlessly off her plating, which had been augmented by hanging chains.[6]

As expected, all this firing alerted Flusser's squadron, and the open-ended gunboats *Miami* and *Southfield* moved up, eager for action. Flusser, in anticipation of such action, had lashed the two vessels together by a heavy chain in hopes of capturing the ram between the two and then pounding her into submission with their big guns.

Wily Captain Cooke dodged the trap by steaming close to the shore and, at the right moment, turning and heading straight for the ships, which were maneuvering to counter his unexpected turn. He had pulled off an end run, in modern parlance.

The *Albemarle* plowed into the *Southfield* amidships and opened a hole clear through to the boiler. The gunboat sank like a chunk of lead, with the loss of most of her crew. But she almost took the ram down with her, because her chains on the foredeck tangled with those of the ram, which was pulled down to such a depth that water began to pour in through her portholes. It began to look critical for the *Albemarle,* but as the *Southfield* settled on the bottom, she turned on her side, freeing her adversary. It was a close call for Cooke and his men.

The *Miami,* meanwhile, had broken free of the *Southfield* and began pouring broadside after broadside at the ram from her big guns, which included 9-inch guns and a 100-pound Parrott rifle. But the missiles bounded off the *Albemarle's* side like so many rubber balls. Then an unexpected thing occurred: One of *Miami's* 8-inch shells ricocheted back and exploded almost at the lanyard of the gun from which it came, killing Captain Flusser and six crewmen. The Federal crewmen tried to board the ram but were driven off by a determined and well-armed crew.[7] In the meantime, the other Union warships, realizing what they were up against, broke off engagement and fled down the river. *Albemarle* was unable to begin pursuit because of her slower speed.

Captain Cooke, now in possession of the river, turned his guns on the Union defenders of Plymouth, in support of Hoke's assault, and bombarded the defenders mercilessly, trying to prevent the Federals from repulsing the Confederate move, but Plymouth continued to punish the attacking Rebels.

In spite of heavy losses to his troops, Hoke took the town, along with 3,000 prisoners, 28 cannons, 5,000 rifles, and 700 barrels of flour, plus 300 tons of coal, which was badly needed by the Confederate navy. Plymouth was once again under Southern control, along with command of the Roanoke River and its entrance. Then the *Albemarle* steamed upriver for further completion. Everyone knew that the Federals would return soon, and with greater numbers and strength.

They didn't have to wait long, for on May 5 the Union fleet once again appeared, this time with four double-enders, the *Mattabesett, Sassacus, Wyalusing,* and *Miami,* along with the gunboat *Whitehead* and the side-wheelers *Commodore Hall* and *Ceres.* Accompanying the fleet were two heavily armed transports with seven guns each. The main body of the fleet had a firepower of thirty-six 9-inch Dahlgrens, eight 100-pound Parrott rifles, and two 14-pound howitzers. The entire flotilla carried a total of 82 guns against the *Albemarle's* two 6.4-inch Brooke rifles.

As this powerful fleet, with the *Mattabesett* in the van, approached the mouth of the Roanoke, witnesses described the scene as being a beautiful morning with a just-risen sun, calm waters, and birds skimming majestically over the water in the sound—an unlikely scene for the carnage about to take place.

Eagerly awaiting them was Cooke and the *Albemarle* with two consorts, the armed steamers *Bombshell* and *Cotton.* The former had been raised and refitted after it was sunk during the first battle off Plymouth in April.

The Union flotilla was under the command of Captain Malancton Smith, and he had issued orders for the double-headers to close on the ram, bombard her, then get out of line as quickly as possible. Then they would close in for another round. The tactic was similar to the bombardment of Cape Hatteras and Port Royal, with ships sailing an elliptical pattern while broadsiding their target. The gunboats and transports were to deliver salvos from below. Some mines had been issued to *Miami* to be delivered if the occasion was offered to her.

But once again, everything seemed to go wrong for the Union. Cooke got off the first shots, which hit the *Mattabesett,* wounding six men. The *Sassacus* opened fire on the ram, but once again, the shots seemed to bounce harmlessly away. Soon five Union ships and the *Albemarle* were furiously slugging it out. At times the smoke was so dense, the Federal ships had to sheer off to prevent being rammed.[8]

The ram's armor seemed impenetrable, and finally Smith ordered the *Sassacus* to give the *Albemarle* a dose of her own medicine by ramming her, in an effort to save the other ships. The heavy double-ender, with a full head of steam and her paddlewheels churning furiously, plowed through the water and plunged head-on into the ram amidships. The *Albemarle* heeled over from the impact, but the citadel held. The ram's gunners threw a shot into the double-ender that hit her boiler and sent steam roaring throughout the doomed vessel, scalding many of her crew.

The scene was out of some inferno, with the damaged ship spouting steam and the cries of the wounded and dying echoing over the sound. Added to that was the gunsmoke obliterating the scene, punctured by orange flashes and the heavy thudding of big guns. For a time, the *Miami* tried to ram the *Albemarle,* attempting to sink her with a mine, but that too was unsuccessful. Crewmen from the ram attempted to board the *Sassacus* but were driven away as the wounded ship veered off. Meanwhile, the *Bombshell,* under heavy fire, struck her colors and surrendered.[9]

As happened before in February when locking horns with the seemingly indestructible ram, the Union squadron decided it had had enough, and Smith ordered a withdrawal. The fleet, with the wounded *Sassacus* and the prize *Bombshell* in tow, withdrew to lick its wounds, again leaving the little ram alone as an illustrious master of the field. As before, the small warship had bested a large and powerful enemy squadron. It was incredible, and the Confederates made the most of it through cheers and accolades. To them, it was a case of David against Goliath once more. The "David" went up to Plymouth and docked, and soon workmen were swarming over her to fix her wounds. It was a great day with a great boost in morale for the Confederacy.

But that was soon to change when General Hoke's forces were recalled from the Plymouth area to Virginia to meet General Grant's Campaign of the Wilderness. The *Albemarle* remained at Plymouth as a deterrent against any further Union naval incursions into Roanoke Sound.

While this struggle was going on, another Confederate ram was trying to make history at Wilmington. The *Raleigh* had been built at Wilmington and commissioned on April 30, 1864. A sister ship, the *North Carolina,* had been launched in October 1862, but never forayed out for battle; her hull had become worm-infested, and she became a floating battery on the Cape Fear River to protect blockade-runners. Eventually she foundered and was sunk on December 27, 1864—an ignominious end for a warship.

The *Raleigh,* however, did challenge the blockading ships in a sortie down the Cape Fear River, crossing the bar and coming face-to-face with *Mount Vernon, Howquah, Britannia,* and *Nansemond.* A brief exchange took place, in which the *Howquah* received a hole in her stack, but the ram was unharmed. Then she broke off the engagement, recrossed the bar, and moved upstream, where she ran hard aground, broke her back, and was later destroyed.[10]

Now the Union high command concentrated once again on the only obstacle still present in either Albemarle Sound or the Roanoke River: the *Albemarle.* She had to be destroyed. But how?

The answer came from Lieutenant William Barker Cushing, a young, dashing career navy man who was given his rank in July 1862 for his daredevil feats. During his short career, he was responsible for the capture of a blockade-runner, the destruction of a salt works in North Carolina, a successful raid on Confederate-held Jacksonville, North Carolina, and a series of night missions behind enemy lines. Cushing volunteered to destroy the *Albemarle* using 15 to 20 handpicked volunteers and specially fitted "torpedo boats." His daredevil reputation quickly won approval for the mission from Admiral Lee and Secretary Welles.[11]

Cushing procured two steam-powered picket boats of 45-foot length and light draft. He fitted the bow of each vessel with a 12-pound howitzer and a 14-foot boom, or spar, at the end of which was mounted a specially designed explosive device. The device was controlled by a series of lanyards mounted on a stanchion in the boat. Each boat was to tow a cutter.

He wasted no time in putting his plan to work. On the night of October 8, 1864, Cushing and his men shoved off from Norfolk and took a complicated and difficult course through a canal and small streams to Albemarle Sound, losing one of the launches along the way. With the remaining boats, he steamed up the sound to the mouth of the Roanoke River, where he joined the Union fleet stationed there, keeping an eye out lest the ram venture out. There, on the night of the 26th, he ventured upstream but ran aground, and the mission was postponed until the next night. When darkness fell on October 27, he again shoved off, this time with a borrowed cutter from the *Shamrock* in tow. He deftly passed the wreck of the *Southfield* on the way, muffling his engine with a heavy blanket and carefully avoiding possible enemy gun sites there. In the event they were spotted as they approached the ram, his plan called for the cutter to race down to the wreck to prevent an alarm rocket from being fired. Everything depended on a surprise raid.[12]

Finally, ahead loomed the dark shape of the ram lying alongside her wharf at Plymouth, surrounded by a boom of logs extending 30 feet out from her side. Cushing had hoped to board and capture the *Albemarle* instead of destroying her, but when a sharp-eyed sentry spotted them and raised an alarm, he decided on a head-on attack using the spar mine. He immediately ordered full speed toward the dark-shrouded vessel. The log boom worried him at first, but he correctly reasoned that the logs would be slippery after being submerged in the water for so long.

A hail of bullets met them, which miraculously hit no one, but some managed to tear his coat and "cut out the sole of his shoe," as he later reported.[13] The steam launch hit the logs and slid over easily into the space of water between it and the ram. Cushing lowered the boom, and the explosive charge went under the *Albemarle*'s overhang at her quarter port. He yanked the lanyard, the device exploded with a roar, and a huge geyser of water poured down on him and his boat, extinguishing the boiler, but at the same time a shot from one of the ram's small guns tore a hole in the bottom of the boat. The ram gave a shudder as it was lifted slightly out of the water by the force of the heavy explosion.

Earlier on board the *Albemarle,* at 3:00 A.M. October 27, the officer of the watch, Lieutenant A. F. Warley, had received a report that an approaching craft was sighted. The alarm bell was given, the crew was beat to quarters, and small-arms fire was directed at the boat. After the explosion, Warley ordered the pumps manned and the boilers fired to activate an auxiliary engine. He reported that "the water gained on us so fast that all exertions were fruitless." Later, after the incident took place, he expressed fury that the launch had not been sighted earlier and that an artillery battery by the vessel was not utilized until it was too late.[14]

The *Albemarle* sank quickly, leaving the top of her shield and stack above water. Sometime later, a captured letter from a crew member revealed that the explosion ripped a gaping hole in her hull some six feet long, and she sank almost instantly. "The crew," he wrote, "lost everything they had, bed, clothing, hats and shoes."[15]

What about Cushing and his men? As his boat sank, he refused to surrender at a command from the deck of the ram, but instead ordered his men to abandon the launch and swim away—a case of every man for himself. He stripped himself of sword, revolver, shoes, and bullet-torn coat and dove into the river, swimming for his life. With his fabulous good luck still holding, he made shore, meeting one of his crew members along the way. Cushing tried to help the exhausted man, but he himself was too weak, and unfortunately the man went down and was lost. Cushing pulled himself up on shore and crawled into a clump of bushes, where he lay exhausted until daylight. The next morning, after a few narrow escapes from searching Confederate soldiers, he managed to steal a boat from under the noses of the enemy and rowed downstream, where he was picked up by a Union picket vessel, the *Valley City*. When the word was spread that Cushing was safe, rockets were fired from the Union fleet and cheers resounded throughout the sound.[16]

Admiral Porter proclaimed that Cushing had displayed "a heroic enterprise seldom equaled and never excelled . . . he has shown an absolute disregard of death or danger." He awarded Cushing with command of a flagship.[17] Congress commended him for his "bravery and enterprise" and promoted him to commander.

With the *Albemarle* gone, the absence of a Confederate army, and the rest of the enemy flotilla routed, Plymouth was once again occupied by the Federals. As for the dreaded ram, it was discovered that after she was sunk, Confederate soldiers destroyed the pilothouse and stack, which were projecting above the water, with explosives. She was afterward raised and towed to Norfolk, where in 1867 she was sold.

With the Confederate naval threat in the Carolina sounds neutralized, the Union ships formerly assigned there were released for blockade duty. Anaconda once again tightened its coils, with a larger number of warships and a steely determination to destroy what vestiges of the Confederate navy remained.

The *Albemarle* incident again points out the weakness of the Confederacy's naval program. With the ram moored to a wharf, only a net of logs protected her. Strikingly absent were more pickets on patrol; had they been on duty, there would have been a better chance of spotting Cushing's small flotilla as it approached. In addition, there were no Confederate navy warships nearby, or within easy call, to come and meet any threat from Union warships venturing up to attack the *Albemarle,* which was helpless at the wharf. So once more we see how the lack of effective shipbuilding facilities, new engines, boilers, and ordnance for their navy continued to dog the Confederates to the end of the war.

Meanwhile, the war with blockade-runners and raiders was still raging along the coasts and on the high seas. The release of Union warships assigned to destroy the *Albemarle* would also greatly help the North in this struggle—particularly when a certain dreaded Confederate raider was taking a toll on Union shipping, demanding immediate attention by the Union Navy Department.

CHAPTER SIXTEEN

KEARSARGE VS. ALABAMA: END OF A RAIDER

On May 15, 1862, at the Birkenhead shipyard of John Laird and Sons, mysterious Hull No. 290 was finally launched, after much speculation concerning her ownership and her destinations. Present at the launching was James Dunwoodie Bulloch, whom we met in Chapter 4. The Confederate agent had signed contracts for two vessels to be used by the Confederacy as a weapon with which to counter the Union blockade, and to sweep Union commerce from the seas. The two vessels, to be named *Florida* and *Alabama*, were to become commerce raiders and were destined to write blazing pages in the naval history of the Civil War.[1]

The first vessel launched was the *Oreto*, ostensibly intended for the Italian government. She was a magnificent ship of 700 tons with an iron hull, two stacks, and a proposed armament of six 6-inch rifles, two 7-inch rifles, and one 12-pound howitzer. She was 171 feet long, with a 28-foot beam and 13-foot draft.

She left Liverpool on March 22, 1862, manned by a British crew, on a course for Nassau. Her armament was shipped separately in the bottom of a British cargo ship, *Bahama*. The two anchored in Nassau, and the armament, stores, and supplies were transferred to light vessels and thence to the *Oreto* in a secluded bay, as was the custom of the Confederacy at that time. Her appointed commander was Captain John Newland Maffitt of the Confederate navy, a career navy man, born at sea, who joined the Confederacy on May 2, 1861. Maffitt renamed the vessel *Florida* and commissioned her in the Confederate navy. (This *Florida* is not to be confused with Semmes' ship C.S.S. *Florida*.)[2]

In spite of Union attempts to have the vessel impounded, Maffitt, on board the *Florida*, slipped out of Nassau and headed for Cuba to take on a crew. Later, she gave the Gulf of Mexico blockading squadrons a real headache, especially when he ran her past a flotilla of enemy ships off Mobile Bay on September 4, 1862. Months later, after repairing his ship, Maffitt once again sailed out of Mobile Bay and past the squadron.[3]

The repercussions from this event, later called the "*Florida* affair" by the press, reverberated throughout the U.S. Navy, the White House, and the halls of Congress. Incriminations flew everywhere, some landing on the heads of Welles and his boss, President Lincoln. But the president stood by his navy secretary, looked the critics in the eye, and that was that.[4]

The one tragic figure to come out of the *Florida* mess was Commander George Preble, captain of the 1,400-ton screw sloop *Oneida*, who first spotted the *Florida* while his own vessel was having boiler problems. Thinking she was a British ship "by the cut of her jib," he hesitated in challenging *Florida*, and in spite of shots fired across her bow, the *Florida* steamed past and entered Mobile Bay safely. Preble was unfairly dismissed from service, but he was later restored to duty, as a result of requests from Admiral David Farragut and the U.S. Senate. Lincoln requested the restoration of Preble to the rank of commander. Welles also stood by Preble in his belief that the approaching ship was British.[5] Meanwhile, Hull No. 290 was christened the *Enrica* as workmen swarmed over her, using huge cranes to install her engines and boilers. No ordnance was installed, per Bulloch's desire to make her appear less like a traditional warship and more along the lines of a merchant vessel.

Mallory decided to appoint Raphael Semmes to take command of the new vessel. Bulloch had desired to be her skipper, but the secretary needed his expertise to obtain ships for the Confederacy. The dynamic Semmes was born in Maryland, entered naval service in 1826, was appointed a lieutenant in 1837, and later was promoted to commander. Between his billets at sea, he read law and was admitted to the bar in 1834. He served in the Mexican War, and in 1849 he settled in Mobile. While there, he wrote his first book, *Service Afloat and Ashore During the Mexican War*. He resigned his commission when his home state of Alabama seceded from the Union, and offered his services to Mallory.

The astute Mallory, knowing unusual ability when he saw it, appointed him a commander in the Confederate navy. As part of his first duties, he spent some unsuccessful weeks scouting the North for ships, but did manage to obtain a great deal of much-needed ordnance. Later, he was given the duties of the LightHouse Bureau. Semmes, with piercing eyes and waxed mustache, became the epitome of authority for his crews.[6]

Semmes, as did Mallory, believed that commerce raiders should be added to the navy in order to weaken the North's overseas commerce. His break came when Mallory sent him to New Orleans to take command of the very first raider, the [first] *Florida*, on April 22, 1862. This vessel was converted from the coastal packet *Havana* at a New Orleans shipyard. Semmes inspected the vessel and pronounced her seaworthy. After overhauling the ship by expanding her coal bunkers and ordnance storage facilities, he added an eight-inch pivot gun and four 32-pound smoothbores. When it was finished, equipped, and crewed to his satisfaction, Semmes, without wasting any time, took her down the Mississippi to the Head of the Passes and a planned run past the Union blockade fleet. His break came when the blockade ship *Powhatan* moved off to investigate a strange sail. He slipped out from under the guns of Fort Jackson and headed into the Mississippi Delta. Semmes was spotted by the screw frigate *Brooklyn* returning from her station; the race was on, but he managed to pull ahead of the slower Union warship, which mysteriously refused to use her superior gunnery.

Upon seeing his command for the first time, Semmes was captivated by her lines. Later, he was to describe her as a beautiful thing to look upon.[7] He was right: Finished and ready for her storied career, the vessel was a magnificent entity, with a 220-foot length, 32-foot beam, and 15-foot draft. She had two engines that produced 300 horsepower to power her single screw at 12 knots, and that screw was rigged to be lowered or raised at will. The engines featured an attached condensing unit for producing fresh water for long voyages. As for her silhouette, she had low but slick lines and was barkentine-rigged with the first mast square-rigged; the second and third were fore- and aft-rigged. This gave her more sails for speed. Semmes decided to name her the *Alabama*.

Alabama's formidable armament consisted of a 110-pound rifle pivoted forward, one 8-inch solid shot gun pivoted abaft the main mast, and six 32-pounders as broadside batteries. In spite of her impressive battery, Executive Officer John McIntosh Kell stated that she was "built for speed rather than battle," but with her imposing armament, it was clear she could hold her own in any ship-to-ship engagement. Her crew consisted of 120 men and 24 officers.[8]

She went first to the Union whaling grounds in the Azores, where she destroyed 10 whaling vessels—one with a dead whale still alongside—then returned to the East Coast of the United States, where she captured and destroyed 11 more ships. Generally, the crews of the captured vessels were taken off, needed provisions and stores were removed, and then the ship was burned. For these actions, Semmes was roundly denounced as a pirate by the Northern press, but he vigorously denied that in his memoirs.

While in the Caribbean, Semmes steered for the Gulf of Mexico, where he heard a Yankee fleet of transports was lying off Galveston, Texas. This would be a rich source of prizes for him and his crew. On January 11, 1863, the *Alabama* approached Galveston, where the transports were spotted. But what was not spotted was a fleet of five Union warships off the city. Semmes decided not to turn and run, but rather fight it out. Quickly, he was challenged by the 1,126-ton iron-hulled side-wheel schooner *Hatteras*. The Union ship cautiously approached the *Alabama* under the impression she was a British vessel. As she drew near the *Hatteras,* her skipper, Homer C. Blake, demanded, "What ship is that?" The answer came back from Kell: "Her Britannic Majesty's steamer *Petrel*." Blake ordered a boat launched, deciding he should row over and palaver with the "British" captain.

When the boat approached within 100 yards of the *Alabama,* Kell shouted, "This is the Confederate steamer *Alabama!*" The guns were then run out, and the unsuspecting *Hatteras* came under fire. The Union gunboat was fatally hit and began to sink; her crew was removed and taken prisoner aboard the *Alabama.* Within 13 minutes, the doomed side-wheeler was head down in the shallow water, with only her top hamper showing. It was to be the only time in the war that a Confederate raider sank a Union warship and escaped to boast about it.

By the time the rest of the Union squadron was alerted and started a chase, Semmes had deftly slipped away for Jamaica, where he discharged his prisoners, made repairs, and provisioned his ship.[9] Then he left Jamaica at night to avoid the Union warships searching for him. He sailed down the coast of South America, where he captured and burned a few more Union ships. From South America he headed for the Cape of Good Hope and into the Indian Ocean as far as Singapore, where he solidified his reputation as a scourge of the seas by destroying Union ships there to the extent that other Union ships refused to leave port. His next visit was off the coast of India, down the east coast of Africa, and then back to South America.[10]

By this time the *Alabama* was badly in need of repairs. Also, the long months at sea had finally had a debilitating effect on Semmes' health. But he took solace in the amazing record of his voyages: 21 months logging 75,000 miles with 64 prizes valued at nearly $6,500,000. A most unusual aspect of her career was the fact that the *Alabama* had never entered a Confederate port for repairs or refueling and replenishing. Most of it had been done at Brazil, Cape Town, and Singapore, among other ports of entry.[11]

The *Alabama* badly needed repairs, so on June 11, 1864, he sailed into the harbor at Cherbourg, France, for repair and replenishment. There he had hoped to request relief from his command because of his failing health. He requested permission to put the *Alabama* in dry dock, inasmuch as Cherbourg was a French naval base and there were adequate repair facilities available.[12]

This was a tough decision to make, because entering a dry dock meant that his presence would be broadcast to every U.S. warship in northern Europe.[13] Fate stepped in, however, in the form of Emperor Napoleon III. Because he was away on vacation, permission for Semmes to put his vessel in dry dock was denied. It was later revealed that had Semmes entered Le Havre, at which there were private dry docks available, he would have been accommodated immediately. Such are the fortunes of war.[14]

Meanwhile, the American vice consul at Cherbourg relayed information on the *Alabama* to the U.S. minister to France, William L. Drayton, in Paris. Drayton in turn relayed it to Captain John Ancrum Winslow, captain of the 1,031-ton, 8-gun sloop of war *Kearsarge,* lying off Vlissingen (Flushing), in the Netherlands. Winslow called his crew together, informed them that the dreaded Confederate cruiser was lying helpless in the harbor at Cherbourg, and that they would set sail immediately. They arrived at Cherbourg on June 14.[15]

Winslow, a career navy man, having been appointed a commander in 1859, had been a roommate and messmate of Raphael Semmes while aboard the U.S.S. *Cumberland*. Winslow had been the captain of the *Benton* in the Mississippi campaign, where he was injured and invalided home until 1862, when he was promoted to captain and given command of the *Kearsarge*. He spent the intervening time searching for Confederate raiders, being unsuccessful until fate handed him the *Alabama* at Cherbourg.[16] He was determined to either take or destroy the dreaded cruiser, either way ridding the seas of that scourge forever.

The wily Semmes realized the situation he was in. If he left port, there would be nowhere to go, because the very reputation of his ship had almost cleared the ocean of Union commerce. If he stayed, he would be eventually bottled up, as other Federal ships would join the *Kearsarge* and he would be unable to engage them in combat. But one-on-one with the Union sloop was a tempting proposition. He wrote that his intention was "to fight the *Kearsarge* as soon as I can make the necessary arrangement."[17] Semmes was unsure the two antagonists were evenly matched, but he would go ahead anyway.

Confederate Flag Officer Samuel Barron in England, who had received Semmes' report after the battle, wrote:

> He [Semmes] saw and calmly and intelligently considered and weighed all the elements of superiority in the enemy, within his knowledge and belief, before going out, and it is proper for me to say that I entirely acquiesced in his determination to meet the *Kearsarge,* believing as I then did that the general greater force of the enemy in number of men and weight of metal was not sufficient to discourage the confident expectation of victory entertained by the officers and crew of the *Alabama*.[18]

Semmes called his executive officer, Kell, to his cabin, and when that worthy had been seated, Semmes said, "I am going out to fight the *Kearsarge*. What do you make of it?"[19] This was most unusual, because Semmes was not in the habit of sharing knowledge of ship's operations with his officers. Kell reminded him that the gunpowder supply was weak, as shown in gunnery practice weeks earlier, and that only one out of three shells exploded on contact. "I will take my chances of one in three," Semmes replied.[20] They also discussed the advantages of the *Kearsarge*'s heavy guns. Both officers agreed that the Union ship was heavier and stronger, having been built and manned for battle, whereas *Alabama*'s advantage was that of speed. But that speed might have been whittled down because of the deteriorating hull.

Still, Semmes must have considered the capabilities of both ships as he studied the black-hulled *Kearsarge* outside the breakwater. The *Kearsarge* was heavier than the *Alabama* and sported two powerful 11-inch Dahlgrens in her armament. The hard, cold fact was that Winslow could hurl 430 pounds of iron in each shot, compared with Semmes' 360 pounds.[21] It is not known if Semmes saw a change in the lines of the Union ship, which revealed the installation of many fathoms of anchor chain along her sides, to protect the engines. These chains were covered with wooden boards painted the same color as the hull. Historians have argued for years over whether or not Semmes knew of these chains before the battle (he was supposed to have been told by an authority in Cherbourg) or learned of it after.[22] Flag Officer Barron, in an official report, declared that "until after the battle neither he [Semmes] nor I knew anything of the complete protection given to her [*Kearsarge*'s] vital sections by the chain armor which she wore."[23]

Semmes was adamant. He would fight the *Kearsarge*, because the very idea of his beloved ship "bride" rotting in a harbor or being captured by the Union was repugnant to him. Better he meet his adversary and slug it out in a display of glory. He called his men together, told them about his decision to fight, then went about getting his ship battle ready. He ordered 150 tons of coal for his bunkers, put ashore captured sextants and gold plus other spoils of war, had the decks holystoned and the brass fixtures polished, and generally gave the ship a fresh look, hiding the fact that she was deteriorating and badly in need of overhaul.

On June 15, he wrote in his journal:

> My crew seems to be in the right spirit, a quiet spirit of determination pervading both officers and men. The combat will no doubt be contested and obstinate, but the two ships are evenly matched, that I do not feel at liberty to decline it. God defend the right and have mercy on the souls of those who fall, as many of us must."[24]

Semmes had already notified his old friend Winslow of his intention to fight, so his present energies were devoted to getting the ship ready and to encouraging his crew. He told them that their ship had become a "household word wherever civilization extends." Then he flung out the challenge: "Shall that name be tarnished by defeat?" The crew, of course, reacted with rousing cheers of "Never! Never!"[25]

Sunday, June 19, 1864, dawned sunny and clear as the *Alabama* weighed anchor and steamed out of the harbor, out of West Pass, and around the breakwater, and stood out to sea to challenge her adversary. She was accompanied by the French ironclad *Couronne* and the yacht *Deerhound,* owned by the wealthy Englishman John Lancaster, plus a fleet of French luggers. Winslow, meanwhile, fearing a question of jurisdiction with the French government, had steamed out to a distance of six to eight miles from the breakwater. The French had sent along the *Couronne* to see that no boundaries were compromised in the coming battle. Excited spectators lined the shores of Cherbourg to witness the struggle—a festive atmosphere prevailed throughout the city and its environs.

Winslow had not been idle during the long wait for Semmes to appear, drilling his crew in close-quarters combat. Part of Winslow's confidence was based on the 150 fathoms of chain mail on the sides of his ship; he was sure it would be enough to deflect any shots from *Alabama*'s guns.

As the *Alabama* drew near her adversary, the *Couronne,* the *Deerhound,* and the luggers veered off and hove to, awaiting the oncoming battle. When she was within full sight of the *Kearsarge,* that vessel wheeled around and headed straight for her. The crew of the *Alabama* loosed the starboard battery, as did the crew on *Kearsarge.*[26]

As they drew to within 1,200 yards, *Alabama* opened with her 100-pound pivot gun, but the shot whizzed over the *Kearsarge.* By this time, both vessels were presenting their starboard sides to each other. Then began a macabre dance of death as both ships began a circular pattern, like two boxers in a ring, always keeping a distance of 900 yards, blasting away at each other with broadsides. During the battle, Semmes became aware that his shots were bouncing off the sides of the *Kearsarge,* while hers were aimed at *Alabama*'s waterline. One shot entered *Kearsarge*'s hull and lodged in her sternpost, where it failed to explode because the percussion cap was faulty. One can only speculate what would have happened if that shell had exploded.[27]

Round and round the ships danced, discharging broadside after broadside, the crews loading, firing, and running guns in and out. Projectiles slammed into bulwarks or whacked through sails. Some thudded in below decks, sending lethal showers of splinters and shrapnel into the crews, creating horrific wounds or killing them outright. Occasionally a gun would explode, wounding or killing those nearby. All around, clouds of gunsmoke, punctured by orange-red flashes, hugged the ships, causing the crews to cough and rub their eyes until a welcome breeze or the forward motion of the ship dissipated it.

Finally, after 60 minutes of continuous gunfire, the superior gunnery of the *Kearsarge* took its toll. The *Alabama* had been fatally wounded, and the battle was over. Water gushed into the hull through many shot holes, and the ship began to list. Semmes, slightly wounded, hauled down the colors. Winslow observed these signs of distress in his enemy, together with a cessation of her fire, and therefore he withheld his own. Semmes had hoped to sail for the safety of the harbor, but the rapidly incoming water put out his boilers and began to force the ship head down in the water. He immediately dispatched a boat to the *Kearsarge* to ask for assistance in removing the dead and wounded from the decks. Winslow sent two boats, including a cutter.[28] At this point, an incident occurred that has puzzled many historians. It has been related that Winslow fired five or six shots at the dying *Alabama* after she struck colors, allegedly thinking it was a Confederate ruse. Winslow denies this in his reports, but Semmes asserted as much in his report to Mallory.[29]

Lancaster in the *Deerhound*, meanwhile, had come up to assist, and Winslow begged him to rescue as many of *Alabama's* survivors as he could, which he did: 42 men, including Semmes and Kell. Semmes declared that he was under "English colors; the sooner you land me on English soil the better."[30] Lancaster obliged, and quickly whisked him and the other crew members away.

The *Alabama*, in her death throes, raised her stern to the sky and plunged into 190 feet of water. As she disappeared beneath the waves, the crew of the *Kearsarge* refused to cheer; instead, they stood silently watching in awe.[31]

The toll of this short but fierce battle was 26 men killed or lost on the *Alabama*, with 63 men taken prisoner; the *Kearsarge* suffered 1 man killed and 3 wounded. Many historians agree that the Confederate ship sank in glory, in spite of her checkered past.[32]

For many years the *Alabama* lay where she had sunk, undisturbed except for the destructive influences of salt water and tides. Only recently was she discovered by a French minesweeper, and later examined by archeologists, who retrieved a number of artifacts from her bones. But at the present time no plans have been made to raise her.

AFTER the battle, comments came from many sources. The sinking of the *Alabama* made Captain Winslow a celebrity. The Lincoln administration considered the triumph "a sweet and moral victory" over the Confederacy and over England, which had built the Confederate cruiser and "provided every assistance in the way of material support."[33] Gideon Welles wrote Captain Winslow, congratulating him on his good fortune in meeting the *Alabama,* which had so long avoided the fastest ships in the service.[34] Winslow eventually received a vote of confidence from Congress and was later promoted to the rank of rear admiral.

Through the years, rumors intimated that Semmes had stood on the quarterdeck of his dying ship and, in a gesture of defiance, thrown his sword into the sea. But recent research indicates that he would not have had time to do so. His own wife denied it in the following years, although Jefferson Davis relates the incident in his work *Rise and Fall of the Confederate Government.*[35]

Southern observers were critical of the *Kearsarge*'s iron armor. E. A. Pollard, editor of the *Daily Richmond Examiner,* carped that the protection "gave *Alabama* scarcely a little chance in her favour." He likened it to a chivalric code of old "when knights had their hands hacked off when concealed armor was discovered."[36]

The New York press, as would be expected, had a field day. The *New York Times* rejoiced that the "pirate [*Alabama*] had at last gone to the bottom of the sea" and that she had at last met her "equal" when she came face-to-face with a Union warship.[37] Other similar comments appeared in various newspapers around the North.

The Confederacy, of course, lauded Semmes in spite of his defeat. After all, he did take on a powerful Union warship in spite of overwhelming odds, and had displayed great skill and daring. He was looked upon as a hero.

Semmes, after his recuperation period in England, returned to the Confederacy, where the Confederate government warmly greeted him and promoted him to rear admiral.[38] In February 1865, he was given command of the James River squadron, which consisted of six ships. He saw little or no action until the evacuation of Richmond in April, when he was forced to destroy his vessels and organize his men into a brigade, for which he was unofficially given the rank of brigadier general.

After the surrender, Semmes was arrested and brought to Washington on a charge of treason against the United States. The charges were soon dropped, and he was allowed to return to his home city of Mobile, where he resumed his law practice. He was appointed a judge of the probate court and remained in this post until his death on August 30, 1877. The entire city of Mobile came to a halt during his funeral as the populace honored its favorite son. His memory is revered to this very day in that city.

Raphael Semmes was a strange combination of legalist, visionary, tactician, poet, and humanitarian. His knowledge of law kept him ahead of his enemies, because that knowledge allowed him to be aware of what was happening around him and at government locations at all times, and stymied even his foreign supporters at times. This knowledge, coupled with a natural shrewdness, enabled him to thumb his nose at stalking Union ships and to boldly sail away under their very noses, as in the incident at the Head of the Passes in the Mississippi Delta, during which he outfoxed superior Union naval forces.

Semmes' humanitarian nature would show from time to time when he removed passengers and crews from captured prize ships. He would burn the ships only because he didn't have enough personnel in his complement for prize crews. In fact, his writings often reflect sorrow at destroying such fine vessels.

However, there is some question in this author's mind as to Semmes' proficiency as a military tactician. Most of the time he dodged combat with enemy ships, except at Galveston, where he was forced into a fight with the U.S.S. *Hatteras,* which was indisputably a vessel inferior to his own. He could also be accused of using stealth in his ruse of declaring his vessel to be British. Furthermore, he had a touch of vanity, and that could have been responsible for his taking on a ship that he knew to be superior to his, the U.S.S. *Kearsarge.*

We will probably never know whether he was cognizant of the armor on that ship, although it is certain that he was well aware of her formidable armament. Arthur Sinclair wrote that Semmes had mentioned it to his crew but made light of it. His ship's surgeon and paymaster, Dr. Francis Galt, wrote that he and other officers on the *Alabama* knew of the chains. Another explanation, one with which this author agrees, is rooted in Semmes' Southern sense of chivalry. He was a man of high honor, and he viewed his challenge to Winslow to fight as an extension of the old dueling code (in that era, duels were not an uncommon event in the South). According to that code, honor demanded that no participant have an advantage over the other such as the *Kearsarge* armor represented. This could be a line of reasoning that Semmes might have followed. Evidence that he was deeply attached to the concept of honor is found in his almost fanatical abhorrence of criticism of his ship and crew; consider also his pep talk before the battle, in which he spoke about the "tarnish" of defeat.

But, as I have said, *we may never know for sure if Semmes was aware of* Kearsarge*'s armor.* Be that as it may, the battle between the *Alabama* and *Kearsarge* has gone down as one of the most thought-provoking events in naval history, and will be discussed and debated for many years still to come. It was a classic sea battle that foreshadowed those that would be fought many generations later.

Meanwhile, back in the United States, the struggle between the Union and the Confederacy went on, with one of the greatest military events of the war about to take place.

CHAPTER SEVENTEEN

CLIMAX AT FORT FISHER, PART 1

Late in 1864, after General George Henry Thomas' victory at Nashville, Union attention once again turned to the South Atlantic sector of the East Coast, where General Sherman had occupied Savannah after his famous (infamous to some) march to the sea. General in Chief of the Army Ulysses Grant suggested that he commence an overland march through South and North Carolina in an effort to cut Confederate supply lines between Richmond and Petersburg, Virginia. Therefore, coordinated naval actions were vital to the plans, especially at such ports as Charleston and Wilmington. These ports were blockaded but not occupied. Of the two, the latter was of more importance to General Sherman, who declared that the port "would give me additional point of security along the seacoast." Furthermore, occupation of Wilmington would give him help from a coastal operations base.[1]

With the closing of the ports of New Orleans and Mobile and a tight blockade of Charleston, Wilmington took on more and more importance to Union planners. The city, often called "the mouth of the Confederate states," was the one operational port through which supplies, munitions, and war materiel that they were unable to manufacture on their own were obtained. Therefore, to lose Wilmington, according to C. B. Denison, a leading Confederate army engineer, was to "receive a fatal blow—a wound which must endanger the life of Lee's army."[2]

Wilmington was also referred to as the "second capital of the Confederacy." It was the site of never-ceasing, bustling activity with wharves groaning under cotton bales to be loaded onto low, sleek blockade-runners ready for runs to Nassau or Bermuda and hence to Europe. The city, located 30 miles from the mouth of the Cape Fear River, was founded as New Town (Newton) in the 1730s and in 1740 was incorporated and renamed Wilmington to honor Spencer Compton, Earl of Wilmington and a British politician and favorite of King George II. During the Revolutionary War, Lord Cornwallis used Wilmington as his headquarters in 1781. With the Civil War, the city burgeoned as a hub of blockade-running activities, supplying Confederate armies and boasting a population of 9,552 people, including whites, free blacks, and slaves. It also had the distinction of being the last Confederate port to be closed by the Union blockade.

To the south of Wilmington, a peninsula named Cape Fear jutted down, flanked by the Atlantic Ocean to the east and south and the Cape Fear River to the west. The peninsula ended at Smith Island, formed when a hurricane created a wide channel called New Inlet, separating the island from the rest of the peninsula. The channel opened to the east and emptied into the Cape Fear River itself, which meandered south and entered into the Atlantic at Old Inlet and the Western Bar Channel.

Cape Fear was so named because of the many storms that hit the area, making navigation dangerous. In fact, during the war, 31 steam and 22 sail blockade-runners, along with Federal and Confederate military vessels, were lost in the Cape Fear regions.[3]

It was through these channels that shallow-draft blockade-runners roamed while on their errands of mercy. Shoal waters prevented deep-water vessels from entering New Inlet and Old Inlet, although the latter at high tide may have admitted shallower-drafted ships, but that site was guarded by three forts, Holmes, Caswell, and Campbell, with Forts Johnston, Lamb, and Anderson 12 miles up the river on the west side. Also, above Fort Fisher on the east side were batteries called Sugar Loaf, Gatlin, and Anderson. Farther up the peninsula, three miles south of Wilmington, Forts Mears, Lee, and Stokes stood guard against any excursions that far upriver. These installations played a vital part in keeping the river and its mouth opened to traffic. In fact, the blockade-runner *R. E. Lee* made 21 unhindered trips in just 10 months.

Revealing the importance of Wilmington to the Confederacy is the fact that during the period from October 1864 through January 1865, 31 blockade-runners brought in over 4,000 tons of meat, 750 tons of lead, 950 tons of saltpeter, 546,000 pairs of shoes, 700,000 blankets, 500,000 pounds of coffee, 69,000 rifles, and 43 pieces of artillery. Of course, all this was paid for by cotton, rice, and naval stores shipped back to European sources.[4]

Of the five forts plus the three batteries on or near the Cape Fear River, Fort Fisher was the most prominent and formidable. Built on the ruins of an old gun emplacement, Battery Boles, Fisher was greatly expanded and made more powerful by Colonel William Lamb, a Virginia native who graduated first in his class at William and Mary College with a law degree. The John Brown affair at Harper's Ferry, in 1859, catapulted him into military life, when he was given a rifle company to command. At the beginning of hostilities, he was appointed to the rank of major and became quartermaster of the Wilmington District. He was commissioned a major, and later a colonel, while serving at old Fort St. Phillip on the Cape Fear River. On July 4, 1862, he was given command of Fort Fisher. With a most unusual instinct and intelligence, without formal training at a military academy, Lamb threw his energies into transforming a small gun emplacement into a formidable works "ready to deter attack and withstand an invasion."[5] The facility was named after Colonel Charles Fisher, an officer of the 6th North Carolina Regiment, killed at the battle of First Manassas in 1861.

When completed, Fort Fisher was a far cry from the ineffectual Battery Boles. It was constructed in the shape of a large 7 and was 2,580 yards long (nearly 1½ miles). Its short bar, or landface, was 682 yards long and contained 22 guns. Radiating off from this landface were three layers of land mines connected to the fort by electric wires. Running along its entire length was a series of 9-foot-high palisades made of sharpened logs pierced at intervals with rifle holes. At the apex, or elbow, of the 7 was the center traverse, 43 feet high.

The 1,898-foot stem of the 7 was the seaface of the fort, which contained a series of 15 traverses or mounds 20 to 30 feet high, containing 20 guns en barbette, or moveable carriages. The seaface ended at a large mound 43 feet high, containing two large guns, a 10-inch Columbiad and an 8-inch Armstrong rifle. Farther down, at the tip of the bifurcated peninsula, facing New Inlet, was Fort Buchanan, bolstered by four guns. Also, Fort Fisher's seaface contained a mixture of ordnance, including 32-pound smoothbores, 7-inch rifles, 10-inch Columbiads, and one 150-pound Armstrong rifle that was rarely used because of lack of proper ammunition.

In the center of the fort, a diagonal line of rifle pits ran from the telegraph station on the seaface to the western end of the fort, almost on the shoreline of the river. All in all, it was a most formidable military installation with a total of around 44 guns, and one that Colonel Lamb reported to contain a complement of 800 to 1,400 troops.[6]

The reducing of Fort Fisher, or its capture, had long been on the minds of the Lincoln administration, and Secretary Welles vainly implored General Henry Wager Halleck, chief of staff, to provide troops and equipment for an assault on Fort Fisher from New Bern. Admiral David Dixon Porter, recently appointed commander of the North Atlantic Blockading Squadron, also considered the capture of Fort Fisher and Wilmington a necessity.

Ulysses S. Grant too viewed this military campaign as a top priority because of General Sherman's Carolinas campaign. Not only did he acknowledge the importance of stopping blockade-running traffic, but he considered the importance of Wilmington to European countries as well. He wrote:

> It was equally important to us to get possession of it [Wilmington] not only because it was desirable to cut off their supplies so as to insure a speedy termination of the war, but also foreign governments, particularly the British Government, were constantly threatening that unless ours could maintain the blockade of that coast, they would cease to recognize any blockade. For these reasons, I determined, with the concurrence of the Navy Department, to send an expedition against Fort Fisher for the purpose of capturing it.[7]

Admiral Porter planned the naval aspect of the campaign with his usual energy. He assembled a fleet strong enough to subdue the enemy facility, which reconnaissance showed to be seemingly impregnable. He divided his

87-ship North Atlantic Blockading Squadron into five divisions, and picked from these 50-odd vessels for the assault. For his flagship, he chose the *Malvern,* a captured side-wheel blockade-runner of moderate size, 1,400 tons, with 500 horsepower, which would allow him to "move about more rapidly."[8]

Around 6,500 troops for the Fort Fisher expedition were to be supplied by Major General Benjamin Franklin Butler, recently appointed as commander of the Army of the James.[9] Butler placed the force under the command of Brigadier General Godfrey Weitzel, a career army officer and former chief engineer for General Butler's New Orleans campaign. Because of bureaucratic bungling, the expedition was delayed, and on October 24, Lamb received word that Fort Fisher was to be assaulted and that Admiral Porter was to command the fleet.[10] Lamb immediately began preparing to counter the attack.

As far as Butler was concerned, the delay did not mean that all was lost. The extra time allowed him to come up with the concept of a huge floating bomb to be exploded near the fort, causing a great deal of damage and demoralizing the garrison. To him, the idea was not as fantastic as it seemed, because there were plenty of old hulks and condemned powder on hand to rig such a floating bomb.

Always the innovator, Butler got the basic idea from an incident that occurred in October 1864 in Erith, on the Thames in England. 104,000 pounds of gunpowder in a warehouse accidentally exploded. The blast killed several people, left a crater 75 feet wide and 30 feet deep on the waterfront, and flung out a shock wave that was reported to have been felt as far as London, 15 miles away.[11]

Butler's plan was to take an old hull, load it with around 200 tons of powder, run it as close as possible to the fort, and detonate it. The explosion would likely level the fort and stun or kill many of its occupants. Butler wrote: "I think the work will be seriously damaged by the explosion of the principle [*sic*] magazines, and the traverses and bombproofs may be shattered or overturned."[12] Although there was much skepticism except on the part of President Lincoln, who expressed mild enthusiasm, Fox and Welles remained confident the plan might work, and they pushed ahead until they received permission from a panel of army and navy ordnance specialists to launch the scheme.

The vessel picked for the floating bomb was a worn-out three-masted schooner, the 438-ton, iron-hulled *Louisiana*, formerly used in the cotton trade. She was 150 feet long, with a 22-foot beam and an 8½-foot draft. The hull was taken to Norfolk to be fitted out, and a quantity of old, condemned gunpowder was located at various armories.

The *Louisiana* was stripped down to the main deck, a wooden housing built over most of her length, which was covered with canvas and painted to waterproof it. The entire hull was painted gray and a fake smokestack was installed behind the real one to give the hull an appearance of being a blockade-runner. It was decided that the powder was to be stowed mainly above the waterline to allow an explosion with a lateral effect. The powder was packed in bags of 50 pounds, the majority of which were packed in the berth deck, with the rest in open barrels in the aft coal bunker.[13] Ignition of the charges was to be accomplished by two slow matches on powder trains and clocklike detonator devices set behind the hold area. As an extra precaution, lest the fuses and detonator fail, a fire was to be kindled in the forecastle.[14]

The scheme called for a daring commander. Butler found him in the person of Commander Alexander C. Rhind of the gunboat *Agawam* and former captain of the ill-fated *Keokuk*. Rhind was a fearless leader and one who distinguished himself in a daring, commandolike raid against a Confederate gun position at Dawho, South Carolina. His ship had been laid up for repairs and not available for the operation, but he was presented to Porter as the perfect man for the job of skippering the *Louisiana*. Rhind had doubts about the plan but accepted the task because he knew it to be important to the entire assault plan on Fort Fisher. The date set for the sailing of the armada was set for December 8, but for unknown reasons Butler delayed the departure until December 12, which turned out to be a cold, windy day.

The *Louisiana* had preceded the fleet on December 15, to Beaufort and was now being loaded with 215 tons of powder. She had sailed ahead partially filled, for fear of becoming top-heavy and thus subject to capsizing in the gale-swept waters. Rhind had done his job well, but the task caused another delay in departure because of more inclement weather that settled in. The transports, meanwhile, had steamed ahead to anchor at Masonboro Inlet, 18 miles north of Fort Fisher. There, Butler made a series of reconnaissances of the fort, but he inadvertently revealed his vessel to the fort, thereby alerting them.

With the *Louisana* towed by the gunboat *Sassacus,* Porter dispatched the fleet to the invasion area on December 20 to rendezvous with the transport vessels, but approaching bad weather forced the transports back to Beaufort, leaving the warships to ride out another bad storm off Cape Fear. Finally December 23 dawned clear, so Porter decided to send in the *Lousiana*. He ordered the fleet 12 miles out to sea, leaving the *Louisiana* to be towed in by the tug *Wilderness*. When the small flotilla neared the shore, Rhind cast off from the tug and proceeded down the coast under *Louisiana's* own steam. For a while they followed in the wake of a blockade-runner, *Little Hattie,* in hopes the Confederates would think the *Louisiana* was a second blockade-runner. When he reached a spot that he thought was 300 yards from the fort, he dropped anchor and prepared the hulk for the coming explosion.

Rhind and his crew set the ignition devices, set a small kindling fire in the forecastle, then abandoned the bomb vessel. Rhind felt a twinge of disappointment—he would have liked to have brought the vessel closer to the fort, but he had pushed his luck far enough, and so he decided that 300 yards was close enough. However, he had misjudged the distance and had dropped anchor 600 yards away instead of the supposed 300 yards.

The explosion took place at 1:50 A.M., December 24, and it proved to be a bitter disappointment. In the log of the *Advance,* a captured converted 1,000-ton blockade-runner, a terse note appeared: "At 1:50 A.M., the explosion of the powder boat took place."[15] Two sharp reports were heard and a brilliant sheet of flame erupted, jarring most of the ships close in and a group of North Carolina junior reserves camping on the beach. The flash was followed by a "low, rumbling sound as if thunder," heard all the way to Wilmington. But in the fort, no one paid much attention to the explosion, except for a few sentries. Colonel Lamb had just retired to his quarters in a brick house formerly owned by the lighthouse keeper, and he had hardly lain down when the house was gently rocked. He described the sound as that of a "report of a ten-inch Columbiad." In the morning, Lamb reported the explosion to General William Henry Chase Whiting in Wilmington and dismissed it as a "blockader got aground near the fort; set fire to herself and blew up."[16] Thus the grandiose scheme of General Butler ignominiously came to naught, a waste of powder, time, and effort.

The fleet returned that morning to deliver its planned bombardment. From the ramparts of the fort, Lamb watched the gathering ships and later wrote: "A grander sight than the approach of Porter's formidable armada toward the fort was never witnessed on our coast. With the rising sun out of the old ocean, there came on the horizon one after another, the vessels of the fleet, the grand frigates leading the van, followed by the ironclads."[17] This excerpt from his diary reveals something about Lamb's character. Here he was, faced with a powerful fleet ready to blast his fort to pieces, yet he took time to philosophize about the grand sight.

The fleet, consisting of over 50 warships of all kinds, frigates, gunboats, and monitors, was the largest armada yet assembled during the war. Porter arranged his ships in concentric arcs, with the monitors, able to take the most punishment, anchored within a quarter of a mile of the beach. The heavier, deep-water ships were farther out, from a mile to a mile and a half, and still farther out were the various support vessels.

Then the big guns were unleashed. Lamb called it a "terrific bombardment." For five hours, the fleet's 619 guns let loose a tremendous hail of shot and shell at the rate of 115 shells per minute.[18] The barrage was so heavy, it filled the air with thunder, with bright flashes piercing almost a solid wall of gunsmoke. The shore, according to an observer, resembled a "desert sandstorm."[19] However, remarkably enough, little damage was done to the fort by this bombardment. Lamb's brick house was demolished, and some flagstaffs were shot down.

The next day, December 25, the transports moved up and unloaded 2,500 of Butler's troops north of the fort. After regrouping, the troops moved down the beach toward the fort, capturing a small battery as they went. But as they approached the fort, they were met with a disconcerting sight—the fort appeared untouched. Confederate troops were spotted manning some of the ramparts and even behind the palisades. Evidently bombardment had been a great fizzle.

But not all was what it seemed. The fort had sent frantic calls to General Braxton Bragg at Wilmington, but for some reason he appeared to ignore them. Perhaps he thought there were more Union troops than were reported to have landed, judging by the huge naval force and the fierce bombardment, and so there was little he could do. However, no one knows for sure.

Of course the Union troops on the beach, under the command of Colonel Newton Martin Curtis, did not know this; neither did Butler, running up and down the coast in a navy tug, observing the situation. He quickly sized up the situation and, after conferring with General Weitzel, decided on a withdrawal. Butler considered the following factors: The fleet was running out of ammunition, the fort was untouched, reinforcements from Bragg could be on their way, and to top things off, a big storm was headed toward the area.

Meanwhile, the troops on shore managed to get closer to the fort, and sharpshooters fired on the fort's personnel. One brave Union officer managed to reach the base of a parapet and to retrieve a Confederate flag; a soldier also managed to get to the edge of the works, kill a courier, and capture his horse.[20]

The damage to the fort was minimal—only two Brooke rifles were disabled, and those by internal explosions—and only 22 men were wounded. Colonel Lamb could never understand why the fleet had concentrated on the landface instead of the seaface, where much damage to his guns could have been done. Perhaps Butler and Porter had decided that a concentration of fire on the landface would have paved the way for the Union troops to carry that section of the fort where there were palisades, traverses, and gun chambers.

Finally, Butler threw in the towel. He sent a dispatch to Admiral Porter in which he gave his reasons for withdrawing the troops. When Curtis' men had advanced to within 50 yards, it became evident that only a siege could eventually take the fort, and that "did not come within my instructions." The rumored presence of a portion of Hoke's division arriving on the scene, plus the prospect of "threatening weather," made it impossible to land more troops. "I see nothing can be done by land forces," he wrote. "I shall therefore sail for Hampton Roads as soon as the transport fleet can be got in order."[21] Butler left the scene so hurriedly that 700 men were stranded on the beach for two days until taken off by naval personnel.

Why General Hoke failed to attack the stranded group with what forces he had at hand is another mystery we will never understand. Perhaps he, too, was awed by the tremendous Union firepower plus the size of the transport fleet and therefore was under the impression that many more troops would be landed. It could have been so had Butler not decided to withdraw, because he did have 6,000 troops on hand.

The failure to capture Fort Fisher set off a firestorm of protest that almost equaled the fierceness of the bombardment. Porter bitterly wrote that he wished Butler's men had followed the example of the officer who "took the flag from the parapet and the brave fellow who brought the horse out from the fort. I think they have found it an easier conquest than supposed."[22] Porter had sent to Beaufort for more ammunition, and he maintained that had Butler waited, he could have laid down an even barrage to keep Confederate heads down while the Federal troops carried the fort. It was no secret that Butler and Porter had long disliked each other, although they were forced to work together in the Fort Fisher campaign.

General Grant wrote to Lincoln and expressed the opinion that the expedition was a "gross and culpable failure . . . who is to blame will, I hope, be known." Grant found out and quickly relieved Butler of command and replaced him with the very able General Alfred Howe Terry, with orders to prepare another expedition against Fort Fisher. Grant spelled out his reasons for relieving Butler of his command in an official report:

> It will be perceived that it was never contemplated that General Butler should accompany the expedition but that Maj. General Weitzel was especially named as the commander of it. . . . My dispatches to General Butler will show his report to be in error where he states that he returned after having effected a landing in obedience to my instructions. On the contrary, these instructions contemplated no withdrawal, or no failure after a landing was made.[23]

Despite all the criticism, Butler may have been right in his observations of the Fort Fisher military situation. For some reason, the army and navy had squandered precious time while Lamb, his troops, and his fort grew stronger. Perhaps Butler underestimated the amount of force needed to carry the fort, counting on the bomb boat and the fleet bombardment to obtain an easy victory.

The *Louisiana* bomb boat incident has been widely covered. But from the outset, it would appear that the plan would have succeeded had the hulk been placed closer to the fort. Of course, had it been closer, the Confederates might have spotted her and blown her out of the water before the powder could have been detonated. All things considered, the idea of getting the *Louisiana* close enough to the fort was absurd. Once again, poor judgment was at fault.

The navy, for its part, was bitter about the abortive campaign. Captain Thomas O. Selfridge, commander of the *Huron,* later stated that "words cannot express the bitter feeling and chagrin of the navy."[24] According to historian Rod Gragg, another naval officer was heard to remark that Butler was "either a black-hearted traitor or an arrogant coward."

A second officer wrote to his wife: "What did he [Butler] go there for? To take possession after we had conquered? We could do that ourselves." And another wrote: "We all believe Butler to be a rank traitor and a coward and everything but a gentleman."[25] Still another complained that Butler "was determined to have his own way and seeing that he could not, he was bent on thwarting everything." Admiral Porter was reported to have declared: "God save me from further connection from such generals."[26]

Such comments indicate the feelings of the fighting men involved in the first assault on Fort Fisher. All indications pointed toward a conquering of the fort rather than a withdrawal, which was looked upon as a defeat. Many of the personnel in the navy in particular were of the opinion that the fort could have been carried, as General Curtis had reached the ramparts and there was no Confederate fire. Also, Curtis believed he could have taken the fort, and subsequent study suggests that he well might have if the rest of Butler's troops had landed. It is also now believed that Hoke's force, had it arrived, would not have been sufficient to repel the full force of the Union troops.

The fleet returned to Hampton Roads stunned by the defeat at Fort Fisher, especially after flinging more than a million pounds of iron at the fort, landing 3,000 troops, and advancing almost to the edge of the fort, only to have victory snatched away from them at the last minute by a combination of a seemingly confused and ill-informed commander and the failure of the boat bomb to do its job.

On the other side, it is not difficult to imagine what joy and celebration went on in Fort Fisher. The Confederates had endured a horrific bombardment and beaten off an assault against their works, and the fort was still in their possession with a minimal amount of damage. Little wonder they considered that they had given the Yankees "a good thrashing and they left."[27]

But no one doubted that the Federal withdrawal was only temporary and that they would soon return.

CHAPTER EIGHTEEN

CLIMAX AT FORT FISHER, PART 2

With General Butler banished to his home in Massachusetts, Grant moved swiftly to prepare another assault on Fort Fisher. But he needed a commander who was efficient, daring, and well liked, unlike Butler. He picked Major General Alfred Howe Terry, a lawyer and native of Connecticut.

Grant's choice of Terry was excellent, if initially a bit puzzling, as Terry, a practicing attorney and clerk of the New Haven County superior court, had never attended West Point and had no formal military training. However, at the outbreak of war, he was commissioned as commander of the 2nd Connecticut Regiment, which fought at the first battle of Bull Run and later assisted in the capture of Port Royal and Fort Pulaski. On April 26, 1862, he was appointed a brigadier general with command of the X Corps of General Butler's Army of the James. It was a meteoric rise, though not unusual for the early days of the war, when commissions were quickly and easily earned.

Grant was greatly impressed with Terry because he was the antithesis of Butler. According to historian Rod Gragg, Terry was a competent, unassuming officer popular with his subordinates and troops alike—qualities Grant badly needed for this all-out campaign to capture the strongest fort in the Confederacy. Even Lincoln was impressed with Terry. Upon meeting him for the first time, the president commented, "Why have we not seen you before?" Terry modestly replied that he was busy fighting the war.[1]

On January 3, 1865, Grant wired Terry that the expedition he was to command had been fitted out "to renew the attempt to capture Fort Fisher, N.C., and Wilmington ultimately, if the fort falls." Terry was to report to Rear Admiral Porter at Fort Monroe, and Grant informed him that "it is exceedingly desirable that the most complete understanding should exist between yourself and the naval commander." Grant was concerned about "unity of action" between the two commanders, given the fiasco with Butler a month before. He informed Terry and Porter that a siege train would be loaded on ships to accompany the expedition if that operation became a necessity. In addition, he informed them that a division of troops would augment those he already had.[2]

General Grant was most anxious to capture Fort Fisher. He reasoned that the Confederate forces there would not be able to defend the fort, defend Wilmington, and fight Sherman's advancing army at the same time. They would be forced to divide their forces and do battle on two fronts, thereby weakening them in both sectors.

As for Porter, he would have preferred to have his old friend General Sherman lead the assault on Fort Fisher, but that worthy general was busy slugging his way through Georgia. The admiral was unsure of Terry's abilities, but he approved of the choice because he did not want to vindicate Butler's trumped-up version of the first assault in December. He trusted Grant's judgment and immediately requested that Grant give Terry the additional troops.[3] Also, Porter took great pains to ensure that his ships would have plenty of ammunition, coal, and provisions this time, because there would be no room for failure and recriminations.

Terry and his command reached Fort Monroe on January 2. After consulting with General Grant, he commenced loading his troops on transports, and on January 6 the force slipped out of Hampton Roads. The destination was known only to a few in the army and navy departments; even Terry did not know where he was headed, because he carried secret orders to be opened only at sea. He had in his command the same troops from the earlier aborted assault, plus two brigades of black troops, under the command of General Charles J. Paine.[4]

The troop fleet reached Beaufort on January 8, and Terry wasted no time consulting with Admiral Porter and planning the assault. Their first departure date had to be postponed, but the time was well spent allowing the commanders to resolve a lot of tactical issues. January 12 dawned with clear skies, moderate winds, and calm seas, allowing the combined fleet to depart for their destination.[5]

Porter had chosen the same naval units as used in the first assault: 58 warships, augmented by a larger supply train. His plan called for three attack and four reserve columns. This time the four monitors would stand in closer to the fort than previously. The monitors *Monadnock, Mahopac, Canonicus,* and *Saugus* would close to within 1,200 yards of the land-face salient of the fort. The first line would contain 13 ships, with the powerful *New Ironsides* and the great screw frigate *Brooklyn* in the van. The second line would consist of 12 warships; and the third, stationed off the Mound Battery, would have 12. To the east, four divisions of 17 ships would be composed of vessels of all types and tonnage. The reserve two divisions farther out would contain supply vessels, colliers, tugs, and dispatch vessels.[6]

In the fort, Colonel Lamb had been closely observing this gathering armada out at sea. "Daylight disclosed the return of the most formidable fleet that ever floated at sea," he wrote, "supplemented by transports carrying 8,500 men, and soon there rained upon fort and beach a storm of shot and shell that caused both earth and sea to tremble."[7] His garrison at the time consisted of 800 men, with 200 unfit for duty, but with reinforcements during the following day and night of 700 troops and a detachment of 50 sailors and marines, boosting the total to 1,350 minus the unfit men. The numbers were lopsided indeed, but Lamb and his men were not cowed by the discrepancy in numbers.

General Whiting, the Confederate commander of the Wilmington District, arrived at the fort to inform Lamb that he had come to share his fate and "that Lamb and his garrison would be sacrificed." But Lamb responded, "Don't say so, General: we shall certainly whip the enemy again." Whiting informed him that General Bragg had been removing stores and ammunition from Wilmington and was looking for a place to fall back to. This news was to have a profound morale effect on the outcome of the battle.[8]

At 4:00 A.M. on January 13, the transports stood in close to the beach while the monitors opened fire on the landface to cover the landing of the

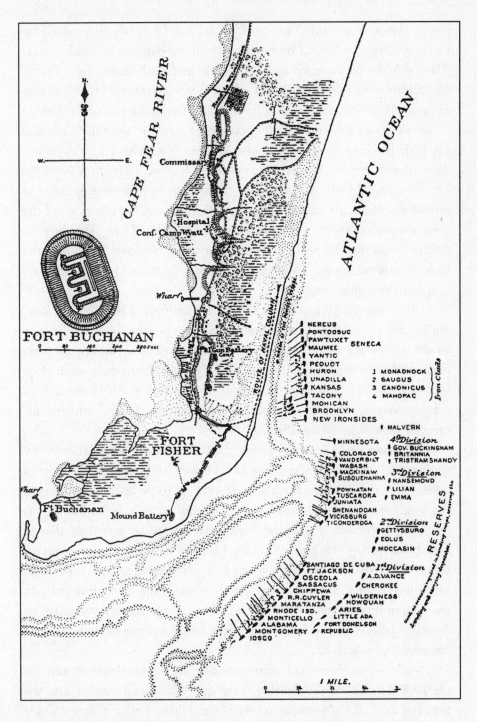

Map of Fort Fisher, revealing the placement of Union naval power and land assault routes. From *Battles and Leaders of the Civil War*.

troops plus a siege train. The *Brooklyn* and her 12 vessels also moved up and commenced a furious bombardment on the parapets of the landface. The rest of the fleet opened up, and "heaven and earth shook" from the relentless barrage of shot and shell. General Whiting estimated that "the rain of projectiles, increasing in the fury, was at times up to 160 per minute."[9]

Terry's troops landed without opposition by 3:00 P.M. on the 13th. On the 14th, pickets were sent out and exchanged shots with Confederate soldiers at outposts, but no serious opposition followed. This was puzzling, because General Hoke had a division nearby, but he mysteriously failed to oppose the landing force. Perhaps, as before, he was apprehensive of the great armada off shore and its massive cannonading. Then Terry threw a defense line across the peninsula from the Atlantic shore to the bank of the Cape Fear River, facing Wilmington, in order to protect his rear from attack from that direction.

As Terry moved his force down the peninsula toward the fort, the leading brigade would dig in for a time, then move on; the following brigade would occupy the abandoned position, then move on to occupy the next position dug by the leading brigade. By nightfall, all troops were in position near the fort and all artillery had been landed.[10] All Union troops finally hunkered down to observe the "grand bombardment," which commenced at daylight on the 15th.

"The firing never ceased," wrote C. B. Denison, a Confederate Army engineer. "All day and night long the 11-inch and 15-inch fiery globes rolled along the parapets; the palisades were cut to pieces and the wires to the [land] torpedoes were plowed up." Denison was told by an English officer who witnessed it that the bombardment was greater than that at Sevastopol during the Crimean War. Denison reported that the barrage was so severe that the defenders in the fort were unable to bury their dead, much less repair damage to the works.[11] A later compilation revealed that the ammunition expended by the fleet in the two assaults amounted to 3 million pounds of projectiles of all sizes, to say nothing of the enormous amount of powder used.

A weak countermove had been attempted by the Confederate navy on the 14th. The C.S.S. *Chickamauga* fired on Union troops dug in near the fort, but the U.S.S. *Monticello* moved up and drove her off the next day.[12] Colonel Lamb repeatedly wired Bragg to attack the landing force, especially two brigades of black soldiers on the land side, but the general never responded.[13] He was no doubt establishing a defense line farther north. Meanwhile, the bombardment increased to "inconceivable fury." The air was hot with burning debris and shells, as all combustible materials in the fort were set afire. A huge pall of smoke hung over the fort like a gigantic blanket.

Admiral Porter, not wanting the army to get the credit, equipped and landed a contingent of 2,000 sailors and marines with instructions to assault the northeast bastion of the fort, in concert with Terry's troops assaulting the west end of the landface, near the river, at a point called Shepherd's Battery. This tactic would later come to be known as a pincer movement.

At 3:25 P.M. on the 15th, when all preparations for the land assault were finished, Porter, at a prearranged signal, shifted the fleet's fire from the landface to the seaface, to take the attacking land forces out of harm's way.[14]

The naval force, armed only with cutlasses and revolvers, rushed down the beach, reaching the water edge of the palisades, then moving around it and toward the parapets of the northeast bastion. In spite of a heavy concentration of fire from troops atop the bastion, some of the naval force managed to reach the berm, but they were cut down by the murderous fire. Then, with their ranks decimated by men dropping "like falling bricks," they were forced to retreat, leaving behind 400 dead and wounded.

A great cheer went up in the fort. Lamb, along with the rest of the garrison, thought the naval assault to be the main one and that they had repulsed it. But their cheers were short-lived. The ill-fated naval attack had accomplished one thing: It left Shepherd's Battery wide open and defended by only a few troops.

In the meantime, while the naval force was being repulsed, three Union brigades had come down the river road, across the bridge, and down the riverside gate to assault the weakly defended Shepherd's Battery while the majority of the fort's defenders were engaged in the northeast bastion fight. Suddenly, the Confederates were amazed to see the Federal flag planted atop the traverse at Shepherd's Battery. They quickly rallied to fight the intruders, but it was too late—they were overwhelmed by the might of the hard-fighting Union troops, and began to fall south toward Battery

Buchanan, engaged in ferocious hand-to-hand fighting. With their backs to the river and no promise of reinforcements, they surrendered. Among the prisoners were the wounded commanders, General Whiting and Colonel Lamb.

After the surrender, Federal troops captured 169 pieces of artillery, 2,000 stand of arms, ammunition, and a great supply of provisions. But the cost was heavy, with 973 Federals killed, wounded, or missing, while Confederate casualties were estimated at 500 killed, wounded, or missing, with over 2,000 troops taken prisoner.

The fleet responded with a great uproar of celebration, with whistles blowing and salute guns fired, along with the victorious troops celebrating in the fort. But the celebrations were cut short by an unexpected catastrophe: A tremendous explosion took place in the fort near the northeastern bastion, sending tons of earth into the air and killing or wounding 200 men, Union and Confederate alike. It seems that some Union sailors had gotten drunk on captured spirits and were pillaging the fort when they happened on the main magazine near the bastion. They went inside to explore the magazine, carrying torches. The fire from the torches touched off 13,000 pounds of powder. The explosion flung dirt, sand, and debris into the air, along with some men sleeping atop the magazine. The fort was quickly covered with a large umbrella of smoke, according to observers in the fleet.[15] Some Union officials thought that the explosion was deliberately set off by a wire leading to someone hiding in the swamp alongside the river, but that theory was soon put to rest.

Soon after the surrender of Fort Fisher, the Confederates abandoned and blew up Forts Caswell, Campbell, and Johnston, thus severing the supply line to Lee's army from the ocean.[16] Soon after the surrender, a blockade-runner came in, guided by the lights and buoys originally set by the Confederates. The surprised captain and his crew were taken prisoners.

The occupation of Wilmington occurred on February 22, 1865, and was uneventful and without serious resistance. In fact, General Terry and his staff rode into the city, dismounted, and shook hands with the mayor, John Dawson. The city was officially surrendered and occupied by the forces of General Joseph Hawley, who was a native of North Carolina. Confederate General Hoke had long since taken his troops and abandoned the city to its fate.

Six weeks after the surrender of Wilmington, General Lee would surrender his army, now ill-equipped, demoralized, and impotent, and the Confederacy would fade into the history books.

THE assault on and capture of Fort Fisher was one of the most intriguing military operations of the Civil War. Once again, it showed that a powerful naval force could pound an installation into submission. Without Porter's fleet, the capture of Fort Fisher by ground troops alone would have taken much more time, because at the outset a careful examination of the fort suggested that it might be impregnable. However, one of its less visible weaknesses was the element of undercomplementing, to coin a phrase. Lamb's repeated calls for reinforcements went unheeded by General Bragg, who sat at Wilmington with sizeable forces of troops during both attacks but hesitated to commit them, because men were standing by to be sent elsewhere in an effort to check Sherman's rapid and seemingly unstoppable push toward the sea through Georgia. It was the capstone to Grant's theory that the Confederates would be unable to fight on three fronts in the Carolinas. Colonel Lamb was highly critical of Bragg after the war, and often wrote and spoke publicly about the controversial general's timidity, as did other members of Lamb's command, including his army engineer, E. C. Denison.

Much blame was placed on Porter for the casualties of the assaulting naval land forces. Outside of the marines, placing naval personnel in harm's way was foolhardy, because they were equipped with only cutlasses and revolvers and were up against enemy troops trained for land warfare. As naval historian Nathan Miller has pointed out, it was as if the contingent were a mere naval boarding party.[17] In addition, the marines who were at the rear of the attacking force failed to cover them with rifle fire. Without that fire cover, to keep the heads of the fort's defenders down, the sailors were like lambs sent to the slaughter. No one has satisfactorily explained why those marines didn't respond in the way they should have.

We have earlier mentioned the criticism of General Bragg's timidity. The general, in his declining years, wrote much about the Fort Fisher affair. His answer to the criticism was well put, and partially explains his hesitancy:

No human power could have prevented the enemy from landing, covered as he was by a fleet of ships carrying six hundred heavy guns. Anywhere beyond the range of our heavy guns in the fort our land force could not approach him. Once landed, our only chance was to keep him from the fort, if possible. With less than half his numbers, had we extended far enough toward the fort to prevent his movement that way, he would have crossed the narrow peninsula north of us and cut us off entirely, when the fort and all must have gone.[18]

Historian Charles M. Robinson wrote that Fort Fisher "was to the Union navy what Appomattox was to the Union army. It was the last great maritime action of the war in which the navy had operated by sea and river, and had learned to work jointly—if not always harmoniously—with the army."[19] This assessment is true in light of the previous amphibious actions of the war, in which amphibious forces supported by warships took Cape Hatteras, Port Royal, and Roanoke Island. In the case of Fort Fisher, the operation was much larger, with an enormous fleet of warships covering the landings of a much larger amount of troops than previously.

The Fort Fisher campaign forever relegated the ancient practice of massed armies facing each other to the scrap pile, along with bows and arrows and blunderbusses. For with naval gunfire support, the fighting was less intense and of shorter duration than previously, relatively speaking. No amount of cannon batteries could match the awesome firepower of a large fleet of warships equipped with the largest guns yet cast.

One can speculate all day about the pluses and minuses of the Fort Fisher campaign, but the stark reality remains that because the fort was taken, the port of Wilmington was closed to Lee's army while he was fighting for his life. According to most historians, this probably hastened the end of the war.

Perhaps naval historian Nathan Miller said it best, concerning the vast implications of the fall of Fort Fisher and Wilmington:

The Capture of Wilmington ended the navy's role in the Civil War—a role which, if not decisive, was vital to the final Northern victory. Command of the sea and inland waters provided the Union armies with a mobility that overcame the Confederacy's interior lines of communication. It provided the Union with the tactical advantage of being able to shift its forces to apply pressure at any given point.[20]

CHAPTER NINETEEN

TWILIGHT OF THE CONFEDERATE NAVY

After the surrender of Fort Fisher, the port of Wilmington was no longer a conduit through which war materiel flowed to Confederate armies in the field. However, the occupation of Wilmington could not occur until the remaining Confederate strongholds in the river were subdued. With shallow-draft gunboats able to enter the river, ship-to-shore bombardments were held against Forts Holmes, Caswell, Campbell, and Anderson farther upstream.

The last of these was a hard nut to crack, so a certain amount of resourcefulness was needed. Porter, taking a leaf out of his Mississippi River fleet book, built a dummy monitor, nicknamed "Old Bogey," out of an old scow, some barrels, and canvas, to ascertain enemy gun positions on the river.

Then, on the night of February 18, 1865, Lieutenant Cushing, in *Monticello,* piloted the fake gunboat upriver and let it flow past the fort with the flood tide, through a file of mines and gunfire. Finally Old Bogey slammed into the eastern bank of the river, scattering the defenders there. The fort's batteries pounded away at the grounded dummy but were puzzled as to why the vessel didn't return the fire.[1]

The gunboats shelled Fort Anderson relentlessly until its surrender on

February 19. Then Porter took his flotilla up the river, past mines and obstructions placed in the river by Confederates, and on to Wilmington on the 22nd. Once there, Porter's flagship, the *Malvern,* tied up to a wharf and was greeted by hundreds of blacks who loudly celebrated the arrival of the Federals. The admiral ordered a salute of 35 guns, and many citizens, thinking a naval fight had broken out, fled from the wharf area.[2]

With the closing of the port of Wilmington and the Confederate evacuation of Charleston on February 16, 1865, the Confederate navy reached its nadir as a viable fighting force. But one area still held the last remnants of that navy: the James River squadron at Chaffin's Bluff below Richmond. On February 23, Porter and the *Malvern* shoved off from the wharf at Wilmington and headed for Hampton Roads, at the head of the James.

The James River, the largest waterway lying wholly within the state of Virginia, has gone down in history as one of the most important rivers in the Civil War, alongside the Mississippi and Red Rivers. It rises in the Allegheny Mountains and flows southeastward for 340 miles until it reaches Hampton Roads and empties into Chesapeake Bay; here it is almost five miles wide and deep enough for oceangoing ships to navigate. Its chief tributaries are the Appomattox and Chickahominy Rivers.

As the river winds and loops southeasterly, it passes spots with such unlikely names as Dutch Gap, Deep Bottom, Bermuda Hundred, City Point, and Flowerdew Hundred before it reaches Hampton Roads. Many of these sites were strategically centered in the struggle for Richmond during the final months of the war. The most prominent of these was City Point, at the confluence of the James and Appomattox Rivers. General Grant established his base of operations there, from which he would launch his assault on Petersburg, a Confederate stronghold to the west. That city was the hub of an important railroad, the Weldon & Petersburg, a vital artery of supplies to Lee's army and to Richmond.[3]

Earlier in June, Grant decided to move his army from a point called White House, located on the Pamunkey River, to the west of the James, already secured by General Butler in May. But crossing the wide river proved to be a problem for his huge army. The solution to the problem was a pontoon bridge built by 450 of his engineers at the river's narrowest point, called Point Wyanoke. The pontoon bridge, which spanned 2,000 feet, was built on over 100 pontoon craft spaced 20 feet apart and secured to schooners anchored upstream. Planks were laid edge to edge to provide a roadway 11 feet wide, and it featured a removable midsection to accommodate river traffic. The entire project was remarkably accomplished in 70 hours, and over it moved 60,000 men with a wagon train of ambulances, artillery, supplies—and all in just 70 hours.[4] This amazing feat was to be the forerunner of many such bridges in Europe built by Allied forces in World War II. The Confederate James River squadron failed to come down and challenge this construction, mainly because of the many obstructions in the river placed by Union naval forces.

Soon City Point was turned from a sleepy port village into one of the busiest sites in the war; it was to become an element in Grant's waterborne supply line for his 11-month Petersburg campaign. The place bustled with stables, a post office, chapel, sutler's or merchant shacks, and a large hospital. Warehouses supplied by river traffic sent goods to a rail line containing 275 railroad cars and 25 locomotives ferried up from Washington, which supplied the Union army headquarters and trenches outside of Petersburg.

Meanwhile, closely watching all this activity was Flag Officer John K. Mitchell, with the remnants of the Confederate James River squadron at Richmond, bottled up by the Union squadrons. Then on January 23, when many of Porter's ships had been pulled for the Fort Fisher campaign, and after a reconnaissance force revealed that his vessels could penetrate the obstacles in the James at high tide and under the cover of darkness, Mitchell saw his opportunity to descend the river and strike a blow at the growing Union base at City Point.

His command was still a powerful force, built around three ironclads, *Richmond, Fredericksburg,* and *Virginia II.* The rest of the flotilla consisted of the gunboats *Roanoke, Hampton, Nansemond, Drewry, Beaufort, Raleigh,* and *Patrick Henry,* the last formerly used as a school ship. Added to the squadron were a tugboat and a mail vessel. The ironclads, of course, were the mainstay of the flotilla, because of their armament. The *Fredericksburg* and *Richmond* each carried four 6-inch rifles. The *Virginia II* was built along the lines of the old *Virginia,* with a casemate of 6-inch armor and two 8-inch and two 6-inch Brooke rifles, and was one of the most powerful vessels in the Confederate navy.[5]

The only Union warship facing this formidable squadron was the powerful, double-turreted *Onondaga,* armed with two 15-inch Dahlgren smoothbores and two 150-pound rifles. The rest of the Union James River division of four ironclads and seven gunboats had been pulled for service at Fort Fisher.[6]

During the night of January 23, 1865, Commodore Mitchell brought the three ironclads, the gunboat *Drewry*, a "torpedo boat," and three "torpedo launches" down the river. At Trent's Reach, the *Virginia II, Richmond, Drewry*, and *Fredericksburg*, plus a torpedo launch, ran aground at the obstructions placed there by the Federals. The *Fredericksburg* managed to pull free but was called back to protect the stranded vessels. A Union battery, using powerful lights, fired on the stranded vessels. The *Ononadaga*, meanwhile, had retired down to the river to "obtain an advantageous position," in order to fight the oncoming enemy vessels.

At the grounding of the enemy ironclads and gunboat, Parker brought the *Onondaga* to within 9,000 yards of the *Virginia II* and opened up on her with 15-inch Dahlgrens. The *Virginia II* was struck between 125 and 150 times, with little effect, but two 15-inch projectiles almost penetrated her armor. The *Richmond* sustained some damage, but the *Drewry* was destroyed at flood tide. Commodore Mitchell, concerned that his vessels would sustain serious and possibly fatal damage, decided to withdraw his force upstream to lick its wounds.[7]

Parker was later reprimanded and removed from command because of his hesitation in coming up; had he done so earlier, he might possibly have destroyed the Confederate fleet while it was helplessly aground. He was replaced by Commodore Edward T. Nichols, a veteran of Farragut's New Orleans campaign.

No more naval action occurred on the James until General Grant invited President Lincoln, his wife, and their son Tad to City Point for a visit. The Lincolns came from Washington and up the James River on the steamer *River Queen*, docking at City Point on the 26th. There they were welcomed with lunches, dinners, and parties of all kinds, and Lincoln even rode out to the Petersburg area with Grant to visit the troops and to witness some of the fighting. Back at City Point with Grant, he conferred with General Sherman and Admiral Porter, who was an old friend of Sherman's. The indefatigable Sherman had just returned from his successful Shenandoah campaign and the isolating of General Johnston's Confederate army in the Carolinas.[8]

Grant was eager for this three-way conference between the leading commanders in order to discuss the fall of Richmond, the destruction of

Lee's army, and the ending of the war. After it, he returned to Petersburg to direct the final push to take Petersburg. Lincoln, Tad, and Porter remained at City Point, on board the *Malvern*, after Mrs. Lincoln returned to Washington. The president was most happy to relax and to be away from the cares of his office for a time.

One night, while discussing the current naval situation, Lincoln asked Porter if the navy could do something at the moment to "make history." When Porter explained that the Confederate fleet was bottled up at Richmond and impotent, Lincoln replied, "But, can't we make a noise?"[9] Porter replied to the request and sent a dispatch to Commander William Ronckendorff, who was in command of monitors that had returned to the area, ordering him to shell the Confederate works above Howlett's Battery near Dutch Gap. "The object," he wrote, "is to make the rebels think we are about to attack. They are prepared to sink their gunboats at the first sign of one . . . the only object is to make noise." The monitors moved up and made their demonstration of pyrotechnics, including rockets, blue lights, and a barrage of 10-inch shells. It managed to shake up the Confederates there, and lowered their morale to the extent that it contributed to the final fall of Richmond.[10]

Then, on April 2, Grant finally captured Petersburg, and General Lee, realizing that the end of hostilities must be drawing to a close, sent a message to President Davis to evacuate Richmond immediately. The president was in church when the message arrived, but he quickly left to begin packing and making plans to leave the city and team up with General Lee at Danville.

Secretary Mallory wired Admiral Raphael Semmes, who was now commander of Confederate naval forces on the James, as to the disposition of his squadron. "Upon you," the secretary wrote, "is devolved the duty of destroying your ships this night and with all the forces under your command joining General Lee."[11] Semmes complied by blowing up all his remaining vessels. According to witnesses, the explosions created a noise not unlike the shock of an earthquake. The air was filled with missiles, and the spectacle was apparently beyond description. The admiral then took his command to Danville, North Carolina, where he remained until General Johnston surrendered his forces. Meanwhile, Richmond was set afire and inhabitants began to stream out of the city in a panic while thunderous explosions rocked the city. In the lower section of the city, on the James, the

Patrick Henry was burning furiously; warehouses were torched and the Tredegar Iron Works was ablaze, as were entire blocks. A canopy of smoke hung over the city. Adding to this nightmare, stored artillery shells—mostly at Tredegar Iron Works—exploded wildly, intensifying the horror of the fleeing inhabitants.

Elizabeth L. "Crazy Beth" Van Lew, a Union spy living in Richmond, wrote about the evacuation in her diary. She described the turmoil within the city before and during the evacuation:

> The constant explosion of shells, the blowing up of the gun boats, and of the powder magazine, seemed to jar, to shake the earth, and lend a mighty language to the scene. All nature trembled at the work of arbitrary work, the consummation of the wrongs of years. The burning bridges, the roaring flames added a wild grandeur to the scene.[12]

After General Godfrey Weitzel's troops occupied the city, President Lincoln decided on a personal visit to Richmond. On April 4, he boarded the *River Queen* and, accompanied by Porter in *Malvern,* sailed up the James toward Richmond. But below the city, the *River Queen* went aground, so Porter had the president and his party transferred to a barge and rowed up to the wharf of Richmond. There Lincoln, accompanied by Porter, Tad Lincoln, and a contingent of armed marines, went ashore and strolled through the now smoldering city.[13] The presidential party walked through the streets, which were empty, until they came upon some black workmen, who immediately recognized the tall figure of the president. One of them fell at his feet, proclaiming Lincoln to be a "great messiah." Lincoln was embarrassed and told the workman that he must "kneel to God only and to thank Him for the liberty you will hereafter enjoy." Soon he was surrounded by joyful black folk who just wanted to touch him.[14]

Lincoln decided to visit General Weitzel's headquarters, located at the former Confederate White House, and spent some time there reminiscing. After a few more hours, Lincoln and his party toured the devastated city and finally returned to the barge and thence to the *Malvern,* much to the relief of Porter and his associates, who had feared for Lincoln's life, lest some renegade Confederate soldier ambush him.

The capitulation of Richmond heralded not only the end of the war but virtually all naval activity along the East Coast as well. But one last exploit of the Confederate navy was yet to come. At Shreveport, Louisiana, Lieutenant Charles W. Reid, who had taken command of the 655-ton, three-gun wooden ram *William H. Webb* and who had been bottled up in the Red River by Union ships and lacking communications, decided to make a run for it. So on April 16, 1865, he slipped down the river, past a Union monitor and two ironclads, and into the Mississippi River. When he approached New Orleans, he hoisted a Union flag as a disguise and boldly ran past the city, taking some shots from shore artillery, which caused little harm. But upon reaching a position 25 miles downriver, he discovered the screw sloop *Richmond* and two gunboats, *Hollyhock* and *Florida,* waiting for him. The big warship had her broadside run out, and the situation for Reid looked gloomy and untenable; he knew he could not outrun the enemy flotilla. Reid decided to run the *Webb* aground and escape, but he was soon surrounded by an armed shore party from the ships; he surrendered with 25 of the crew.[15] The incident occurred just 16 days after Lee's surrender at Appomattox.

A Confederate raider, the *Shenandoah,* fell victim to the lack of communication concerning the end of the war. This remarkable raider was built in England and purchased by the Confederacy in September 1864. After being equipped and her command taken by Captain James Waddell, she set out for the Pacific, where she raised havoc with Union seaborne commerce. During her career, she captured or destroyed over 36 ships, many of them whalers, and managed to log over 40,000 miles. When ships were destroyed, prisoners were kept in the *Shenandoah's* forecastle and were humanely treated. When Waddell learned of the surrender on November 5, 1865, he set sail for England by way of Cape Horn. There, at Liverpool, he surrendered to British authorities, and his ship was later turned over to the United States, which sold her at auction to the sultan of Zanzibar. A footnote to this story is that the *Shenandoah* had the distinction of being the only Confederate ship to circumnavigate the globe.[16]

Thus ended the last exploits of the Confederate navy and particularly her rogue raiders, which were never a part of the navy but nevertheless contributed much to the war effort.

CHAPTER TWENTY

A GLANCE BACKWARD

The importance of naval activity during the Civil War is underlined by one important fact: As with land actions, it began on the East Coast and ended on the East Coast.

Some historians have challenged the assumption that the blockade weakened the Confederate armies by denying them vital war matériel to sustain them in the field, arguing instead that the blockade-runners got sufficient supplies through. This assumption is based on the argument that Lee's army held its own against the Union in the final year of the war. But it overlooks the fact that Lee's army was demoralized and ill equipped, especially during the Carolina campaigns. Many of his troops were without necessities such as shoes, proper clothing, and good ammunition. By the time of the fall of Richmond, they could not have fought much longer, even if they had been able to team up with Johnston's army. While it is true that many blockade-runners got through, what they were able to supply was not enough to make a difference.

When Lincoln declared the blockade, the major ports of the South were Norfolk, Charleston, Wilmington, Savannah, Pensacola, Mobile, New Orleans, and to a lesser extent Galveston. Through these avenues intercourse with England and Europe flourished, financed by the enormous output of cotton. Furthermore, the Confederacy had been blessed with deep-water channels, harbors, and major railroad connections inland. The leaders of the Confederacy exploited these avenues; the Union, at the same time, was well aware of them—thus the necessity of the Anaconda Plan and the blockade.

Under the Buchanan administration, however, the splendid U.S. Navy of the War of 1812 had been reduced to a floating junk pile, of which many were in ordinary and others were rotting in harbors. The Home Squadron centered around six steam frigates and six fast screw sloops, plus two store ships and a steam tender, that were available at the outbreak of hostilities. These vessels were barely able to cover the 3,000-mile coastline of the Confederacy with its 189 or more waterways along the Atlantic and Gulf states. Remarkably, the Union managed to maintain a blockade of sorts until its enormous industrial capacity shifted into high gear.[1]

Another remarkable achievement was the declaration of the blockade, which of itself brought up an international dilemma. The very act of declaring a blockade entails war, because the recipient is labeled as a belligerent nation; in the case of the Confederacy, that would validate its claim of being an independent nation. They desired this state of being, because it opened the possibility that England and the rest of Europe would recognize the Confederacy as a separate country and would become customers of its major crop, King Cotton. But when the queen of England declared her country's neutral attitude toward the Civil War in May 1861, the South's hopes for intervention by England were dashed. It then became obvious to the Confederate government that its only remaining option was to find a means to penetrate the blockade and thereby provide a flow of vital goods from overseas. This could only be accomplished by the use of special vessels with low silhouettes, low top hampers, powerful engines, and spacious hold capacities, some outfitted at home, others built in English and Scottish shipyards.

At first, the blockade-running activities were remarkably successful. In four years, through the port of Wilmington alone, 2,000 Enfield rifles, 250,000 pairs of shoes, 50,000 blankets, wool cloth for 250,000 gray uniforms, 100,000 pounds of bacon, 500 sacks of coffee, $50,000 worth of medicines, and other items of vital necessity to the Confederate war effort were brought in. But these impressive figures were soon to diminish as the blockade tightened its coils, especially after the fall of Fort Fisher and the closing of the Cape Fear River in 1865.[2]

In early 1861, the Union navy had to be whipped into some sort of shape for the gigantic and arduous task of blockading the vast coastline of the Confederacy. Lincoln's choice as his secretary of the navy, Gideon Welles, was a splendid stroke. Even with a limited knowledge of naval affairs, the man from Connecticut quickly grew into his task and brilliantly managed the affairs of an expanding navy, especially with his choice of an assistant, Gustavus Fox, and the findings of the astute Blockade Board appointed by Welles himself.

His was an awesome task, but Welles was up to it. In what seemed to be record time, through his efforts the navy grew from roughly 42 serviceable ships in 1861 to over 600 ships of all kinds by the end of the war. Those vessels were produced in major shipbuilding facilities in New York, Philadelphia, Baltimore, Washington, Boston, and Norfolk. The shipyards featured magnificent equipment backed by unlimited resources, which of course gave the Union a decided advantage from the very beginning.

Other innovations of the Civil War Union navy were the "ninety-day wonder" craft, which foreshadowed the assembly lines of warships produced by Henry Kaiser in World War II. But the most fascinating innovation was the introduction of the famous *Monitor* and the turreted gun, foreshadowing the mighty battleships, cruisers, and destroyers of a later era. It would seem that technology played not a little part in the evolving Union navy.

On the other hand, the Confederate naval secretary, Stephen Mallory, faced the herculean task of building a navy from practically nothing but a few river steamers, some coastal packets, and some navy vessels confiscated by southern coastal states after they seceded from the Union. But, from the perspective of 140 years later, it is remarkable that a nation devoid of heavy industry and shipyards was able to produce a fleet of ships, including ironclads. This navy grew in spite of a shortage of skilled mechanics and the fact that at the start, the South had only three rolling mills and one foundry, the Tredegar Iron Works. But with amazing ingenuity, diligence, and hard work, the Confederacy built foundries and rolling mills at Atlanta, Selma, Macon, and Richmond, plus smelting and chemical plants at Petersburg, a powder mill, and a chain of arsenals from Virginia to Alabama.

In the field, the Confederacy doggedly fought on, in some instances winning skirmishes and battles over an enemy with superior numbers and armament. But attrition set in, and with the Confederacy unable to replenish its troops with essential supplies, defeat was inevitable. Truly, it was a struggle of brave people against insurmountable odds.

Some apologists for the Confederacy have maintained that if the South had had even one-third of the amount of warships the Union had, the war would have ended differently. But other historians hold different opinions. While it is true that the war would have gone on for a longer time, it is an irrefutable fact that the Confederate navy, regardless of size, could not have been sustained for long. As we have maintained throughout, the lack of shipyard facilities with a vast industrial base behind them would eventually have rendered the Confederate navy impotent.

The Southerners, however, did introduce a new element to naval warfare—underwater weapons. The innovation of mines to be used in shallow inland waters (interestingly, the mines were ineffective in larger and deeper bodies of water because of anchoring problems) took a toll on Union warships—58 were destroyed—and managed to divert others in order to counter the new threat, thereby keeping Federal fleets out of many rivers and harbors.

Other Confederate innovations in underwater warfare were the spar torpedo boat and an underwater explosive-carrying craft, the submarine. The former was a steam-powered boat featuring a torpedo mounted on the end of a long spar protruding from the bow. It was designed to run into its target and explode the torpedo on contact. However, the former group did not inflict any fatal damage on Union warships, and the latter managed to sink a Union warship, the *Housatonic,* but was destroyed along with the warship. That event, however, was a trumpet call for the emergence of the modern submarine used so effectively in the Atlantic during World War I and in both the Atlantic and Pacific during World War II.

The modern battleship, cruiser, and destroyer owe their ancestry to the innovation of the six city-class ironclad gunboats built by James Eads. These gunboats were used effectively by General Grant in his Mississippi River campaign. Speaking generally, these vessels featured armor-plate citadels punctured by gunports through which protruded heavy guns of various calibers. They were propelled by centerline paddlewheels powered by incline engines. The most famous of these was the U.S.S. *Cairo*, sunk in the Yazoo River (later raised and put on display at Vicksburg Military Park). The Confederates built some twenty ironclads during the war, the most famous of which were the *Arkansas* and the *Tennessee*. The fascinating stories of these vessels are told in the previous volumes in this series.[3]

Civil War naval technology was never more effectively demonstrated than in the introduction of the ironclad and *Monitor*-class war vessels. In the latter group, the prototype was the U.S.S. *Monitor*, invented and built by John Ericsson. This unconventional vessel steamed into Hampton Roads and fought the seemingly impregnable Confederate ironclad *Virginia* to a standstill. At the same time, it sounded a resounding death knell for the wooden warship that had dominated the naval world for many, many generations.

In fact, the later *Milwaukee*-class monitors featured guns that were lowered into the hull for loading, run out, elevated, and trained by steam power. It was one of the most important technological advances in iron warships.

Along with these technological advances in the navies were the careers of great leaders on both sides of the conflict. The Federal navy boasted such stellar lights as Admirals Farragut, Lee, Dahlgren, and Porter, plus such brave commanders as Henry Walke, Andrew Hull Foote, Charles Ellet, Charles Davis, and A. M. Pennock, to name a few. Of these, David Glasgow Farragut stands head and shoulders above the rest. His brilliant and daring tactics in conquering New Orleans and Mobile Bay forever closed those vital ports to the Confederacy, as did the exploits of Admirals du Pont, Porter, and Dahlgren in closing the ports of Charleston, Wilmington, and Savannah, as well as assaulting the enemy bastions at Hatteras, Port Royal, and Fort Fisher. But, to use examples from modern naval history, Farragut combined the brilliant strategy of a Nimitz with the bold exploits of a Halsey. Dahlgren, of course, deserves special mention for his invention of the big gun that bears his name—weapons used so effectively by the Federal navy in its monitors.

On the Confederate side were a host of brave naval fighting men: Franklin Buchanan, who courageously fought Farragut's great armada at Mobile Bay; Raphael Semmes, of Confederate raider fame; and Catesby ap Roger Jones and John Worden of the *Virginia*. There are also Captain

William "Dirty Bill" Porter and Izaac N. Brown, who took the *Arkansas* to Vicksburg, past a powerful Union fleet on the Mississippi.

It would be unforgivable not to mention the daring commanders of the Confederate raiders, which plagued the seas and almost wiped Union shipping from the seas: John Newland Maffitt, Charles W. Reid, John Taylor Wood, and others. These men destroyed or captured a substantial number of ships and obtained enormous prizes.

Aside from the technological advances in the Civil War that gave us ironclads, rifled guns, monitors, submarines, and mines, there were the advances in warfare itself. The most interesting innovation was that of amphibious warfare. This tactic allowed great numbers of seaborne troops to land on enemy shores under a bombardment umbrella of a great number of warships. Early in the war, Grant used this technique on the Mississippi with land troops in his attempt to pass Vicksburg for an end run around the city to assault it from the rear. He landed his 50,000 troops under heavy bombardment from the Mississippi squadron gunboats. The same method was employed by Commodore Porter in the assault and capture of Cape Hatteras, Roanoke Island, Port Royal, and Fort Fisher, at the last of which the largest and most powerful fleet ever assembled covered the landings with massive bombardments. This type of engagement was to be duplicated almost a hundred years later at Normandy and at Japanese-held Pacific islands during World War II.

An important factor in the failure of the Confederate navy was a lack of coordinated command. In such cases as the struggle for New Orleans, the Confederates' potentially potent flotilla was crippled by this lack of central command structure. It was under civilian, army, and navy commands at different times, a situation that was unhappily common to the Confederate navy during the war.

Of course, this was not all Mallory's fault. He was a fine, intelligent leader, rich in naval knowledge, and resourceful. But he lacked the necessary resources to fully implement his ability. He had a plethora of officers for his fledgling navy but a dreadful lack of enlisted seamen. Too often he had to draw from the army, and these men had no expertise in fighting on water.

On the Union side, Lincoln's decision to consider the bombardment of Fort Sumter as an act of war prevented the spectacle of a paralyzed country wringing its hands over the unprovoked attack but doing nothing about it.

Historians have agreed that if there had not been a strong presidency in 1861, the Union might have been fragmented long before any serious battlefield action occurred. Also essential were his decision to suspend the writ of habeas corpus in and around Baltimore and his sending in of Federal troops to prevent Maryland from seceding from the Union and isolating Washington from the rest of the country.

At first, his choice of army leaders was flawed—consider General George McClellan, who would much rather have paraded his army than used it to fight. After choosing more leaders who were seriously incompetent, he found what he needed in General Grant, who not only fought but eventually won the war for him.

His choice of Gideon Welles as secretary of the navy was also brilliant, as was the selection of Edwin Stanton as secretary of war. Although both men at times disagreed with their boss, they nevertheless served him efficiently and faithfully.

Jefferson Davis, on the other hand, had none of the great qualities of Lincoln, although he did his best with what he had. He managed to see his new country, poor in resources and industrialization, through a long and difficult fight with a country superior in those qualities. Davis was a highly opinionated man who believed himself to be superior to members of his cabinet and some of his military leaders, including the able Joseph E. Johnston and Pierre G. T. Beauregard, who were two of his most efficient generals.

In all fairness to him, Davis did make intelligent choices in Robert E. Lee and Stephen Mallory. Both men served him honorably and with precision in the Confederate cause and were responsible for their country lasting as long as it did, in spite of Davis' weaknesses and intractability. It is a proven maxim that a country is only as efficient as its leaders.

But when all is said and done, the stark fact remains that the Federal navy had supremacy almost from the beginning of the war, was backed by unlimited resources, and was used efficiently and powerfully. The Federal navy had the edge in developing new concepts in warships, developing rifled guns, and debuting amphibious warfare.

The advantage of naval supremacy to a country is succinctly pointed out in the Civil War Naval Chronology. I quote it here in conclusion to this work:

Employing the mobile heavy artillery of ships, their carrying capacity, range and speed of operations, armies gained the advantages of the sea. They could strike by surprise, swiftly, and massively. They could promptly shift the heavy artillery of ships or concentrations of troops to attack where the foe was vulnerable or their own lines weak. Ships could strike on the flank or break through and roll up the most powerful position. They could pour in supplies or reinforcements to a key base or shift it at will.[4]

ABBREVIATIONS

B&L   *Battles and Leaders of the Civil War.* 4 vols. New York: Thomas Yoseloff, 1956.

CWD   *The Civil War Dictionary,* ed. Mark M. Boatner III. New York: Vintage Books, 1991.

CWNC   *Civil War Naval Chronology, 1861–1865.* 6 vols. Washington, DC: Government Printing Office, Naval History Division, 1971.

DAFS   *Dictionary of American Fighting Ships.* 9 vols. Washington, DC: Government Printing Office, Naval History Division, 1959–1991.

HTECW   *Historical Times Illustrated Encyclopedia of the Civil War,* ed. Patricia Faust. New York: Harper & Row, 1986.

ORA   *The War of the Rebellion: A Compilation of the Official Records of the Union and Confederate Armies.* 128 vols. Washington, DC: U.S. Government Printing Office, 1880–1901.

ORN   *Official Records of the Union and Confederate Navies in the War of the Rebellion.* 31 vols. Washington, DC: U.S. Government Printing Office, 1894–1922.

WCWN   *Warships of the Civil War Navies,* by Paul Silverstone. Annapolis: Naval Institute Press, 1989.

NOTES

CHAPTER ONE Fort Sumter and the U.S. Navy

1. Welles to Fox, ORA, ser. 1, vol. 1, pp. 240–41.

2. Fox to Cameron, ORA, ser. 1, vol. 1, p. 11; Ivan Musicant, *Divided Waters* (Annapolis: U.S. Naval Institute Press, 1995). Musicant is one of the foremost of naval historians, in this author's opinion.

3. There is no available biography on Major Robert Anderson. However, there is an excellent short bio in *Historical Times Illustrated Encyclopedia of the Civil War,* ed. Patricia L. Faust (New York: HarperCollins Publishers, 1996) hereafter referred to as HTIC. See also Mark Mayo Boatner III, *Civil War Dictionary* (New York: Vintage Books, 1991), p. 15, hereafter referred to as CWD.

4. John J. Nicolay, *The Outbreak of the Rebellion* (New York: Scribner's, 1992 [1883]), pp. 29–30.

5. Ibid., p. 22; *Fort Sumter: Anvil of War* (Washington, DC: Division of Publications, National Park Service, U.S. Department of the Interior). Nicolay's description of Fort Sumter differed from official sources, but preference is with this official source.

6. William C. Davis, Brian C. Pohanka, and Don Troiani, *The Civil War Journals: The Battles* (Nashville: Rutledge Hill Press, 1998). A new, excellently illustrated book.

7. The unhappy story of the *Star of the West* is told in detail in Jack D. Coombe, *Thunder Along the Mississippi* (New York: Bantam Books, 1996), chap. 1. Other accounts may be found in B&L, vol. 1, and Musicant, *Divided Waters,* chap. 1.

8. The whole puzzling affair over the *Powhatan* can be read in ORN, ser. 1, vol. 1.

9. Chestnut to Anderson, ORN, s.1, vol.1, p. 14.

10. ORA, ser. 1, vol. 1, p. 36. There has been some controversy over who fired the first shot at Fort Sumter. Traditionally it was thought that a wild-eyed secessionist, Edward Ruffin, had pulled the lanyard at the Iron Battery on Morris Island.

Other sources say it was Captain James. A rather spirited defense of James is presented by Stephen B. Lee, C.S.A., in *Southern Historical Society Papers*, vol. 11, November 1883. This defense of James was challenged by Ruffin in an article in the same publication.

11. Joe H. Kirchenberger, *Eyewitness History of the Civil War* (New York: Facts on File, Inc., 1991), p. 55.

12. Mary Chestnut, *A Diary from Dixie* (New York: D. Appelton & Co., 1928); Kirchenberger, ibid.

13. Doubleday quote from Kirchenberger, p. 55.

14. Fox to Welles, ORN, ser. 1, vol. 4, pp. 250–53.

15. Fox to Welles, ibid., p. 252. Also see Coombe, *Thunder Along the Mississippi*, chap. 9, for detailed description on fire rafts and how Farragut dealt with them.

16. Fox to Welles, ibid., p. 249: E. Milby Burton, *The Siege of Charleston, 1861–1865* (Columbia: University of South Carolina Press, 1970), p. 70.

17. ORA, ser. 1, vol. 1, p. 22; Burton, p. 15.

18. Anderson to Beauregard, ORN, ser. 1, vol. 1, p. 15.

19. Beauregard to Anderson, ORN, ser. 1, vol. 1, p. 15.

20. Gillis to Gillis, ORN, ser. 1, vol. 1, p. 252.

21. Ibid., p. 5.

22. Anderson letter, courtesy Chicago Historical Society.

23. Anderson to Crittenden letter, courtesy Chicago Historical Society Archives. Box xe-8.

24. Carl Sandburg, *Abraham Lincoln: The War Years, 1864–1865* (New York: Dell, 1954), vol. 3, p. 65.

25. Nathan Miller, *The U.S. Navy* (Annapolis: NI Press, 1997), p. 17.

CHAPTER TWO A Navy Yard Falls

1. John Niven, *Gideon Welles, Lincoln's Secretary of the Navy* (Baton Rouge: Louisiana State University Press, 1973), p. 339.

2. Donald L. Canney, *Lincoln's Navy: The Ships, Men and Organization, 1861–65* (Annapolis: Naval Institute Press, 1998), p. 48.

3. Niven, *Gideon Welles,* p. 340; Canney, *Lincoln's Navy,* pp. 48–49; Nathan Miller, *The U.S. Navy* (Annapolis: NI Press, 1997), p. 110.

4. HTECW; Musicant, *Divided Waters,* pp. 29–30.

5. Niven, *Gideon Welles,* p. 340; Welles to McCauley, ORN, ser. 1, vol. 4, p. 274; Musicant, *Divided Waters,* pp. 30–31.

6. Welles to McCauley, ORN, ser. 1, vol. 4, pp. 277–78.

7. Welles to McCauley, ORN, ser. 1, vol. 4, p. 275; Robert Collins Suhr, "Firing the Norfolk Navy Yard," *America's Civil War,* November 1996, p. 54.

8. Isherwood to Welles, ORN, ser. 1, vol. 4, pp. 280–81.

9. *Confederate Military History,* Guild Press of Indiana, Inc., vol. 3, chap. 8, pp. 124–25.

10. ORN, ser. 1, vol. 4, p. 308; *America's Civil War,* p. 56.

11. Paulding to Welles, ORN, ser. 1, vol. 4, p. 305; Niven, *Gideon Welles,* p. 344; *Confederate Military History,* vol. 3, chap. 8, pp. 125–26.

12. Wright to Townsend, ORN, ser. 1, vol. 2, pp. 22–23; *Confederate Military History,* pp. 125–26.

13. Robert Collins Suhr, "Firing the Norfolk Navy Yard," *America's Civil War,* p. 57. It is interesting to note that McCauley had completely lost his nerve and holed up in his office. It was only through the pleadings of his younger son that he was able to move out to safety on the *Pawnee.*

14. Paulding Report, ORN, ser. 1, vol. 4, p. 305.

15. Suhr, "Firing the Norfolk Navy Yard," p. 56; Musicant, *Divided Waters,* pp. 36–37.

16. Paulding Report, ORN, ser. 1, vol. 4, p. 305.

17. Wright to Townsend, ORA, ser. 1, vol. 2, pp. 21–22.

18. Wright Report, ORA, ser. 1, vol. 2, pp. 21–22; Suhr, "Firing the Norfolk Navy Yard," p. 56; ORN, ser.1, vol. 4, pp. 305–306.

19. "The Raw Confederate of 1861," *Southern Historical Society Papers,* vol. 21, 1894, pp. 346–47.

20. Trenchard to du Pont, ORN, ser. 1, vol. 4, p. 303.

21. Welles Report, *Confederate Military History,* vol. 3, chap. 8; vol. 12, p. 29.

22. Quoted in O. H. Hoehling, *Thunder at Hampton Roads* (New York: Da Capo Press, 1933), p. 35; CWNC, vol. 1, p. 42.

CHAPTER THREE The Blockade and the Blockade-Runners

1. *The Civil War at Charleston* (Charleston, SC: Post-Courier), pp. 2–3.

2. *Lincoln, Speeches and Readings, 1859–1865,* 2 vols. (New York: Library of America, 1974), pp. 223–24; Sandburg, *Abraham Lincoln,* pp. 38–39.

3. HTECW, pp. 208–9; CWD, pp. 225–26; Bill Riley, foreword, in Jefferson Davis, *Rise and Fall of the Confederate Government,* (New York: Joseph Yoseloff, 1958), foreword to vol. 1.

4. Harry Hansen, *The Civil War: A History* (New York: Penguin Books, 1991), p. 50.

5. Sandburg, *Abraham Lincoln,* pp. 38–39.

6. E. B. Potter and Chester W. Nimitz, *Sea Power: A Naval History* (Englewood Cliffs, NJ: Prentice-Hall, 1970), pp. 250–51. This, in the author's estimation, is the definitive work on naval history. See also Howard P. Nash Jr., *A Naval History of the Civil War* (New York: A. S. Barnes and Co., 1972), pp. 15–16; Coombe, *Thunder Along the Mississippi,* pp. 8–9. It was unconscionable of the Buchanan administration to allow the once magnificent U.S. Navy to fall into disrepute. It was a stark sign of an administration of undue caution and inaction.

7. Welles kept a diary during his tenure in office. Two editions of it have been published: *Diary of Gideon Welles,* 3 vols., introduction by John J. Morse Jr. (Boston: Houghton Mifflin Co., 1911) and *The Diary of Gideon Welles,* 3 vols., ed. Howard K. Beales (New York: W. W. Norton, 1960). An excellent biography is Richard West's *Gideon Welles: Lincoln's Navy Department* (Indianapolis: Bobbs-Merrill, 1943). The author's favorite is John Niven's *Gideon Welles.* The diaries themselves must be read with caution, because Welles was greatly opinionated and tended to reflect glory on himself.

8. Niven, *Gideon Welles,* p. 324.

9. An excellent biography of Scott is to be found in David W. Jordan, *Winfield Scott: A Soldier's Life* (Bloomington: Indiana University Press, 1988). A short but succinct biography appears in HTECW, p. 813, and *Who's Who in the Civil War* (New York: Facts on File, Inc., 1998).

10. The struggle to open the Mississippi River to the Gulf of Mexico, along the lines of the Anaconda Plan, is fully covered in Coombe, *Thunder Along the Mississippi.*

11. Niven, *Gideon Welles,* p. 357.

12. The subject of viable warships at the beginning of the blockade is aptly covered in Canney, *Lincoln's Navy.* Another good source is Nash, *Naval History of the Civil War.*

13. The long, tedious board reports are found in ORN, vols. 12 and 16. William Fowler offers a fine explanation of the board and its reports in his banner work *Under Two Flags: The American Navy in the Civil War* (New York: Avon Books, 1990).

14. Privateering is adequately covered in Potter and Nimitz, *Sea Power,* pp. 256–57; HTECW; and Horner, David, *Blockade Runners* (New York: Dodd Mead & Co., 1968), p. 14. See also *The Blockade: Runners and Raiders* (New York: Time-Life Books, Inc., 1983).

15. *The Blockade: Runners and Raiders,* pp. 14–16; Hansen, *The Civil War: A History,* pp. 49–51; Musicant, *Divided Waters,* chap. 4; Davis, *Rise and Fall of*

the Confederacy, pp. 343-44. Even though it was written later, Davis shows his total frustration with a recalcitrant Britain.

16. Philip Van Doren Stern, *The Confederate Navy: A Pictorial History* (New York: Da Capo Press, 1992); John C. Wideman, *Civil War Chronicles: Naval Warfare* (New York: Metro Books, 1997), pp. 30–33. The latter is a new book rich in information and original illustrations.

17. Horner, *The Blockade Runners,* p. 13. This is a very fine book on blockade-running, in spite of its age.

18. Ibid., p. 13.

19. Bern Anderson, *A Naval History of the Civil War* (New York: Da Capo Press, 1962), p. 222. Although the Confederate naval officers didn't receive extra pay for the dangerous work, they were compensated in gold.

20. The amazing story of the *Hattie* is related in Horner, *The Blockade Runners,* chap. 11.

21. Ibid., pp. 204–6. My research assistant and I were allowed to examine many of the artifacts from this vessel at the U.S. Archaeological Underwater Unit at Fort Fisher during our visit there.

22. Niven, *Gideon Welles,* pp. 347–48; Canney, *Lincoln's Navy,* pp. 30–33; *The Blockade Runners and Raiders,* p. 20.

23. Potter and Nimitz, *Sea Power,* p. 251.

CHAPTER FOUR A New Navy Is Born

1. Davis, *Rise and Fall of the Confederate Government,* p. 241. In his introduction to the two volumes, Bill I. Riley paints a picture of Davis as a most complicated man who was admired by some, disliked by others. The president did, nevertheless, fulfill his job with all the energy and intelligence he could muster.

2. For Mallory, the student is advised to consult Joseph T. Durkin, *Stephen Mallory: Confederate Naval Chief* (Chapel Hill: University of North Carolina Press, 1954); capsule biographies are available in *Who Was Who in the Civil War; Dictionary of American Biographies,* 22 vols. (New York: Scribner's, 1928–1932), vol. 1; and HTECW, p. 471.

3. William N. Still Jr., *Iron Afloat* (Columbia: University of South Carolina Press, 1971), pp. 7–9; 1971, *Confederate Military History,* vol. 12, chap. 2, pp. 8–9.

4. Confederate Navy Correspondence, 1861–1865, ORN, ser. 2, vol. 2, p. 40.

5. WCWN, pp. 199–200. This work remains the most comprehensive account of both Confederate and Union navies. Coombe, *Thunder Along the Mississippi,* p. 44; Musicant, *Divided Waters,* p. 68; B&L, vol. 1, pp. 624–25.

6.   Confederate Navy Correspondence, ORN, ser. 2, vol. 2, p. 64.

7.   U.S. Naval Chronology, part 3, p. 89.

8.   Ibid., p. 74.

9.   *Confederate Military History*, vol. 12, chap. 2, p. 9.

10.   CWNC, part 3, p. 151; Stern, *The Confederate Navy*, p. 233.

11.   CWNC, part 3, p. 151; Stern, *The Confederate Navy*, pp. 198–99; 233–34; HTECW, p. 521. When Richmond was evacuated, on April 3, 1865, the *Patrick Henry* was burned by the Confederates to prevent capture.

12.   Confederate Navy Correspondence, ORN, ser. 2, vol. 2, p. 64.

13.   Bulloch to Mallory, ORN, ser. 2, vol. 2, p. 85.

14.   HTECW, p. 89; see also CWD, p. 98.

15.   Stern, *The Confederate Navy*, p. 19.

16.   The planning and construction of the Eads ironclads is extensively covered in Coombe, *Thunder Along the Mississippi*, chap. 2; see also Nash, *A Naval History of the Civil War*, chap. 1; and USNC, ser. 2, vol. 2.

17.   WCWN, p. 229.

18.   For the saga of the star-crossed *Manassas*, consult Coombe, *Thunder Along the Mississippi*, chap. 9; see also Fowler, *Under Two Flags*, chap. 6.

19.   For an excellent account of the concept and construction of *Mississippi* and *Louisiana*, consult Raimondo Luraghi, *A History of the Confederate Navy* (Annapolis: Naval Institute Press, 1996), p. 598. Luraghi, an Italian-born historian, has written a classical and definitive history of the Confederate navy, compiled over many years. See Jack Coombe, *Gunfire Around the Gulf*, (New York: Bantam Books, 1999), chap. 9. It is this author's opinion that Mr. Luraghi has been largely underrated by historians.

20.   For an account of the amazing *Arkansas* story, consult Coombe, *Thunder Along the Mississippi*, pp. 153–60. Most of this material, gathered at the source of construction, Yazoo, Mississippi, was hitherto unreleased; the official account is found in ORN, ser. 1, vols. 18, 19, and 22. The serious student should also consult B&L, vol. 3, p. 556.

21.   A complete list of Confederate ironclad histories is listed in WCWN, pp. 200–209; see also DAFS, in 9 volumes.

22.   USNC, vol. 2, p. 91.

23.   Luraghi, *History of the Confederate Navy*, p. 346.

24.   Richard Wheeler, *Voices of the Civil War*, (New York: Thomas Y. Crowell, 1976), p. 56.

25.   Quoted in Musicant, *Divided Waters*, p. 75.

CHAPTER FIVE The First Amphibious Operations, Part 1: Cape Hatteras

1. Fowler, *Under Two Flags,* p. 60; Musicant, *Divided Waters,* chap. 6; Nash, *A Naval History of the Civil War,* p. 50; ORN, ser. 1, vol. 6, p. 9.

2. Welles to Stringham, ORN, ser. 1, vol. 6, p. 110.

3. ORN, ser. 1, vol. 6, p. 199. The board, however, recommended the sinking of old hulks filled with stone ballasts in the strategic waterways of this region, namely, Hatteras, Cape Henry, and Cape Lookout. Interestingly, they skirted the use of military force.

4. Godfrey Report, ORN, ser. 1, vol. 6, p. 111. N. P. Godfrey, who submitted this report, made the comment that the Federal government must have their sharpest agents in various Confederate forts.

5. This controversial figure's biography is covered in Richard W. West Jr., *Lincoln's Scapegoat General: A Life of Benjamin F. Butler, 1818–1893* (Boston: Houghton Mifflin, 1965). His correspondence is covered in *The Private and Official Correspondence of General Benjamin Butler,* 5 vols. (Norwood, MA: Plimpton, 1917). Good capsule summaries are found in *Who Was Who in the Civil War* and in HTECW, p. 27.

6. There appears to be no definitive biography of Flag Officer Stringham. Much has been written about him, and excellent biographies are found in *Who Was Who in the Civil War* and HTECW, p. 27.

7. Wool, Special Orders No. 13, ORN, ser. 1, vol. 6, p. 112.

8. HTECW; Musicant, *Divided Waters,* pp. 78–80; B&L, vol. 1, p. 6634; Fowler, *Under Two Flags,* pp. 62–63; ORN, ser. 1, vol. 6, p. 120. The two steamers *George Peabody* and *Adelaide* were originally purchased as block ships but were used as transports in his expedition.

9. Log of U.S.S. *Minnesota,* ORN, ser. 1, vol. 6, p. 140.

10. Col. Martin Report, ORN, ser. 1, vol. 6, p. 140.

11. Gillis to Welles, ORN, ser. 1, vol. 1, p. 140.

12. Col. Martin Report, ORN, ser. 1, vol. 6, p. 140.

13. Ibid., p. 140.

14. Log of U.S.S. *Minnesota,* ORN, ser. 1, vol. 6, p. 122. Stringham took notice of the fort gunners' failure to respond effectively because they were outranged.

15. Stringham to Welles, ORN, ser. 1, vol. 6, p. 124.

16. Fox to Stringham, ORN, ser. 1, vol. 6, p. 166: Musicant, *Divided Waters,* pp. 82–83.

17. Col. Martin Report, ORN, ser. 1, vol. 6, p. 141; Anderson, *A Naval History of the Civil War,* p. 49.

18. Andrews Report, ORN, ser. 1, vol. 6, p. 144; Rush Hopkins, "East Coast

Operations in Carolina," B&L, vol. 1, pp. 632–33; Log of *Monticello,* ORN, ser. 1, vol. 6, p. 123.

19. Anderson, *A Naval History of the Civil War,* p. 51; ORA, ser. 1, vol. 6, p. 583; ORN, ser. 1, vol. 6, p. 120.
20. Stringham to Welles, ORN, ser. 1, vol. 6, p. 126.
21. Davis, *Rise and Fall of the Confederate Government,* vol. 1, p. 77.
22. *Confederate Military History,* vol. 12, chap. 3, p. 17.

CHAPTER SIX The First Amphibious Operations, Part 2: Port Royal
1. ORN, ser. 1, vol. 12, pp. 201–6; B&L, vol. 1, pp. 672.
2. Welles to du Pont, ORN, ser. 1, vol. 12, pp. 214–15.
3. Davis, *Rise and Fall of the Confederate Government,* vol. 2, pp. 77–78; Nash, *A Naval History of the Civil War,* pp. 56–57.
4. B&L, vol. 1, p. 691; Musicant, *Divided Waters,* p. 97.
5. Niven, *Gideon Welles,* p. 359; C. Vann Woodward and Elisabeth Muhlenfeld, eds., *The Private Mary Chestnut: The Unpublished Diaries* (New York: Oxford University Press, 1984), p. 359. It is interesting to note that Mary Chestnut, in her diary for October 24, 1861, said she was told by authorities that the Yankees would attack Bull's Bay and Port Royal simultaneously, to prevent the Confederates from concentrating their forces.
6. Of Goldsborough, there are excellent capsulated biographies in HTECW and CWD. For obvious reasons, du Pont is covered more widely: H. A. du Pont, *Rear Admiral Samuel Francis du Pont* (New York: National American Society, 1956), and John D. Hays, *Samuel Francis du Pont: A Selection from His Civil War Letters,* 3 vols. (Ithaca, NY: Cornell University Press, 1969).
7. James C. Bradford, ed., *Captains of the Old Steam Navy* (Annapolis: Naval Institute Press, 1986), p. 149; ORN, ser. 1, vol. 12, pp. 208–209.
8. *Confederate Military History,* vol. 5, chap. 2, p. 30.
9. It has always been a mystery as to why these furtive traitors in the Federal government were never tried for treason after the war.
10. ORN, ser. 1., vol. 12, pp. 220–21; Potter and Nimitz, *Sea Power,* p. 252. These historians maintain that 13,000 troops were under Sherman's command, instead of 12,000.
11. WCWN, p. 27; DAFS, p. 128; B&L, vol. 1, p. 691. Many of these vessels were scattered at various stations and were to be brought in while the force was at Hampton Roads.
12. Musicant, *Divided Waters,* p. 95.
13. Miller, *The U.S. Navy,* p. 117; Canney, *Lincoln's Navy,* p. 189.

14. Du Pont Report, ORN, ser. 1, vol. 12, p. 259; B&L, vol. 1, p. 674; Potter and Nimitz, *Sea Power*, p. 242.

15. Sherman Report to Adjutant General, ORN, ser. 1, vol. 12, p. 288.

16. B&L, vol. 1, p. 691; *Savannah Republican*, Nov. 12, 1861.

17. Wagener Report, ORN, ser. 1, vol. 12, pp. 262–65.

18. Du Pont's Action Report, ORN, ser. 1, vol. 12, p. 262.

19. Log of *Susquehanna*, ORN, ser. 1, vol. 12, p. 275.

20. Log of *Pawnee*, ORN, ser. 1, vol. 12, p. 275.

21. Du Pont Report, ORN, ser. 1, vol. 12, p. 262.

22. Wagener Report, ORN, ser. 1, vol. 12, p. 262.

23. Elliot Report, ORN, ser. 1, vol. 12, pp. 315–17.

24. Pickens Report, ORN, ser. 1, vol. 12, p. 414: Burton, *The Siege of Charleston*, p. 75.

25. Davis, *Rise and Fall of the Confederate Government*, p. 79.

26. Musicant, *Divided Waters*, p. 101; B&L, vol. 1, pp. 689–90.

27. Quoted in "Life After Occupation," *The Blockade: Runners and Raiders*, p. 34.

CHAPTER SEVEN The *Trent* Tribulation

1. There are no definitive biographical books on Mason and Slidell. However, excellent short bios are found in HTECW, pp. 479 and 682, and CWD, pp. 516 and 765.

2. Mason to Hunter, ORN, ser. 1, vol. 1, p. 149.

3. Wilkes to Welles, ORN, ser. 1, vol. 1, p. 149.

4. Wilkes to Welles, ORN, ser. 1, vol. 1, pp. 129–30; Bern Anderson, *By Sea and By River: A Naval History of the Civil War* (New York: Da Capo Press, 1962), p. 182; B&L, vol. 1, p. 135.

5. Log of *San Jacinto*, ORN, ser. 1, vol. 1, pp. 132-33.

6. Wilkes, "Captain Wilkes Seizes Mason and Slidell," in Henry Steele Commager, *Blue and Gray*, 2 vols. (New York: Meridian, 1973), vol. 1, p. 530.

7. Fairfax Report, ORN, ser. 1, vol. 1, pp. 133–34; *Confederate Military History*, vol. 1, ch. 15, pp. 425–26. Fairfax was well aware this was a most unusual circumstance.

8. A. E. Pollard, *The Lost Cause* (New York: Gramercy Books, 1994), p. 175; B&L, vol. 2, p. 139.

9. D. M. Fairfax, B&L, vol. 2, p. 134. Fairfax later fought with Farragut and in the siege of Charleston. He was named a rear admiral in 1880.

10. Niven, *Gideon Welles*, p. 445.

11. Fairfax, B&L, vol. 2, p. 135.

12. *New York Times,* November 20, 1861.

13. Earl Russell to Lord Lyons, ORN, ser. 1, vol. 1, pp. 160–61; also Allan Nevins, *The War for the Union: The Improvised War, 1861–1862* (New York: Charles Scribner's Sons, 1959), pp. 388–99.

14. Seward's long letter can be found in its entirety in ORN, ser. 1, vol. 1, pp. 177-87; see also Niven, *Gideon Welles,* pp. 445–46; Nevins, *The War for the Union,* p. 388; and B&L, vol. 2, pp. 141–42.

15. Diary of Maria L. Daly, quoted in Kirchenberger, *Eyewitness to the Civil War,* p. 146.

16. Woodward and Muhlenfeld, eds., *Private Diary of Mary Chestnut,* pp. 203, 204-5.

17. Quoted in Wheeler, *Voices of the Civil War,* p. 57.

18. *Confederate Military History,* vol. 1, chap. 15, p. 426.

19. CWNC, vol. 1, p. 40.

20. Geoffrey Smith, "Charles Wilkes: The Naval Officer, Explorer and Diplomat," in James Bradford, ed., *Captains of the Old Steam Navy* (Annapolis: Naval Institute Press, 1986), pp. 65–66.

CHAPTER EIGHT Mopping Up the Sounds: Roanoke

1. Matthew Fontain Maury, "A vindication of Virginia and the South," in *Southern Historical Society Papers,* vol. 1, no. 2, pp. 104–105. These papers, issued after the war, are valuable in that one gets a retrospective on the weaknesses of the Confederacy from many of those who participated in the war.

2. McClellan to Burnside, ORN, ser. 1, vol. 6, p. 508; Anderson, *The Naval History of the Civil War,* p. 62.

3. McClellan to Burnside, ORN, ser. 1, vol. 6, p. 508; "Invading the Island Sea," in *The Coastal War* (New York: Time-Life Books, 1984), pp. 17–19.

4. Musicant, *Divided Waters,* p. 125; Stern, *The Confederate Navy, A Pictorial History,* p. 68.

5. *The Coastal War,* p. 18.

6. John G. Barrett, *The Civil War in North Carolina* (Chapel Hill: University of North Carolina Press, 1963), pp. 70–72.

7. Henry Van Brunt, Flag Secretary, Rough Notes on Naval Expedition to Roanoke Island, ORN, ser. 1, vol. 6, pp. 581–83.

8. Ibid., p. 588; *The Coastal War,* p. 24; Barrett, *The Civil War in North Carolina,* p. 74–76.

9. Burnside Report, ORN, ser. 1, vol. 9, pp. 76–77; Nash, *A Naval History of the Civil War*, p. 75; *The Coastal War*, p. 24; B&L, vol. 2, pp. 642–43. The similarity to World War II landings with troops storming ashore under the protecting curtain of fire from naval guns is astounding. Another is in Goldsborough's plan for a series of signals between himself and the field commanders in order to prevent bombardment of friendly troops and to shell particular locations as specified by the field commanders.

10. Flag Officer Lynch Report, ORN, ser. 1, vol. 9, p. 594.

11. ORA, ser. 1, vol. 9, p. 75; Goldsborough Report to Welles, ORN, ser. 1, vol. 9, p. 550.

12. Lynch Report to Mallory, ORN, ser. 1, vol. 9, pp. 594–97. Lynch was shackled with an inferior naval force, as opposed to the Union's, but he was determined to do the best he could with what he had.

13. Ibid., p. 596; B&L, vol. 2, p. 645; *Confederate Military History*, vol. 4, chap. 3, p. 38. The C.S.S. *Ellis* was captured in spite of the commander's order to blow her up. The move was thwarted by a black coal heaver who wanted it captured by the Union.

14. *Confederate Military History*, vol. 4, chap. 4, p. 38; *The Coastal War*, p. 34.

15. Quoted in *The Coastal War*, p. 37. For a detailed description of the New Bern battle, consult B&L, vol. 2, pp. 647–52; Nash, *A Naval History of the Civil War*, chap. 11; and also HTECW, p. 524.

16. Quoted in Kirchenberger, *Eyewitness History of the Civil War*, p. 99.

17. First Session, 1st Confederate Congress, *Southern Historical Papers*, vol. 6, ser. 44, p. 28.

18. Ibid.

19. Ibid., p. 29.

CHAPTER NINE *Monitor* vs. *Merrimack*, **Part 1: The Antagonists**

1. Confederate Navy Department Correspondence, ORN, ser. 2, vol. 2, pp. 67–68.

2. Ibid., p. 68; John V. Quarstein, *The Battle of the Ironclads* (Charleston, NC: Arcadia Publishing, 1999), p. 27. Quarstein is the director of the Virginia War Museum in Newport News and a nationally recognized authority on the *Monitor* and *Merrimack*.

3. Fletcher Pratt, *A Short Naval History of the Civil War* (New York: Pocket Books, Inc., 1956), pp. 65–66.

4. Confederate Navy Correspondence, ORN, ser. 2, vol. 2, p. 40; Quarstein, p. 29.

5. John M. Brooke, "The *Virginia* or the *Merrimac:* The Real Projector," *Southern Historical Society Papers,* vol. 19 (19), pp. 5–6.

6. WCWN, p. 27. This is still best and far away the most authoritative work on Civil War navies.

7. The specifications of the *Merrimack (Virginia)* were obtained from many sources, including DAFS, vol. 4, p. 338; "The *Merrimack* and the *Monitor:* Report of the Committee on Naval Affairs," *Southern Historical Society Papers,* vol. 13, pp. 91–92; Musicant, *Divided Waters,* pp. 139–41; *Comparing the Ironclads,* U.S.S. *Cairo* Museum, Vicksburg Military Park; Still, *Iron Afloat,* pp. 23–26; B&L, vol. 1, pp. 692–93; Stern, *The Confederate Navy,* p. 81. Most agree, with minor exceptions, on the accepted dimensions on the configuration of *Merrimack.* Also, recent underwater archeological work on the wreck of the *Monitor* verifies the configuration of that vessel, with only minor variations.

8. Catesby ap R. Jones, *"Monitor* and *Merrimac,"* courtesy of the archives of the Maritime Museum, Newport News, Virginia. See also "Battle of Hampton Roads," in Jack Sweetman, ed., *Great American Sea Battles* (Annapolis: Naval Institute Press, 1998), pp. 110-11.

9. Quarstein, *The Battle of the Ironclads,* p. 35; Jones, *"Monitor* and *Merrimac,"* p. 66.

10. William Cline, "The Ironclad Ram *Virginia:* The Story of Her Launching Accomplishments," *Southern Historical Society Papers,* vol. 32, p. 243.

11. For biographies on Buchanan, consult Charles Lee Lewis, *Admiral Franklin Buchanan: Fearless Man of Action* (Baltimore: Norman Remington Co., 1929); Bradford, ed., *Captains of the Old Steam Navies,* pp. 87–112. For short bios, consult HTECW, p. 86, and CWD, p. 94.

12. Quoted in Musicant, *Divided Waters,* p. 144; see also Robert J. Schneller, *A Quest for Glory: A Biography of Rear Admiral John A. Dahlgren* (Annapolis: Naval Institute Press, 1996), p. 194. It was this report by which Buchanan expressed the impossibility of the *Virginia's* sailing out of Hampton Roads. Mallory's lack of knowledge concerning the capabilities of the ironclad are astounding, considering his naval background. The only answer is that, like everyone else, he did not understand the ironclads, untried and new on the world naval scene.

13. CWNC, vol. 1, p. 26.

14. Brooke, "The *Virginia,* or *Merrimack:* Her Real Projector," *Southern Historical Society Papers,* vol. 19, p. 31.

15. Quoted in Hoehling, *Thunder at Hampton Roads,* p. 84.

16. Quoted in Kirchenberger, *Eyewitness History of the Civil War,* p. 99; Wheeler, *Voices of the Civil War,* p. 36.

17. Niven, *Gideon Welles,* p. 364.

18. Ibid., pp. 336–37; Musicant, *Divided Waters,* pp. 158–59; Quarstein, *The Battle of the Ironclads,* pp. 40–41.

19. Anderson, *By Sea and by River,* pp. 7–8; B&L, vol. 1, pp. 730–31; Edward Beach, *The United States Navy: 200 Years* (New York: Henry Holt & Company, 1986), pp. 250–55; Nimitz and Potter, *Sea Power,* p. 265.

20. Quarstein, *Battle of the Ironclads,* p. 42.

21. "Report on the Committee on Naval Affairs," *Southern Historical Society Papers,* vol. 12, p. 91.

22. The one definitive work on Ericsson and the *Monitor* is, of course, William Church, *Life of John Ericsson* (New York: Scribner's, 1911).

23. See James Turtius de Kay's excellent work, *Monitor* (New York: Walker and Company, 1997); Beach, *The United States Navy,* pp. 265–66; HTECW, p. 246. Additional material on the *Monitor* is from Hoehling, *Thunder at Hampton Roads,* chap. 2; Musicant, *Divided Waters,* chap. 12; Quarstein, *Battle of the Ironclads,* pp. 40–44; Statistical Data of Ships, ORN, ser. 2, vol. 1. The author is most indebted to the *Monitor* National Marine Sanctuary, Newport News, for its series of pamphlets and some unpublished data generously presented to the author, along with many charts of all sizes, plus a model of the ship. For Ericsson's own descriptive account, see B&L, vol. 1, pp. 730–44. Some of Ericsson's dimensions on the *Monitor* are substantiated by the NOAA from the wreck of the *Monitor.* See also William C. Davis, *Duel Between the First Ironclads* (New York: Doubleday, 1975), pp. 46–47; Donald Canney, *Mr. Lincoln's Navy,* chap. 5; also consult WCWN, p. 4.

24. For information on Fort Pickens and Pensacola Naval Station, see Coombe, *Gunfire Around the Gulf,* chap. 3. For biographical material on Worden, consult Clarence Edward Macartney, *Mr. Lincoln's Admirals* (New York: Funk & Wagnalls, 1956). The best bio, in the author's opinion, is "John Lorimer Worden" in *Ironclad Captains,* Monitor National Marine Society Report Series (Washington, DC: U.S. Government Printing Office, 1998).

25. Some of the accounts of the *Monitor's* voyage to Hampton Roads err in that the *Seth Low* did not take her in tow until they were well clear of New York Harbor and not from the Brooklyn Navy Yard as first reported. I followed an account of the voyage in a letter by Samuel Dana Greene to his parents dated March 16, 1862, courtesy Mariners' Museum archives, Newport News, Virginia. Another source I followed is an undated letter to his father from John J. N. Webber, acting master of the *Monitor,* available in both the Chicago Historical Society and the Fort Monroe Historical Archives.

26. Greene letter; Webber letter; see also Hoehling, *Thunder at Hampton Roads,* p. 88. The executive officer seemed to have been the calmest one and a take-

charge person on board the *Monitor* on her near-fatal journey to Hampton Roads, during which even the captain was seasick. Greene's calm demeanor would also benefit him in the struggles to come. Perhaps he was the one person who single-handedly guided the stricken ironclad to safety when all seemed to be hopeless.

27. Monograph *The Monitor and the Merrimack,* Tales of Old Fort Monroe, no. 12., Fort Monroe Archives. The small size of the ironclad failed to instill much confidence from observers in the fleet that night, after they had witnessed the awesome size and power of the *Virginia* and the carnage and destruction she engendered.

28. Greene letter; de Kay, *Monitor,* p. 183; John Wideman, *Naval Warfare: Courage and Conflict on the Water* (New York: Friedman/Fairfax Publishers, 1997), p. 76. The plucky ironclad steamed out to meet her larger antagonist in what has been described by some writers as an "iron David against an iron Goliath."

CHAPTER TEN *Monitor* vs. *Merrimack,* Part 2: The Conflict

1. Unfortunately, for some unknown reason, no photo of the *Virginia* exists. However, some sketches exist based on eyewitness reports, and a reasonable likeness of the craft has been created. The author has been especially captivated by paintings of the vessel by Tom W. Freeman in Wideman, *Naval Warfare,* p. 70. Freedman did intensive research before painting his impressions of the famous ironclad.

2. CWNC, vol. 2, p. 5.

3. Quoted in de Kay, *Monitor,* p. 133.

4. Quoted in Davis, Pohanka, and Troiani, *Civil War Journal: The Battles,* p. 103.

5. For those interested in the Peninsula Campaign, consult the excellent account by Alexander Webb, *The Peninsula: McClellan's Campaign of 1862,* vol. 3 of Scribner's Campaigns (New York: Scribner's Sons, 1882). Some original copies of this work are still available. J. Miller's three-volume work on the campaign will be reissued, but no further information was available at press time. For short accounts, consult HTECW, p. 571, and ORN, ser. 1, vol. 11.

6. E. V. White, "The First Iron-Clad Naval Engagement in the World," courtesy of the Casemate Museum archives, Fort Monroe. White was an officer in the Engineer Corps of the Confederate Army. When the call came for volunteers to man the *Virginia,* he responded and became an engineer on board. His narrative is one of the first and most factual Confederate accounts consulted by the author.

7. "The Ram *Merrimack*," *Richmond Dispatch*, Feb. 21–22, 1892, in *Southern Historical Society Papers*, vol. 20, p. 20–25; Buchanan Report to Mallory, courtesy of the Mariners' Museum Library archives, Newport News.

8. All information on Union ships culled from WCWN and DAFS.

9. Beach, *The United States Navy: 200 Years*, p. 282. The *Virginia's* painfully slow turnaround did give the Union ships an opportunity to set battle conditions, but as events proved, it was for the most part a futile effort because of the startled Union crews' perception on the apparent invulnerability of the enemy.

10. Quarstein, *Battle of the Ironclads*, p. 60; de Kay, *Monitor*, p. 161; Still, *Iron Afloat*, p. 29.

11. Van Brunt to Welles, courtesy National Archives, Great Lakes Division Record Group 45: Microfilm 89. The *Minnesota* received a shot from a Confederate battery on Sewell's Point that "crippled her mainmast."

12. Pervaiance Report, courtesy National Archives, Great Lakes Division Record Group 45: Microfilm 89.

13. William Morrissett, "A Confederate Eyewitness Account of the *Merrimack* Battle," compiled by Weldon B. Heston, courtesy Mariners' Museum archives.

14. E. J. White, "The First Iron-Clad Naval Engagement in the World," p. 110, courtesy Casemate Museum, Fort Monroe.

15. Wheeler, *Voices of the Civil War*, p. 66.

16. Quoted in "The Ram *Merrimack*," *Southern Historical Society Papers*, vol. 20, pp. 8–9.

17. Quarstein, *The Battle of the Ironclads*, p. 61; Wheeler, *Voices of the Civil War*, p. 67; Musicant, *Divided Waters*, pp. 150–51. The last of these includes a description of the carnage on the dying *Cumberland* that is the best this author has seen.

18. Buchanan to Mallory, courtesy Mariners' Museum archives. Buchanan praised Commodore Tucker's flotilla for its successful run past Union shore batteries, and described the run as "miraculous." See also "Ram *Merrimack*," *Southern Historical Society Papers*, vol. 20, pp. 8–9; Buchanan to Mallory, ORN, ser. 1, vol. 7, p. 44, and Davis, *Rise and Fall of the Confederate Government*, pp. 197–98.

19. John Taylor Wood, "The First Fight of Iron-Clads," in B&L, vol. 1, pp. 700–701. One observer on the *Congress* describes his walking along the decks on the arms, legs, heads, and organs of shattered crewmen.

20. Buchanan to Mallory, courtesy Mariners' Museum archives. Buchanan did not admit being wounded, but merely stated he passed the command on to Jones; Pendergrast to Welles, ORN, ser. 1, vol. 7. The *Cumberland's* executive officer maintained that in view of the carnage and damage to his ship, and the fact that

there could be no relief from the *Minnesota,* he hauled down the colors "without any further loss of life on our part." See also Wood, "The First Fight of the Ironclads," for a graphic description of the surrender of the *Congress.*

21. Rev R. C. Foute, "Echoes from Hampton Roads," *Southern Historical Society Papers,* vol. 19, p. 247. Foute, a midshipman on the *Virginia,* maintained that the "victorious" vessel was received with "the wildest shouts of joy."

22. The incidents of Stanton's behavior at Lincoln's cabinet meeting is covered in Niven, *Gideon Welles,* p. 406, and in Hoehling, *Thunder at Hampton Roads,* chap. 11.

23. Worden Report to Welles, courtesy Mariners' Museum archives.

24. Marston's decision to circumvent orders is discussed in Dana Greene, "In the *Monitor* Turret," in B&L, ser. 1, vol. 7, p. 721.

25. Ibid., p. 722; Worden report to Welles, Mariners' Museum archives, p. 5; Straubing, *Civil War Eyewitness Accounts,* p. 146.

26. Greene Report, Mariners' Museum archives; Greene, "In the *Monitor* Turret," p. 722.

27. Quoted in Quarstein, *The Battle of the Ironclads,* p. 76.

28. Greene Report, Mariners' Museum archives, p. 6; John J. N. Letter, p. 2; courtesy, Casemate Museum, Fort Monroe.

29. Wood, "The First Fight of the Ironclads," pp. 701–702.

30. Greene Report, Mariners' Museum archives, p. 6; Greene, "In the *Monitor* Turret," p. 723.

31. Van Brunt Report, courtesy National Archives, Great Lakes Division Record Group 45, M 125.

32. William Frederick Keeler, "How the *Merrimack* fought the *Monitor,*" quoted in Straubing, *Civil War Eyewitness Accounts,* pp. 148–50.

33. Greene letter, Mariners' Museum archives, p. 7.

34. Wood, "The First Fight of the Ironclads," p. 702.

35. Greene letter, Mariners' Museum archives, p. 7; Greene, "In the *Monitor* Turret," p. 727; Sweetman, *Great American Sea Battles,* p. 125.

36. Van Brunt Report to Welles, courtesy Mariners' Museum archives, p. 5.

37. Jones to Mallory, ORN, ser. 1, vol. 7, p. 46; "The Ram *Merrimack,*" *Southern Historical Society Papers,* vol. 20, p. 16.

38. Greene letter, Mariners' Museum archives, p. 8; Worden Report to Welles, Mariners' Museum archives, p. 6; John Webber letter, Casemate Museum archives, Fort Monroe, p. 3.

39. Quoted in Quarstein, *The Battle of the Ironclads,* p. 92.

40. de Kay, *Monitor,* p. 198.

CHAPTER ELEVEN *Monitor* vs. *Merrimack,* Part 3: The Aftermath

1. Welles to Hale, May 30, 1864, courtesy Mariners' Museum Archives.

2. Davis to Confederate Congress, April 10, 1862, ORN, ser. 1, vol. 7, p. 43; Bruce Catton, *Reflections on the Civil War* (New York: Berkeley Books, 1982), p. 137.

3. At this writing, there is no newly published biography of Tattnall. One old biography is Charles C. Jones, *The Life and Services of Commodore Josiah Tattnall* (Savannah: Morning News Steam Printing House, 1878). Excellent bios are to be found in HTECW, CWD, and *Who Was Who in the Civil War.*

4. Extracts from the Court-Martial of Flag Officer Josiah Tattnall, C.S.N., ORN, ser. 1, vol. 7, pp. 751–99.

5. Quoted in "The Ram *Merrimack,*" *Southern Historical Society Papers,* vol. 20, p. 20.

6. Ibid., p. 21; Stern, *The Confederate Navy,* p. 88: Still, *Iron Afloat,* pp. 38–39.

7. William Still Jr., *Ironclad Captains: The Commanding Officers of the U.S.S. Monitor* (Washington, DC: U.S. Government Printing Office, 1988). Biographies of six captains of the famous ironclad during her short career are found in this excellent work.

8. Ibid., p. 173.

9. Greene letter, Mariners' Museum archives. Greene continued his naval career after the *Monitor* was gone. Unfortunately, he committed suicide in December 1884. It is believed that a brain tumor, plus untiring, carping criticism, contributed to his death.

10. Tattnall General Order, ORN, ser. 1, vol. 7, p. 760.

11. Quarstein, *The Battle of the Ironclads,* p. 106; Stern, *The Confederate Navy,* p. 88.

12. The Goldman brothers' Civil War letters, transcribed by Bobby Goldman. The author is indebted to Mark Hopkins of Houston for these letters. The Goldman brothers served in the war, but not together. Jasper's letter presents a different view of the reasons Tattnall could not take the *Virginia* up the James. The presence of a sunken hulk in midstream is not mentioned in other research material.

13. Quoted in Still, *Iron Afloat,* p. 40. Tattnall was court-martialed in 1862 for the destruction of the *Virginia.* The court gave him an honorable acquittal, stating that the destruction of the ram was justified.

14. Mark Nesbitt, *Rebel Rivers* (Mechanicsburg, PA: Stackpole Books, 1993); Fowler, *Under Two Flags,* pp. 91–92; Still, *Ironclad Captains,* p. 45.

15. Still, *Ironclad Captains,* p. 68.

16. Quoted in Hoehling, *Thunder at Hampton Roads,* p. 188; Still, *Ironclad Captains,* p. 69.

17. Lee to Trenchard, ORN, ser. 1, vol. 8, p. 318.

18. Lee to Welles, ORN, ser. 1, vol. 8, pp. 344–46.

19. Helmsman Francis Butts, quoted in Quarstein, *The Battle of the Ironclads,* p. 122; Lee to Welles, ORN, ser. 1, vol. 8, p. 344.

20. Paymaster William Frederick Keeler, *Aboard the U.S.S. Monitor, 1862: The Letters of Paymaster William Frederick Keeler, U.S. Navy, to His Wife, Anna* (Annapolis: Naval Institute Press), pp. 253–60.

21. Keeler, *Aboard the U.S.S. Monitor,* p. 260.

22. The story of the *Monitor*'s discovery is covered in *A Look at the Monitor National Marine Sanctuary: Past, Present and Future,* published by the *Monitor* National Marine Sanctuary, Sanctuaries & Reserve Division, National Oceanic and Atmospheric Administration, September 1994. The author and his research assistant were privileged to view at close hand some of the artifacts, through the kind permission of NOAA personnel at Newport News. We were privileged to view fragments of armor plates and the propeller of the famous ironclad on display at the Mariners' Museum.

CHAPTER TWELVE Fort Pulaski Falls

1. Detailed narratives of the Mississippi River and Gulf of Mexico campaigns are covered in Coombe, *Thunder Along the Mississippi* and *Gunfire Around the Gulf.*

2. Howard Blair, *Adventure Guide to Georgia* (Edison, NJ: Hunter Publishing, 1997), pp. 198–99; Stern, *The Confederate Navy,* p. 74; Michael J. Varhola, *Everyday Life in the Civil War* (Cincinnati: Writer's Digest Books, 1999), p. 249. The latter is a new book that, in spite of its title, supplies an amazing amount of military information.

3. Musicant, *Divided Waters,* p. 104; *Confederate Military History,* vol. 6, chap. 4, p. 89.

4. *Confederate Military History,* vol. 6, chap. 4, p. 89.

5. Ibid., p. 83; Lee Report, ORN, ser. 1, vol. 12, pp. 505–506.

6. Short biographies on Gillmore are found in HTECW, p. 310, and CWD, p. 343. Gillmore's own narrative of the assault on Fort Pulaski is found in B&L, vol. 2, pp. 1–12.

7. Commander Rodgers Report, U.S.S. *Wabash,* ORN, ser. 1, vol. 12, pp. 730–31. Information on the James rifle is from Dean S. Thomas, *Cannons: An Introduction to Civil War Artillery* (Gettysburg: Thomas Publications, 1985), p. 42.

8. *Confederate Military History,* pp. 89–90; Gillmore Report, ORA, ser. 1, vol. 6, chap. 15, pp. 145–46.

9.   Gillmore Report, ser. 1, vol. 6, chap. 15, p. 9.

10. As quoted in Robert J. Schneller Jr., *A Quest for Glory: A Biography of Rear Admiral John A. Dahlgren* (Annapolis: Naval Institute Press, 1996), p. 253.

11. Hunter to Stanton, ORA, ser. 1, vol. 6, p. 134.

12. Gillmore Report, ORA, ser. 1, vol. 6, p. 146.

13. Schneller, *Quest for Glory,* p. 254. Schneller wrote that Gillmore went on to play a major role in the reduction of Charleston in July.

CHAPTER THIRTEEN Fort Sumter Revisited

1.   For detailed studies of the Mississippi River and Gulf of Mexico campaigns, consult Coombe, *Thunder Along the Mississippi* and *Gunfire Around the Gulf.*

2.   Musicant, *Divided Waters,* p. 369.

3.   Inside front cover, *The Civil War at Charleston;* Burton, *The Siege of Charleston,* pp. 156–57; Anderson, *By Sea and by River,* pp. 156–59; Stern, *The Confederate Navy,* p. 163; *Confederate Military History,* vol. 5, chap. 5, p. 98.

4.   *Charleston Courier,* March 12 and 13, 1862; Still, *Iron Afloat,* pp. 81–82.

5.   WCWN, p. 295; HTECW, pp. 139, 555.

6.   B&L, vol. 4, p. 6.

7.   ORN, ser. 1, vol. 13, pp. 590–99; *Confederate Military History,* vol. 5, chap. 10, p. 193; CWNC, part 3, pp. 18–19; Burton, *Siege of Charleston,* pp. 126–30; B&L, vol. 4, pp. 6–7; Davis, *Rise and Fall of the Confederate Government,* p. 205.

8.   B&L, vol. 4, p. 7; Musicant, *Divided Waters,* p. 381.

9.   ORN, ser. 1, vol. 13, pp. 589–623. The entire engagement is covered in this volume, including individual ship reports.

10. WCWN, p. 8. It is interesting to note how these vessels closely resemble the configurations of the *Monitor.*

11. CWNC, part 3, p. 19.

12. Admiral John Rodgers, "DuPont's Attack on Charleston," B&L, vol. 4, p. 33.

13. WCWN, pp. 15, 18; Canney, *Mr. Lincoln's Navy,* p. 194. This vessel, designed by Charles W. Whitney, was often confused with true monitors because of her appearance. The absence of rotating turrets was a fatal weakness, in addition to her light armor.

14. Abstract log of the *Keokuk,* Tuesday, April 6, 1862, ORN, ser. 1, vol. 14, p. 24; Rodgers, "Du Pont's Attack on Charleston," B&L, vol. 4, p. 35; Davis, *Rise and Fall of the Confederate Government,* pp. 208–209. Davis maintains there were 123 mines in Charleston Harbor.

15. Rear Admiral du Pont Report, ORN, ser. 1, vol. 14, p. 3. Because of the confused line ahead, du Pont was reluctant to use the big guns of his flagship, for fear of hitting his own vessels.

16. Milton F. Perry, *Infernal Machines* (Baton Rouge: Louisiana State University Press, 1965), p. 51; CWNC, part 3, p. 59; Musicant, *Divided Waters*, p. 389.

17. The remarkable story of the recovery of these guns is told in "Confederates Salvage Guns of *Keokuk*," in *The Civil War at Charleston*, p. 45.

18. Du Pont Report, ORN, ser. 1, vol. 14, pp. 13–14; CWNC, part 3, p. 61; Schneller, *A Quest for Glory*, p. 237.

19. Niven, *Gideon Welles*, p. 434.

20. Quoted in O.H. Hoehling, *Thunder at Hampton Roads* (New York-Da Capo Press, 1933), p. 35; CWNC, vol. 1, p. 42.

21. Niven, *Gideon Welles*, p. 345.

22. WCWN, p. 203.

23. Littlepage to Jones, ORN, ser. 1, vol. 13, p. 820.

24. Commander Rodgers Report, ORN, ser. 1, vol. 14, pp. 265–67.

25. Jefferson Davis, *Rise and Fall of the Confederate Government*, p. 205.

26. CWNC, part 3, pp. 95–96.

27. CWNC, part 4, p. 148; Still, *Iron Afloat*, pp. 215–16.

28. CWNC, part 3, p. 98; Fowler, *Under Two Flags*, p. 258.

29. CWNC, part 3, pp. 10–11; Fowler, *Under Two Flags*, p. 258; HTECW, p. 46.

30. CWNC, part 3, pp. 10–11; Burton, *Siege of Charleston*, pp. 166–67.

31. Dahlgren Report, ORN, ser. 1, vol. 14, p. 502.

32. "Union Builds Marsh Battery," *The Civil War at Charleston*, pp. 53–54.

33. "City Shelled—Grim New Epoch of War," in *The Civil War at Charleston*, p. 55.

34. Smyth Letter, courtesy South Carolina Historical Society archives, Smyth Letter Collection.

35. Ibid.

CHAPTER FOURTEEN The *Hunley* and Underwater Warfare

1. CWNC, part 1, p. 105.

2. On Maury, see Diana Fontaine Maury Corbin, *The Life of Matthew Fontaine Maury, U.S.N. and C.S.N.* (London: S. Low, Marsten, Searle, and Rivington, 1888). See also Bradford, ed., *Captains of the Old Steam Navy*, pp. 46–63.

3. CWNC, part 2, p. 106; "Damn the Torpedoes, Full Speed Ahead," courtesy of Vicksburg Military Park, National Park Service, Department of Interior. For a

detailed discussion of mines first used in the Mississippi campaign, consult Coombe, *Thunder Along the Mississippi,* chap. 14.

4. Most of these devices are covered in detail in Perry, *Infernal Machines;* see also Isaac N. Brown's treatise "Confederate Torpedoes in the Yazoo," B&L, vol. 3, p. 580, for a discussion of the common types of mine devices that sank the *Cairo* and *Baron de Kalb* in the Yazoo River. In addition, CWNC features accounts of mines being used. Stern's *Confederate Navy* features an interesting and informative discussion of Confederate mines, pp. 182–83.

5. Davis, *Rise and Fall of the Confederate Government,* vol. 2, p. 208.

6. Hunter Davidson, "Electrical Torpedoes as a System of Defense," *Southern Historical Society Papers,* vol. 2, no. 1, pp. 1–6. Davidson suffered from constant criticism of his work, which plagued him throughout his life.

7. Gen. G. J. Rains, "Torpedoes," *Southern Historical Society Papers,* vol. 3, nos. 5, 6, pp. 255–60.

8. A fine description of *Pioneer* is found in Stern, *The Confederate Navy,* pp. 174–75; see also HTECW, p. 586.

9. There are many accounts of the *David*'s attack. One of the most interesting is General Beauregard's own story, to be found in "Torpedo Service in the Harbor Defenses of Charleston," *Southern Historical Society Papers,* vol. 4, no. 4, pp. 145–52.

10. Luraghi, *A History of the Confederate Navy,* pp. 252–54. Luraghi is a professor of American history at the University of Genoa, Italy, and an author of several books on military and naval history. See also W. A. Alexander, "The Story of Captain Hunley and His Brave Assistants—How the *Housatonic* Was Destroyed in Charleston Harbor," from the *Richmond Dispatch,* July 21, 1902, in *Southern Historical Society Papers,* vol. 30, p. 165.

11. W. A. Alexander, "Work of Submarine Boats," *Southern Historical Society Papers,* vol. 30, pp. 165–67; Luraghi, *A History of the Confederate Navy,* pp. 254–56; Perry, *Infernal Machines,* pp. 98–99; CWNC, part 2, p. 244.

12. Alexander, "Work of Submarine Boats," p. 168; Perry, *Infernal Machines,* p. 100; HTECW, p. 364.

13. F. J. Higgins Report, ORN, ser. 1, vol. 15, pp. 328–29; Abstract Log of the *Canandaigua,* ORN, ser. 1, vol. 15, p. 332.

14. Captain Greene Report, ORN, ser. 1, vol. 15, p. 331. The officer's report states that the *Housatonic* was sunk by a "David," which clearly shows he and his colleagues knew nothing about the existence of the *Hunley.*

15. Mark K. Ragan, *Union and Confederate Submarine Warfare in the Civil War* (Mason City, IA: Cevas Publishing, 1999). This book, just published, is a remarkable work on Civil War submarine warfare, featuring a foreword by novelist/

explorer Clive Cussler, through whose work the remains of the *Hunley* have been found. See also ORN, ser. 1, vol. 15, p. 338.

16. Lewis Lord, "Up from a Briny Grave," *U.S. News & World Report,* June 28, 1999; Brayton Harris, *Navy Times Book of Submarines* (New York: Berkley Publishing Group, 1997), p. 95. This is another new book on underwater warfare, and presents an excellent coverage of the exploits of the *Davids* and the *Hunley.*

17. Ragan, *Union and Confederate Submarine Warfare,* pp. 196–97.

18. Schneller, *A Quest for Glory,* p. 276.

19. The *Charleston News and Courier,* quoted in *The Civil War at Charleston,* p. 73.

20. Quoted in Ragan, *Union and Confederate Submarine Warfare,* p. 202. Professor Hortsford had earlier designed a submarine with a periscope and lock chamber, which would be the first such innovations of underwater craft in history and were to become essential features of such. But no record of its being built and tested exists.

21. *Army and Navy Journal,* March 19, 1864, quoted in Ragan, *Union and Confederate Submarine Warfare,* p. 204.

22. Harris, *Navy Times Book of Submarines,* p. 95. Allowing that much comment would occur in the United States, it should be remembered that the exploits of the *Hunley* were watched closely by European navies as well.

23. A new work, R. Thomas Campbell's *The C.S.S. Hunley, Confederate Submarine* (Shippensburg, PA: Burd Street Press, 2000), arrived too late to be included in this work. It is an excellent account of the *Hunley* story and contains much information on the recent discovery of the submarine. See also a new book by Clive Cussler and Craig Dirgo, *The Sea Hunters* (New York: Simon & Schuster, 1996).

NOTE: It was recently disclosed that the remains of one member of the crew on the *Hunley* is missing. How he got out of the vessel, or the supposition that she may have sailed short of one crew member is a mystery (This information courtesy of Dr. Bil Regan, of the Charleston committee working on the restoration of the submarine).

CHAPTER FIFTEEN The *Albemarle* Saga

1. Stern, *The Confederate Navy,* pp. 68–70; HTECW, pp. 524–636.

2. B. P. Loyall, "Capture of the *Underwriter,*" *Southern Historical Society Papers,* vol. 27, 1899, pp. 136–44, is an excellent account from one of the participants in the raid. See also Allen to Graves, ORN, ser. 1, vol. 9, p. 228.

3. WCWN, p. 205; Index, Confederate Naval Vessels entry, ORN, ser. 2, vol. 1, p. 247.

4. For a description of the yards in which the *Arkansas* and her sister *Tennessee* were

built, see Coombe, *Thunder Along the Mississippi,* chap. 10. The *Tennessee* was destroyed while on the stocks at the shipyard 12 miles below Memphis, as the Union fleet approached. The *Arkansas,* partially completed, was towed up the Yazoo River to a makeshift shipyard near Yazoo City, Mississippi. The book also contains a photo of the site of the yard at which she was completed.

5. CWNC, part 4, p. 44; Luraghi, *History of the Confederate Navy,* p. 293.

6. "The Confederate Ram *Albemarle,*" *Southern Historical Society Papers,* vol. 30, 1902, pp. 207–209; CWNC, part 4, p. 44.

7. "The Confederate Ram *Albemarle,*" p. 210; Holden, "First Battle of the Confederate Ram *Albemarle,*" B&L, vol. 4, p. 627. Few accounts of the battle mention the attempted boarding of the *Albemarle* by *Miami's* crew.

8. "Confederate Ram *Albemarle,*" p. 212; Holden, "The *Albemarle* and the *Sassacus,*" B&L, vol. 4, p. 627.

9. Musicant, *Divided Waters,* p. 415; "The *Albemarle* and the *Sassacus,*" Holden, p. 214.

10. The entire *Raleigh* engagement is found in detail in ORN, ser. 1, vol. 10, pp. 18–25.

11. HTECW, p. 199. One cannot overlook the voluminous, fine material on the Civil War in this fairly new publication.

12. Cushing's own account of the raid is found in "The Destruction of the *Albemarle,*" B&L, vol.4, pp. 634–40. Also, his report to Admiral Porter is found in ORN, ser. 1, vol. 10, pp. 611–13.

13. Cushing, "The Destruction of the *Albemarle,*" p. 637; CWNC, part 4, p. 126.

14. Warley Report, ORN, ser. 1, vol. 10, p. 613.

15. "E.K.L." Letter, quoted in ORN, ser. 1, vol. 10, p. 616. The unknown writer cynically called "Captain" Warley's determination to fight as long as there was a man left "all gas."

16. Warley Report, ORN, ser. 1, vol. 10, p. 612; B&L, vol. 1, p. 640; Abstract Log of the U.S.S. *Shamrock* for October 28, 1864, ser. 1, vol. 10, pp. 621–22.

17. Porter, General Orders #34, ORN, ser. 1, vol. 10, p. 618; Chester Hearn, *Admiral David Porter* (Annapolis: Naval Institute Press, 1996). This new book by historian Hearn is an excellent work on Porter. See also CWNC, part 4, p. 126.

CHAPTER SIXTEEN *Kearsarge* vs. *Alabama:* **End of a Raider**

1. Chester Hearn, *Confederate Raider* (Baton Rouge: Louisiana State University Press, 1992), p. 54; Anderson, *By Sea and by River,* pp. 180–81; Stern, *The Confederate Navy,* p. 34. The British-built *Florida* is not to be confused with the

reconstructed coastal packet *Havana* at New Orleans, renamed *Florida* and skippered by Raphael Semmes as his first command.

2. For biographical information on Maffitt, see Emma Maffitt, *The Life and Services of John Maffitt* (New York: Neal Publishing, 1906); HTECW, p. 467. Also consult his own journal in ORN, ser. 1, vol. 1, pp. 766–67.

3. ORN, ser. 1, vol. 1, pp. 436, 437, 459. See Coombe, *Gunfire Around the Gulf,* chap. 12 for a detailed description of the *Florida* affair and the subsequent embarrassment of the U. S. Navy.

4. Lincoln to Congress, ORN, ser. 1, vol. 1, p. 439; Welles to Preble, ORN, ser. 1, vol. 1, pp. 437, 459; Coombe, *Gunfire Around the Gulf,* chap. 11; Musicant, *Divided Waters,* pp. 335–37.

5. Preble was unjustly accused, because he was aware of the sensitivity between the United States and England as a result of the *Trent* affair and was reluctant to take hostile action against what he considered to be an English ship.

6. See Semmes' own memoirs: *My Service Afloat During the War Between the States* (Baltimore: Kelly Piet & Co., 1886). The newest biography of Semmes is John M. Taylor, *The Confederate Raider* (McLean, VA: Brassey's, 1994). This is an excellent study of the amazing Semmes and his amazing ship. Other works include Semmes, *The Confederate Raider Alabama* (Greenwich, CT: Fawcett, 1972) and "Raphael Semmes," in Bradford, ed., *Captains of the Old Steam Navy,* p. 211.

7. Semmes, *My Service Afloat During the War Between the States,* p. 404; CWNC, part 1, p. 93.

8. John McIntosh Kell, "Cruise and Combats of the *Alabama,*" B&L, vol. 4, p. 600; Chester Hearn, *Gray Raiders of the Sea* (Baton Rouge: Louisiana State University Press, 1996), pp. 155–56. Kell was Semmes' executive officer and close friend.

9. Kell, "Cruise and Combats of the *Alabama,*" p. 600; Stephen Foster.

10. Semmes, *The Confederate Raider Alabama,* pp. 34–35; ORN, ser. 1, vol. 17, pp. 507–10. See also Coombe, *Gunfire Around the Gulf,* chap. 12; Kell, "Cruise and Combats of the *Alabama,*" p. 604; CWNC, part 3, p. 8; Hearn, *Gray Raiders of the Sea,* pp. 188–89; Donald S. Frazier, *Cottonclads! The Battle of Galveston and the Defense of the Texas Coast* (Fort Worth, TX: Ryan Place, 1996), pp. 93–98. The last is an excellent read on the actions around Galveston.

11. Taylor, *Confederate Raider,* chap. 13.

12. HTECW, p. 3.

13. Semmes to Barron, ORN, ser. 1, vol. 3, p. 651; Bradford, ed., *Captains of the Old Steam Navy,* p. 214; Musicant, *Divided Waters,* p. 349.

14. Luraghi, *History of the Confederate Navy,* p. 315.

15. Taylor, *Confederate Raider,* p. 197.

16. Excellent short bios on Winslow can be found in HTECW, p. 836, and *Who Was Who in the Civil War*, p. 724. Winslow was an unhappy man. Because he had complained so often, he was given command of a third-rate vessel.

17. CWNC, part 4, p. 75.

18. Flag Officer Barron Report, ORN, ser. 1, vol. 3, p. 649. Writing after the battle, Barron intimated that Semmes was confident of victory. The records do not show this confidence. Some historians believed that it was a case of the victory-or-going-out-in-glory syndrome.

19. John McIntosh Kell, *Recollections of a Naval Life* (Washington, DC: The Neale Company, 1900), p. 245; Kell, "Cruise and Combats of the *Alabama*," B&L, vol. 4, p. 607.

20. Kell, *Recollections*, p. 245; Luraghi, *History of the Confederate Navy*, p. 317; Bradford, ed., *Captains of the Old Steam Navy*, p. 215.

21. Hearn, *Gray Raiders of the Sea*, p. 225. This book is an excellent account of the Confederate cruisers, based on the latest research.

22. Kell comments on this in his *Recollections* but is ambiguous in his article for B&L; historian Luraghi claimed he did know; others are not so sure.

23. Flag Officer Barron Report, ORN, ser. 1, vol. 3, p. 649.

24. Log of *Alabama*, ORN, ser. 1, vol. 3, p. 677.

25. Semmes, *Service Afloat*, p. 756; Bradford, *Captains of the Old Steam Navy*, p. 215; Hearn, *Gray Raiders of the Sea*, p. 227.

26. John M. Browne, "The Duel Between the *Alabama* and the *Kearsarge*," B&L, vol. 4, p. 616. Browne's account is full of details not found in other sources. He even described what the sailors on the *Alabama* wore as they sailed out to combat. This article is the most vivid account of the battle.

27. Ibid., p. 624; Winslow Report, ORN, ser. 1, vol. 3, p. 63. The crew of the *Kearsarge* failed to discover the unexploded shell in their sternpost until they reached Boston for repairs. The sternpost, with the shell still in it, is currently on display at the U.S. Navy's museum at the Washington Navy Yard. Some historians, including Taylor, maintain that the shell was the result of a ricochet rather than a direct hit and would not have caused serious damage to the ship.

28. Log of the *Kearsarge*, ORN, ser. 1, vol. 3, p. 65.

29. Ibid.; Semmes to Mallory, ORN, ser. 1, vol. 3, p. 650. Nothing is said about this in the official accounts, including the reliable CWNC account, pp. 77–78. The Federals countered by stating that the *Alabama* had fired rounds after the surrender. No one knows for sure.

30. Kell, *Recollections*, p. 270.

31. Semmes to Mallory, ORN, ser. 1, vol. 3, p. 650; B&L, vol. 4, pp. 618–19. In October 1984, a team of French archeologists discovered the remains of the

Alabama in the English Channel. She was so deteriorated after 120 years that she will never be raised. The only artifacts recovered were the steering wheel and some English china.

32. Musicant, *Divided Waters*, p. 353.

33. HTCEW, p. 836.

34. CWNC, part 4, p. 78.

35. Davis, *Rise and Fall of the Confederate Government*, p. 257. For a footnote on comments by Mrs. Semmes, see Taylor, *Confederate Raider*, p. 208.

36. Pollard, *The Lost Cause* (New York: Gramercy Press, 1974), p. 552. This is a new edition of the venerable work by the prolific Southern editor, writing from 1861 to 1867 about the Civil War.

37. *New York Times*, July 6, 1864.

38. HTECW, p. 666; CWD, p. 731; Bradford, ed., *Captains of the Old Steam Navy*, pp. 218–19; Taylor, *Confederate Raider*, chap. 20.

CHAPTER SEVENTEEN Climax at Fort Fisher, Part 1

1. Henry Davenport Northrup, *Life and Deeds of General Sherman* (Cleveland: Cleveland Publishing Company, 1891), p. 432. This book is an excellent biography of the great general by one of his contemporaries. See also Allan Nevins, *The War for the Union: The Organized War to Victory, 1864–1865* (New York: Charles Scribner's Sons, 1971), vol. 4, p. 188.

2. "Being an Address by C. B. Denison, of the Engineer Service of the Confederate Army," Raleigh, NC, May 10, 1895, courtesy Fort Fisher Historical Site, Kure Beach, NC. Denison, an army engineer, was present at Fort Fisher at the time of the Union assaults.

3. Information from U.S. Department of Interior, National Park Service's *National Register of Historic Places Inventory*, courtesy Fort Fisher Historic Site, Kure Beach, NC.

4. "An Address by C. B. Denison," p. 37; Musicant, *Divided Waters*, p. 416.

5. Address by Colonel William Lamb to the United Veterans of Wilmington, June 22, 1893, reported in *Weekly Messenger*, Wilmington, NC, *Southern Historical Society Papers*, vol. 21, p. 260. See also Rod Gragg, *Confederate Goliath: The Battle of Fort Fisher* (Baton Rouge: Louisiana State University Press, 1991), p. 17. This is the first of two recent, great books on the battle for Fort Fisher. It has become a classic.

6. Many sources were used for the reconstruction of Fort Fisher—too many to be listed here. I have relied heavily on Colonel Lamb's description quoted in "An Address by C. B. Denison," plus a detailed account in Gragg's *Confederate*

Goliath, pp. 19–21. I have also used Musicant's excellent description in his *Divided Waters;* "Fort Fisher," in *Confederate Military History,* vol. 4. The best and most informative map of the fort is found in Gragg's *Confederate Goliath,* p. 20; U.S. Department of Interior, *National Register of Historical Places,* Item #8, p. 17; Address by Colonel William Lamb, pp. 260–63. A fine, almost three-dimensional map of the fort is found in Chris Bishop, Ian Drury, and Tony Gibbons, *1,400 Days: The Civil War Day by Day* (North Dighton, MA: J. G. Press, Inc., 1998), pp. 218–19. This is a new book featuring not only a chronological account of the war, but many original paintings of Civil War actions.

7. Ulysses S. Grant, *Personal Memoirs of U. S. Grant* (New York: AMS Press, 1972 [1894]), vol. 2, p. 570. This excerpt from Grant's own memoirs refutes some of the sources that maintain Grant's indifference to the campaign against Fort Fisher.

8. Hearn, *Admiral David Dixon Porter,* p. 273.

9. General Butler's controversial occupation of New Orleans after its capture in 1862 is discussed in Coombe, *Thunder Along the Mississippi,* chap. 10. He was labeled with the sobriquet "Spoons" because of his habit of stealing silverware from his hosts. However, in all fairness to him, the accusation is unsubstantiated by historical research.

10. Address by Colonel William Lamb, p. 266. Lamb also received word that his men were expected to "spike the guns, cut telegraph wires and pilot the enemy to the city." He vehemently denied this.

11. John D. Peltzer, "Ben Butler's Powder Boat Scheme," in *America's Civil War,* January 1995, pp. 38–44; Charles M. Robinson III, *Hurricane of Fire: The Union Assault on Fort Fisher* (Annapolis: Naval Institute Press, 1998), p. 88. This work is the latest on Fort Fisher since Gragg's work. Robinson writes from the naval perspective, Gragg from the army's.

12. Robinson, *Hurricane of Fire,* p. 90.

13. Porter Report to Welles, ORN, ser. 1, vol. 2, pp. 234-36; Engineer Report, ORN, ser. 1, vol. 2, pp. 207-209; Robinson, *Hurricane of Fire,* p. 104; Musicant, *Divided Waters,* p. 442; Peltzer, "Ben Butler's Powder Boat Scheme," p. 42.

14. A detailed description of the clock device can be found in Porter Report to Welles, ORN, ser. 1, vol. 2, pp. 207–209. It is too detailed to include here.

15. Log of the U.S.S. *Advance,* ORN, ser. 1, vol. 2, p. 241.

16. Address by Colonel William Lamb, p. 290; Lamb, "Defense of Fort Fisher," in B&L, vol. 4, pp. 642-57. For years, the remains of the powder boat were not found; it was assumed to have been blown to pieces by the blast. But the *Louisiana* wreck site was recently discovered and explored by an underwater

archeological team. It lies 250 yards out from the shore and contains the propeller shaft, machinery, and boiler. The iron hull plating remains remarkably intact.

17.   Address by Colonel William Lamb, p. 271.

18.   *Confederate Military History,* chap. 17, p. 274.

19.   Stern, *Confederate Navy,* p. 236; "An Address by C. B. Denison," p. 39; Fowler, *Under Two Flags,* p. 269.

20.   Porter to Welles, ORN, ser. 1, vol. 11, p. 258; Address by Colonel William Lamb, p. 276; Butler Report, ORA, vol. 81, part 1, p. 968. Lamb denied that any Union soldier reached the ramparts on the landface. He maintains the flag had been dislodged from the bombardment and that the courier had already left the fort and was stopped en route to his destination. Mrs. Lamb, awaiting the outcome of the battle in Wilmington, later confirmed that her husband had sent the courier to some troops outside of the fort. There has been a surprising amount of disagreement over these two incidents.

21.   Butler to Porter, ORN, ser. 1, vol. 11, p. 251; Butler to Grant, ORA, vol. 81, part 1, p. 968. In these reports, Butler steps nearer to admitting his failure.

22.   Butler to Porter, ORN, ser. 1, vol. 11, p. 252.

23.   *Personal Memoirs of U. S. Grant,* vol. 2, p. 575.

24.   *Confederate Military History,* vol. 4, chap. 17, p. 276.

25.   Quoted in Robinson, *Hurricane of Fire,* p. 140.

26.   Gragg, *Confederate Goliath,* p. 97.

27.   Ibid.

CHAPTER EIGHTEEN Climax at Fort Fisher, Part 2

1.   Gragg, *Confederate Goliath.*

2.   Grant order to Terry, ORA, ser. 1, vol. 45. p. 25; Grant to Terry, ORN, ser. 1, vol. 11, p. 404; Grant to Porter, ORN, ser. 1, vol. 11, p. 405.

3.   Porter to Grant, ORN, ser. 1, vol. 11, p. 405.

4.   *Personal Memoirs of U. S. Grant,* pp. 575–76; Thomas Selfridge, "The Navy at Fort Fisher," B&L, vol. 4, pp. 655–60.

5.   Hearn, *Admiral David Dixon Porter,* p. 292; Selfridge, "The Navy at Fort Fisher," p. 658.

6.   Hearn, *Admiral David Dixon Porter,* p. 292; Grant, *Personal Memoirs of U. S. Grant,* p. 576; Selfridge, "The Navy at Fort Fisher," p. 658.

7.   Address of Colonel William Lamb, p. 277.

8.   Ibid. In this report, Lamb stops short of criticizing Bragg for his inaction in opposing the landing of Union troops. Whiting, however, spent a great deal of

time after the war blaming Bragg for the fall of Fort Fisher. Lamb later wrote a scathing rebuke of Bragg.

9. C. B. Denison, "Being an Address in Raleigh, N.C., on Memorial Day, May 10, 1895," courtesy Fort Fisher Museum Archives.

10. Terry Report, January 25, 1865, ORA, ser. 1, vol. 25, p. 396.

11. C. B. Denison address. While Denison stated that the English officer was at the fort, research shows no such officer present after the surrender. However, at the Confederate veterans' gathering at Wilmington in 1893, he was present.

12. CWNC, vol. 4, p. 11: Hearn, *Admiral David Dixon Porter*, p. 304.

13. William Lamb, "Fort Fisher," *Philadelphia Times*, Nov. 12, 1881, courtesy Fort Fisher Archives.

14. CWNC, vol. 4, p. 12; Terry Report, ORA, ser. 1, vol. 25, p. 398; Address of Colonel William Lamb, p. 280; Selfridge, "The Navy at Fort Fisher," p. 658.

15. Hearn, *Admiral David Dixon Porter*, p. 302; Robinson, *Hurricane of Fire*, p. 184.

16. Porter to Welles, ORN, ser. 1, vol. 11, p. 441.

17. Miller, *The U.S. Navy*, p. 141.

18. Braxton Bragg, "Defense and Fall of Fort Fisher," *Southern Historical Society Papers*, vol. 10, p. 346.

19. Robinson, *Hurricane of Fire*, p. 191.

20. Miller, *The U.S. Navy*, p. 141.

CHAPTER NINETEEN Twilight of the Confederate Navy

1. Hearn, *Admiral David Dixon Porter*, p. 306; Abstract Log of U.S.S. *Malvern*, ORN, ser. 2, vol. 12, pp. 174–76.

2. Abstract Log of U.S.S. *Malvern*, ORN, ser. 2, vol. 12, p. 175; Hearn, *Admiral David Dixon Porter*, p. 306.

3. *Personal Memoirs of U. S. Grant*, pp. 607–608; HTECW, pp. 577–79.

4. Nesbitt, *Rebel Rivers*, pp. 115–17. It is puzzling as to how this remarkable engineering feat has been ignored by so many Civil War historians, considering its use many times by Allied forces in Europe.

5. Mitchell to Semmes, ORN, ser. 1, vol. 12, p. 185; Russell Soley, "Closing Operations in the James River," B&L, vol. 4, p. 706; Stern, *Confederate Navy*, p. 240.

6. Soley, "Closing Operations," p. 706; HTECW, p. 546.

7. Hearn, *Admiral David Dixon Porter*, p. 306; Soley, "Closing Operations," p. 707; Musicant, *Divided Waters*, p. 430; "Operations on the James River," in

Confederate Military History, vol. 12, pp. 93–94; Eggleston Report, ORN, ser. 1, vol. 12, p. 190.

8. David Herbert Donald, *Lincoln* (New York: Simon & Schuster, 1995), pp. 571–74; W. Fletcher Johnson, *Life of Wm. Tecumseh Sherman* (Edgewood Publishing Company, 1891), pp. 435–36.

9. Hearn, *Admiral David Dixon Porter*, p. 311.

10. Porter to Ronckendorff, ORN, ser. 1, vol. 95.

11. Mallory to Semmes, ORN, ser. 1, vol. 12, p. 190.

12. David D. Ryan, *A Yankee Spy in Richmond* (Mechanicsburg, PA: Stackpole Books, 1996), p. 105. A remarkable diary of a remarkable woman who lived in Richmond during the war and supplied the Union with important information, both civilian and military.

13. Abstract Log of U.S.S. *Malvern*, ORN, ser. 1, vol. 12, p. 176.

14. Donald, *Lincoln*, p. 576; Hearn, *Admiral David Dixon Porter*, p. 311; Sandburg, *Lincoln*, vol. 3, pp. 804–806.

15. *Confederate Military History*, vol. 12, p. 94.

16. Stern, *The Confederate Navy*, pp. 250–53; Log of *Shenandoah*, courtesy Chicago Historical Society archives.

CHAPTER TWENTY A Glance Backward

1. *National Register of Historic Places Inventory*, U.S. Department of the Interior, National Park Service, courtesy Fort Fisher Archives.

2. James Sprunt, "Vance Kept N.C. Soldiers Well Provided," *Southern Historical Society Papers*, vol. 24, pp. 24–25.

3. Coombe, *Thunder Along the Mississippi*, chap. 13; *Gunfire Around the Gulf*, chap. 13–17.

4. CWNC, vol. 4, p. 3. The tenacity, endurance, and resourcefulness of the Union navy in pursuing the blockade with the few ships of a weakened U.S. Navy was to be matched in 1942 when a handful of destroyers and cruisers and one aircraft carrier faced a formidable fleet of 125 destroyers, 12 battleships, and 10 aircraft carriers of the Imperial Japanese navy. That handful of ships held off the mighty enemy armada until America's industrial capacity began to turn out ships and aircraft at an awesome rate.

BIBLIOGRAPHY

GOVERNMENT SOURCES

Civil War Chronology, 1861–1865. 6 vols. Washington, DC: U.S. Government Printing Office, Naval History Division, 1971.

Dictionary of American Fighting Ships. 8 vols. Washington, DC: U.S. Government Printing Office, Naval History Division, 1959–1981.

Message and Documents: Message of the President of the United States, Accompanying Documents at the 2nd Session of the 38th Congress. Washington, DC: U.S. Government Printing Office, U.S. Navy Department, 1864.

National Register of Historic Places Inventory. United States Department of the Interior, National Park Service. Washington. DC: U.S. Government Printing Office, 1987.

Official Records of the Union and Confederate Navies in the War of the Rebellion. 31 vols. Washington, DC: U.S. Government Printing Office, 1864.

Report of the Secretary of the Navy in Relation to Armed Vessels. Washington, DC: U.S. Government Printing Office, 1864.

War of the Rebellion: A Compilation of the Official Records of the Union and Confederate Armies. 128 vols. Washington, DC: U.S. Government Printing Office, 1880–1901.

JOURNALS

Southern Historical Society Papers

Confederate Military History

Cheesebox—Monitor National Marine Sanctuary

Activities Reports—National Oceanic and Atmosphere Administration, Washington, DC

The Goldman Brothers' Letters Journal

NEWSPAPERS

Charlotte Observer
Charleston News and Courier
Charleston Evening Post
New York Times
Richmond Dispatch
Wilmington Weekly Register
Philadelphia Times
Liverpool Daily Post
Savannah Republican

MAGAZINES

Civil War Times Illustrated
America's Civil War
U.S. News & World Report
Military History
National Geographic
Army and Navy Journal
Civil War Chronicles

BOOKS

American Heritage Battle Maps of the Civil War. Tulsa, OK: Council Oaks Books, 1992.

Anderson, Bern. *By Sea and by River: The Naval History of the Civil War.* New York: Alfred A. Knopf, 1962.

Andrews, J. Cutler. *The North Reports the Civil War.* Pittsburgh: University of Pittsburgh Press, 1955.

Angle, Paul M. *A Pictorial History of the Civil War Years.* Garden City, NJ: Doubleday & Company, Inc., 1967.

Barrat, John G. *The Civil War in North Carolina.* Chapel Hill: University of North Carolina Press, 1963.

Battles and Leaders of the Civil War. 4 vols. New York: Thomas Yoseloff, 1956.

Beach, Edward L. *United States Navy, 200 Years.* New York: Henry Holt & Co., 1986.

Bishop, Chris, Ian Drury, and Tony Gibbons. *1,400 Days: The U.S. Civil War Day by Day.* North Dighton, MA: J. G. Press, 1998.

The Blockade: Runners and Raiders. New York: Time-Life Books, 1983.

Boatner, Mark M. *The Civil War Dictionary.* New York: Vintage Books, 1991

Bradford, James C., ed. *Captains of the Old Steam Navy.* Annapolis: Naval Institute Press, 1986.

Burton, E. Milby. *The Siege of Charleston, 1861–1865.* Columbia: University of South Carolina Press, 1970.

Campbell, R. Thomas. *The CSS Hunley, Confederate Submarine.* Shippensburg, PA: Burd Street Press, 2000.

Canby, Courtland, ed. *Lincoln and the Civil War.* New York: Dell Publishing Co., 1958.

Canney, Donald L. *Lincoln's Navy.* Annapolis: Naval Institute Press, 1998.

Catton, Bruce. *The American Heritage New History of the Civil War: A Guide for Writers, Students and Historians.* Ed. James M. McPherson. New York: Penguin Books, 1996.

———. *Grant Takes Command.* Boston: Little, Brown and Company, 1968.

———. *Reflections on the Civil War.* Ed. John Leekley. New York: Berkley Books, 1982.

———. *This Hallowed Ground.* New York: Pocket Books, 1967.

Chaiten, Peter M. *The Coastal War: Chesapeake Bay to the Rio Grande.* Civil War Series. New York: Time-Life Books, 1984.

Church, William C. *The Life of John Ericsson.* New York: Scribner's, 1911.

The Civil War at Charleston. Charleston: The News Courier and the Evening Post, 1997.

Clinton, Sir Henry. *The American Rebellion.* Ed. William B. Wilcox. New Haven: Yale University Press, 1954.

Commager, Henry Steele. *The Blue and the Gray.* 2 vols. New York: Meridian Division of Penguin Books, 1983.

Coombe, Jack D. *Gunfire Around the Gulf.* New York: Bantam Books, 1999.

———. *Thunder Along the Mississippi.* New York: Bantam Books, 1996.

Cussler, Clive, and Craig Dirgo. *The Sea Hunters.* New York: Simon & Schuster, 1996.

Davis, Jefferson. *The Rise and Fall of the Confederate Government.* 2 vols. New York: Thomas Yoseloff, 1958.

Davis, Kenneth C. *Don't Know Much About the Civil War.* New York: William Morrow and Company, Inc., 1996.

Davis, William C. *The Civil War.* New York: Smithmark Publishers, 1996.

———. *Duel Between the First Ironclads.* Garden City, NY: Doubleday, 1975.

———. *The Fighting Men of the Civil War.* Norman: University of Oklahoma Press, 1998.

Davis, William C., Brian C. Pohanka, and Don Troiani, eds. *Civil War Journal: The Battles.* Nashville: Rutledge Hill Press, 1998.

de Kay, James Tertius. *Monitor.* New York: Walker & Company, 1997.

Donald, Daniel, ed. *Why the North Won the Civil War.* New York: Macmillan, 1960.

Donald, David Herbert. *Lincoln*. New York: Simon & Schuster, 1995.

Durkin, Joseph T. *Stephen Mallory: Confederate Naval Chief*. Chapel Hill: University of North Carolina Press, 1954.

Eisenschiml, Otto. *Why the Civil War?* Ed. Richard B. Morris. New York: Bobbs-Merrill, 1958.

Fowler, William M., Jr. *Under Two Flags: The American Navy in the Civil War*. New York: Avon Books, 1990.

Gallagher, Gary. *The Confederate War*. Boston: Harvard University Press, 1997.

Gragg, Rod. *The Confederate Goliath: The Battle of Fort Fisher*. Baton Rouge: Louisiana State University Press, 1991.

Gruppe, Henry. *The Frigates*. Alexandria, VA: Time-Life Books, 1997.

Hagen, Kenneth J. *This People's Navy: The Making of America's Sea Power*. New York: The Free Press, 1991.

Hansen, Henry. *The Civil War: A History*. New York: Penguin Books, 1991.

Harris, Brayton. *The Navy Times Book of Submarines*. New York: Berkley Books, 1997.

Hattaway, Herman, and Archer Jones. *How the North Won: A Military History of the Civil War*. Urbana: University of Illinois Press, 1983.

Hearn, Chester G. *Admiral David Dixon Porter*. Annapolis: Naval Institute Press, 1996.

———. *Gray Raiders of the Sea*. Baton Rouge: Louisiana State University Press, 1992.

Historical Times Illustrated Encyclopedia of the Civil War. Ed. Patricia Faust. New York: Harper & Row Publishers, 1986.

Hoehling, A. A. *Thunder at Hampton Roads*. New York: Da Capo Press, 1993.

Horner, Dave. *The Blockade Runners*. New York: Dodd, Mead & Company, 1968.

Howarth, Stephen. *To Shining Sea; A History of the United States Navy*. New York: Random House, 1991.

Jones, Virgil Carrington. *The Civil War at Sea*. 3 vols. New York: Holt Rinehart Winston, 1961.

Katchor, Philip. *The Civil War Source Book*. New York: Facts on File, 1992.

Klein, Maury. *Days of Defiance*. New York: Alfred A. Knopf, 1947.

Leifermann, Henry. *South Carolina*. New York: Fodor's Travel Publications, Inc., 1998.

Lincoln, Abraham. *Speeches and Writings, 1859–1865*. 2 vols. New York: Library of America, 1974.

Long, E. B., and Barbara Long. *The Civil War Day by Day: An Almanac 1861–1865*. Garden City, N.Y.: Doubleday & Co., 1971.

Lovett, Leland P. *Naval Customs: Traditions and Usage*. Annapolis: United States Naval Institute Press, 1939.

Luraghi, Raimondo. *The History of the Confederate Navy*. Trans. Paolo E. Coletta. Annapolis: Naval Institute Press, 1996.

Mahan, Alfred Thayer. *The Influence of Seapower upon History.* Englewood Cliffs, NJ: Prentice-Hall, 1980.

McCormick, Robert R. *The War Without Grant.* New York: Bond Wheelwright, 1950.

McPherson, James, ed. *Atlas of the Civil War.* New York: Doubleday & Company, Inc., 1994.

Miller, Edward Stokes. *Civil War Sea Battles: Sea Fights and Shipwrecks in the War Between the States.* Mechanicsburg, PA: Combined Books, 1995.

Miller, Nathan. *The U.S. Navy: A History.* Annapolis: Naval Institute Press, 1996.

Morison, Samuel Eliot. *John Paul Jones: A Sailor's Biography.* Boston: Little-Brown and Company, 1959.

Nash, Howard P., Jr. *A Naval History of the Civil War.* New York: A. S. Barnes & Co., 1972.

Nesbitt, Mark. *Rebel Rivers.* Mechanicsburg, PA: Stackpole Books, 1993.

Nevins, Allan. *The War for the Union: The Impoverished War, 1861–1862.* 4 vols. New York: Charles Scribner's Sons, 1959.

Nicolay, John. *Outbreak of the Rebellion.* New York: Charles Scribner's Sons, 1992 [1881].

Niven, John. *Gideon Welles: Lincoln's Secretary of the Navy.* New York: Oxford University Press, 1973.

Noel, John V. *The VNR Dictionary of Ships & the Sea.* New York: Van Nostrand Reinhold, 1981.

Perry, Milton F. *Infernal Machines: The Story of Confederate Submarines and Mine Warfare.* Baton Rouge: Louisiana State University Press, 1961.

Pollard, A. E. *The Lost Cause.* New York: Gramercy Books, 1994.

Potter, E. B., and Chester W. Nimitz. *Sea Power: A Naval History.* Englewood Cliffs, NJ: Prentice-Hall, 1960.

Pratt, Fletcher. *A Short History of the Civil War.* New York: Pocket Books, 1956.

Quarstein, John V. *The Battle of the Ironclads.* Charleston, SC: Arcadia Publishing, 1999.

Ragan, Mark. *Union and Confederate Submarine Warfare in the Civil War.* Mason City, IA: Savas Publishing Company, 1999.

Reynolds, Clark G. *Command of the Sea.* New York: William Morrow & Co., 1974.

Robinson, Charles M. *Hurricane of Fire: The Union Assault on Fort Fisher.* Annapolis: Naval Institute Press, 1998.

Ryan, David D. *A Yankee Spy in Richmond.* Mechanicsburg, PA: Stackpole Books, 1996.

Sandburg, Carl. *Abraham Lincoln: The War Years, 1864–1865.* 3 vols. New York: Dell, 1954.

Scharf, J. Thomas. *History of the Confederate States Navy.* New York: Rogers & Sherwood, 1887.

Schneller, Robert J. *A Quest for Glory: Biography of Rear Admiral John A. Dahlgren.* Annapolis: Naval Institute Press, 1996.

Stern, Philip Van Dorn. *The Confederate States Navy: A Pictorial History.* New York: Da Capo Press, 1992.

Still, William N., Jr. *Ironclad Captains: The Commanding Officers of the U.S.S. Monitor.* Washington, DC: U.S. Government Printing Office, 1988.

————. *Iron Afloat: The Story of the Confederate Ironclads.* Columbia, SC: University of South Carolina Press, 1985.

————. *Confederate Shipbuilding.* Athens, GA: University of Georgia Press, 1969.

Taylor, John M. *Confederate Raider: Ralph Semmes of the Alabama.* McLean, VA: Brassey's, 1994.

Varhola, Michael J. *Everyday Life During the Civil War.* Cincinnati: Writer's Digest Books, 1999.

Wells, Tom Henderson. *The Confederate Navy: A Study in Organization.* Huntsville: University of Alabama Press, 1971.

West, Richard S., Jr. *Mr. Lincoln's Navy.* New York: Longmans, Green & Company, 1907.

Wheeler, Richard. *Voices of the Civil War.* New York: Thomas Y. Crowell Company, 1976.

Who Was Who in the Civil War. New York: Facts on File, 1998.

Wideman, John C. *Naval Warfare: Courage and Combat on the Water.* New York: Metro Books, 1997.

Woodward, C. Vann, and Elisabeth Muhlenfeld. *The Private Mary Chestnut: The Unpublished War Diaries.* New York: Oxford University Press, 1984.

Woodworth, Stephen. *Jefferson Davis and His Generals.* Lawrence: University of Kansas Press, 1990.

LETTERS, DIARIES, PRIVATE PUBLICATIONS, AND JOURNALS

"A Confederate Eyewitness Account of the *Merrimac* Battle." Mariners' Museum, Newport News.

A Look at the Monitor. National Marine Sanctuary, Sanctuaries & Reserve Division, National Oceanic & Atmospheric Administration, Newport News.

"An Address by C. B. Denison at the Engineer Service of the Confederate Army." May 10, 1895. Fort Fisher Historic Site, Kure Beach, NC.

Robert Anderson, Letters, Chicago Historical Society.

Buchanan Letter to Mallory. Mariners' Museum Archives.

"Cheese Box" Series. National Oceanic Atmospheric Administration. Newport News.

Wylie J. Clark Letters. Chicago Historical Society.

Comparing the Ironclads. U.S.S. *Cairo* Museum, Vicksburg Military Park.

"Damn the Torpedoes!" Vicksburg Military Park, National Park Service, U.S. Department of the Interior.

Goldman Brothers' Civil War Letters. Transcribed by Bobby Goldman. Mark Hopkins, Houston, TX.

Samuel Dana Greene Letter. Mariners' Museum Archives, Newport News.

Holcomb, Robert. "Ernest Hemingway and the Confederate Navy" and "Another Confederate Ironclad." *Liverpool Daily Post*. Chicago Historical Society.

Louis Ashfield Kimberly Letters. Chicago Historical Society.

Lamb, William. "Fort Fisher." Fort Fisher Museum archives.

Log of U.S.S. *Shenandoah*. Chicago Historical Society.

Matthew Fontaine Maury Letters. Chicago Historical Society.

National Register of Historical Places Inventory. U.S. Department of Interior, Fort Fisher Historical Site.

Pervaiance Report. National Archives, Great Lakes Division.

Francis Wilson Pickens Letters. Chicago Historical Society.

"Reports on Cape Fear Wrecks." U.S. Underwater Archaeology Division. Fort Fisher Historical Site.

Smith, Willette. "Search for Confederate Torpedo." *Wreck Diver*, vol. 3, no. 6. Charleston Historical Society.

John Smyth Letters. Chicago Historical Society.

Straubing, C. W. "Eyewitness Accounts." Mariners' Museum Archives.

Van Brunt Report. Mariners' Museum Archives.

Tales of Old Fort Monroe. "The *Monitor* and the *Merrimack*." Casemate Museum, Fort Monroe.

Views of Fort Sumter. South Carolina Historical Society.

John L. Worden Letter. Mariners' Museum Archives, Newport News.

John Webber Letters. Casemate Museum Archives, Fort Monroe.

White, E. V. "The First Ironclad Engagement in the World." Casemate Museum Archives, Fort Monroe.

Gideon Welles Letter to Hayes. Mariners' Museum Archives, Newport News.

John L. Worden Report. Mariners' Museum Archives.

Maps

U.S. Department of Interior Geological Survey, U.S. Govt. Printing Office, Washington, DC.

U.S. Underwater Archaeology Division, Department of the Interior, Fort Fisher, NC.

Casemate Museum, Fort Monroe Archives.

INDEX